*Atlantic Environments
and the American South*

environmental
history
and the
american
south

Atlantic Environments and the American South

Edited by Thomas Blake Earle and
D. Andrew Johnson

The University of Georgia Press

Athens

This publication was made possible in part by a grant from
the Rice University Department of History.

Most University of Georgia Press titles are
available from popular e-book vendors.

Printed digitally

Library of Congress Cataloging-in-Publication Data

Names: Earle, Thomas Blake, editor. | Johnson, D. Andrew, editor.
Title: Atlantic environments and the American South / edited by Thomas Blake Earle,
    D. Andrew Johnson.
Other titles: Environmental history and the American South.
Description: Athens : The University of Georgia Press, [2020] | Series: Environmental history
    and the American South | Includes bibliographical references and index.
Identifiers: LCCN 2019041392 | ISBN 9780820356488 (hardback) | ISBN 9780820356693
    (paperback) | ISBN 9780820356471 (ebook)
Subjects: LCSH: Human ecology—Southern States—History. | Human ecology—West
    Indies—History. | Slavery—Southern States—History. | Slavery—West Indies—History. |
    Southern States—History. | West Indies—History.
Classification: LCC GF13.3.S6 A75 2020 | DDC 975—dc23
LC record available at https://lccn.loc.gov/2019041392

CONTENTS

Part IV. Empire and Expertise

FOREWORD

There are many ways to kick-start a field.

In 2009, one of the first volumes to appear in this book series was a collection that bore its name, *Environmental History and the American South*. Editors Paul S. Sutter and Christopher J. Manganiello pulled together the best writing in the nascent scholarship on southern environmental history to show how a field obsessed with wilderness might help recast the history of a region almost continuously shaped by the presence of humans. The incredible growth of U.S. environmental history over the late twentieth century had largely bypassed the South and its agrarian landscape, perpetuating the stereotype that the region was somehow peculiar, unique. The South was "American with a difference," U. B. Phillips said. But it was another famous phrase uttered by Phillips—"Let us begin by discussing the weather"—that had launched an environmentally deterministic view of the South's troubled past that haunted scholars of the southern environment decades later. Sutter and Manganiello effectively banished the ghost of Phillips by gathering innovative environmental work on oft-studied "southern" subjects from plantations to civil rights.

Alongside a provocative and definitive introduction, the articles, culled from top journals where they had appeared over the previous fifteen years, took on fresh meanings from their new juxtaposition. Taken as whole, the articles signaled the rise of a new way of understanding the South and demanded new questions of environmental history generally. Indeed, the collection came to serve as a guide of sorts to where the growing subfield had been and where it was headed. In the decade since, the books that have appeared in this series have more than added to the debate; they have pushed its edges in new directions. The clearest sign that the field is still healthy is that recent books in our series have argued directly with the conclusions of the first books. Sutter and Manganiello's book lit the match.

Atlantic Environments and the American South is an anthology with a similar purpose and possibility. Much like the earlier book, this volume elegantly and persuasively puts together two fields that have mostly looked past each other. In this case the offending disciplines are environmental history and Atlantic history, although the combination of the two seems a natural one. Both fields developed along the same timeline, only reaching maturity in recent years. Both fields seek to escape the rigid boundaries of the nation-state to create fresh spatial and temporal contexts. And both fields eschew disciplinary and historiographical divisions, preferring more innovative perspectives that can accommodate multiple layers of analysis, geographical orientations, and chronologies. Indeed, the way the Atlantic Ocean acted as a "watery highway" for plants, animals, diseases, people, and ideas of extraordinarily disparate ecosystems almost demands an environmental perspective, as successive waves of navigation, colonization, settlement, and displacement completely transformed all four landmasses surrounding it. Nevertheless, the fields have grown independently over the past two decades and have done so within different historiographical orbits. This collection is all the more pathbreaking as a result.

Whereas the earlier collection brought together previously published journal articles, this book started from scratch. Thomas Blake Earle and D. Andrew Johnson began not with a book proposal but with a conference invitation. The goal was to make people who had not talked to one another do so. The symposium amounted to what Earle and Johnson modestly call "a practical example" of field cross-pollination, but the resulting book is so much more.

In the introduction, nine chapters, and afterword, the authors stake claim to questions and arguments that should be at the heart of new environmental examinations of the Atlantic world. But what these scholars do so well is not simply pore over the Atlantic with an environmental lens. Rather, they build a new vision of the Atlantic world with the environment as one of the main building blocks. Slavery, colonialism, and empire do not go away. Rather, they are questioned here as material, ecological projects as much as social, economic, and political ones. The domination and subordination of colonial lands and peoples initiated massive programs of extraction and exploitation that removed natural and human resources from the periphery for the benefit of the metropole. As this volume makes clear, the history of European imperialism is inseparable from global environmental change and, more specifically, the creation of the American South. Earle and Johnson divide the essays into four categories that keep at the heart of the book Atlantic studies' foundational insights but put the natural world in tandem: Slavery and Climate, Slavery and Landscape, Empire and Infrastructure, and Empire and Expertise.

The results are striking. The authors reveal the mines, plantations, and trade routes that have been crucial to Atlantic world historiography not only as places dependent on the natural world but as locations for the exchange of ideas about the environment. While landscapes as battlegrounds of cultural mediation and environmental knowledge suffuse the anthology, the settings for the essays are not limited to landscapes. Human bodies, diaries, and policy all become sites of negotiation between the physical and human worlds. Disease and climate, on the one hand, and writings and drawings about the South's environment on the other are comparably powerful agents when it comes to colonialization, slavery, and resistance.

Earle, Johnson, and all the authors in this collection push forward each of these respective historiographies by forcing engagement in new and meaningful ways. Atlantic world studies and southern environmental history are better for it.

James C. Giesen and Erin Stewart Mauldin
Editors, Environmental History and the American South Series

ACKNOWLEDGMENTS

This volume has its origins in a symposium held at Rice University in the spring of 2016. We extend our deep appreciation to the people and institutions that made both that event and this resulting collection conceivable. None of this would have been possible without the generous support of Rice University's History Department, the School of Humanities, and the Humanities Research Center. Special thanks go to History Department chair Alida Metcalf and School of Humanities dean Nicolas Shumway for supporting this project. The History Department at Rice was an excellent intellectual community that nurtured our initial idea to bring together scholars to discuss ideas that were in many ways born from our own research. It was humbling to have the support of so many other people who were so deeply invested in the same kinds of questions we were. Intellectually we owe much to Randal Hall and James Sidbury for their support and advice throughout the process. We would be remiss not to acknowledge that we followed in the footsteps of Rice graduate students before us who conceived, planned, and hosted similar symposiums. We extend our gratitude to Ben Wright and Zachary Dresser, and Whitney Nell Stewart and John Garrison Marks for providing models so worthy of emulation.

This book is the culmination of a conversation that started that weekend. We are grateful for all those who participated in the symposium, including those whose work we were unable to accommodate in this collection: Katherine Johnston, Christopher Willoughby, Christopher M. Church, Daniel S. Margolies, Andrew Patrick, Christopher Blakley, William Thomas Okie, Abby Schreiber, Christopher Morris, Georgia Carley, and Craig Colten. We also extend our gratitude to everyone else who participated in the symposium, including April Lee Hatfield, Kristin Wintersteen, Mark Goldberg, Andrew C. Baker, Alan Gallay, W. Jeffrey Bolster, and Paul S. Sutter, and our fellow Rice graduate students, Maria R. Montalvo, David Ponton, Cami Beekman, Christina Regelski, Keith D. McCall, Lauren Brand, and Cara Rodgers. Mart Stewart gave us excellent feedback on an early version of the manuscript. We also would like to thank Tara Johnson for her logistical and planning prowess and support.

We express gratitude to the contributors to this collection not only for sharing their work with us but also for their forbearance as this project has found its way through the review and editing process. Finally, we extend our warmest thanks to Environmental History and the American South series editor James C. Giesen, UGA Press editor Mick Gusinde-Duffy, and the staff at the University of Georgia Press who have made this book a reality.

*Atlantic Environments
and the American South*

Atlantic, Environmental, Southern

Toward a Confluence

THOMAS BLAKE EARLE AND D. ANDREW JOHNSON

In 1523 the king of France, Francis I, tasked the Italian navigator Giovanni da Verrazzano with exploring the eastern coast of North America in the hopes of finding a new route to the Pacific Ocean. Although Verrazzano never found the elusive passage to the Pacific, he did explore many of the coastal regions of North America between Cape Fear and Newfoundland. As with many European conquistadors and colonists, Verrazzano's early writings described the foreign environment the Europeans entered. Along the Carolina coast, just beyond the sandy shore, there were "fields and plains full of great forests" that were "so beautiful and delightful that they defy description." Trees such as palms, cypresses, and "other unknown varieties emit a sweet fragrance over a large area." Verrazzano was taken with the fauna as well, writing, "There is an abundance of animals, stags, deer, hares; and also, lakes and pools of running water with various types of bird, perfect for all delights and pleasures of the hunt." North Carolina was a western Eden.[1]

Similarly, in 1654, a decade before the first attempts to colonize Carolina, English Virginian Francis Yeardley described the lands of "South Virginia or Carolina" as "a most fertile, gallant, rich soil, flourishing in all the abundance of nature, especially in the rich mulberry and vine, serene air, and temperate clime." This "new world" rivaled "any place for rich land and stately timber of all sorts; a place indeed unacquainted with our Virginia's nipping frosts, no winter, or very little cold to be found there." Not to be outdone by successful Spanish and English colonial forays into the Southeast, the French also had designs on the southern reaches of North America. Following the 1682 expedition of René-Robert Cavelier, Sieur de La Salle, who traveled from New France down the Mississippi River to the Gulf of Mexico, Pierre Le Moyne d'Iberville tried to find the mouth of the river, but this time from the gulf. In 1699 d'Iberville attempted to find the main channel of the Mississippi without knowing precisely where his expedition was at any given time. Instead of sailing straight to modern Louisiana, the expedition followed the northern coastline of the Gulf of Mexico and explored locales along the way. Like Yeardley and Verrazzano, d'Iberville found flora worthy of note. In Mobile Bay he "found all kinds of trees, oak, elm, ash, pines, and other trees I do not know, many creepers, sweet-smelling violets, and other yellow flowers, horse-beans like those in

St. Domingue, hickories of a very thin bark, birch." At Biloxi Bay, fauna were added to his description: "tracks of turkeys; partridges, which are no bigger than quail; hares like the ones in France; some rather good oysters." No matter the European background, from the very beginning the denizens of the new, yet-to-be-conceived Atlantic world were keenly interested in its environments.[2]

Europeans, however, were not content to merely write about these "new" environments in such rhapsodic terms. Instead they set to work altering, using, exploiting, and commodifying the "pristine nature" that seemed to unfold before them. These processes, wrought by human agency, environmental context, and historical contingency, are ones that, while ubiquitous to the creation of the Atlantic world, are at times obscured in the literature by a focus on large-scale political and social transformations.[3] Even when historians find individual actors who offer fine-grained readings of these changes, they are most often employed in narratives that emphasize mobility and connections across political and legal boundaries, in addition to stories of cultural continuity and rupture across time and space.[4] Often ignored are the ecological factors that remained relatively immune to the construction of transatlantic empires and the displacement of millions of individuals whether by force or consent.[5]

This anthology places itself at the intersection of Atlantic, environmental, and southern historiographies. However, in doing so we must explore the divergent development of these fields in order to understand why so little historical scholarship exists at this confluence. The fields of Atlantic, environmental, and southern history developed in response to specific contexts and certain questions that have largely forestalled cross-field pollination. After reviewing the historiographical developments that left these fields estranged, we turn our attention to the benefits and crucial insights that a self-consciously Atlantic-environmental history of the American South could offer, closing with a detailed description of the logic and structure of this collection. By centering this project on a region, the American South—defined as the southeastern reaches of North America and the Caribbean—we can interrogate how European colonizers, Native Americans, and Africans interacted in and with the (sub)tropics, a place foreign to Europeans. This anthology is a practical example of what this kind of scholarship offers.

Two critical elements—inexorably intertwined—in the creation of a new Atlantic world beginning in the fifteenth century were the growth, however halting and uneven, of European colonial empires, and the attendant expansion of systems of coerced labor, epitomized most brutally by the transatlantic slave trade. An overwhelming historiographical focus on these entwined phenomena is in no way unexpected. These historical phenomena were astoundingly complex as historians still struggle to firmly grasp the myriad connections that spanned the ocean as easily, and frequently, as they did political, economic, and cultural borders. But this rich and ever-growing historiography often elides the environment as a central unit of analysis. On the face of it, the contention that these fields intersect very little may seem astounding. Over the last forty years, scholars of the Atlantic and the environment have offered some of the most dynamic and theoretically rich works the historical discipline has witnessed. Yet they remained largely estranged for reasons that are numerous and often genealogical. Atlantic history frequently embraces a wider optic that makes on-the-ground readings more difficult. And the focus on race and its construction is not always an obvious area of environmental inquiry. Furthermore, environmental history as a field is a child of the environmental movement of the twentieth century and has largely been concerned with topics such as conservation, preservation, public lands, and other distinctly American questions. Institutional and structural factors also inhibit the growth of a possible Atlantic environmental subfield as one would be hard-pressed to find journals, book series, or institutions to explicitly support the development of Atlantic, or even early modern, environmental history. These two fields have slowly inched toward each other and in doing so have generated a small but growing corpus of important works. This anthology continues this trend while calling for an explicitly self-identified environmental history of the Atlantic.[6]

Atlantic history, so often concerned with connections across the Atlantic Ocean in the aftermath of the Columbian accident of 1492, has been a driving force in the attempt to decenter nationalist narratives and better understand structural changes central to the four continents touching its shores. But Atlanticists have, to a large extent, been less interested in using environmental history as a central analytical tool than as a small piece in writing multivalent, sociocultural histories. Perhaps the most popular of these types of works are commodity histories where the site of resource extraction, whether Central American forests for mahogany, Caribbean islands for sugar, or Madeira for wine, offers the initial context from which goods traveled across the Atlantic and in the process acquired various cultural meanings. Yet such a trend is not indicative of the melding of environmental and Atlantic historiographies. Our goal is to emphasize this dialogue. Both fields are well situated to view historical processes and events from a broad perspective. Both fields follow stories that often, and necessarily, transgress economic, political, and cultural boundaries. And both fields have the ability to scale historical inquiry up or down (or up and down) depending on the questions under consideration. We are arguing that the divergent paths of environmental and Atlantic historiographies are due to intellectual inertia from decades past where scholars in each burgeoning field were interested in different problems.[7]

Focusing on cultural histories of groups either flung across the Atlantic or attempting to survive and reconstitute themselves in the face of colonialism, Atlanticists have long been more likely to study the origins of race or the changing ideas of Atlantic religions than to study fisheries in the North Atlantic or the political ecology of pearl divers in colonial Venezuela. Likewise, many environmental histories, following a separate genealogy, embraced a particularly materialist bent, and in many cases employed a scientifically derived archive that had little to add to the Atlantic discourse. But since the 1980s, these fields have matured such that there have been important, though not systematic, intersections. Scholars such as Richard Grove, Marcy Norton, Virginia DeJohn Anderson, and Elinor Melville have managed to bridge these discourses, but in sum, little work has explicitly been Atlantic environmental history.[8]

Both environmental and Atlantic historical fields, however, share a genealogical precedent in the magisterial work of Fernand Braudel. By thinking of the Mediterranean as a system, Braudel offered a compelling intellectual forebear to later Atlantic histories, whether "consciously or subconsciously," as Nicholas Canny has written. Likewise, by grounding his entire two-volume study of "the Age of Philip II" in geography and environmental cycles, Braudel also was a precursor to the more explicitly materialist strands of environmental history as practiced by scholars such as Alfred Crosby and Donald Worster; indeed, the first part of *The Mediterranean* was titled "The Role of the Environment." In this *historie totale*, time was to be measured on three scales: geographical, social, and individual. But although incipient environmental and Atlantic historians concentrated on aspects of the work of Braudel—and other participants in the *Annales* historiography—their historical inquiries diverged. More recently, however, they have fallen back into each other's orbit.[9]

To foster this dialogue, two traditional focuses of Atlantic history—slavery and empire—can particularly benefit from environmental perspectives. The activities carried out by Atlantic agents—mineral extraction, plantation agriculture, commercial exchange—were at their base environmentally oriented endeavors that depended on enslaved or otherwise coerced labor and imperial and transimperial frameworks. Tobacco farms in Virginia, sugar plantations in Jamaica, silver mines in Mexico, and wharves in Baltimore were but a few of the sites where enslaved labor and colonial processes were applied in ways that required environmental knowledge and consequently created environmental transformations. While certainly the complexity of the Atlantic or the environment cannot be so easily contained within such pithy, if extraordinarily complex, framings as slavery and empire, these processes brought peoples, societies, cultures, economies, and political structures into direct contact with specific environmental circumstances. This anthology explicates that confluence.

Like other places in the Atlantic, the American South was shaped by enslaved labor and imperial regimes. But the unique environments of the American South guided what shape the region would take. European colonizers, particularly the English, French, and Dutch, realized that as they approached the tropics, the environments of North America deviated from more familiar boreal environs that approximated their European homelands. More southerly regions gave colonists more to learn environmentally, but also more exotic possibilities than did areas farther north. Claimed by British, French, Spanish, and later American imperial systems; inhabited by a diverse array of Native American peoples; and home to African and African American populations, the overwhelming majority of whom were enslaved, the southeastern reaches of North America came to possess a unique ecology. As goods, commodities, and peoples moved into and out of this expansive region—with intellectual traditions and cultural assumptions as unavoidable stowaways—the cultural and physical ecologies were subject to various transformations. Understandings of how the bodies of enslaved peoples fit into American contexts shifted with understandings of American climates. Places far removed from the ocean's littoral, like the lower reaches of the Mississippi River valley, were incorporated, in fits and starts, into the Atlantic economy. Even commonly accepted names of environmental features shifted with colonial masters. The early South was indeed a place well suited to examining the collision of Atlantic processes and varied environmental contexts, even if the literature has not kept apace.

Historians of the Atlantic have often planted their stories in the South.[10] Environmental historians, however, until recently have been less likely to do so.[11] The reasons for this are varied. For one, the animating spirit of much early environmental history was contemporary politics, yet the South was a late comer to environmentalism.[12] Or perhaps, more appropriately, the environmental movement was a latecomer to the South, being concerned instead with maintaining the beauty of "wild" or "pristine" lands in the West, protecting various charismatic megafauna, or stemming the tide of the world's exploding population. Furthermore, southern historians have been slow to embrace environmental analyses, as such a lens seemed, until recently, to offer little new insight into the mainstays of the field—slavery, the Civil War, the Jim Crow era, and civil rights. But southern histories have shunned the environmental label because many of them have, paradoxically enough, always been environmental. On the seventy-fifth anniversary of the *Journal of Southern History*, Christopher Morris offered an appraisal of the state of nature in the discipline. From one vantage, so little work claimed the environmental mantle because the importance of the region's environment was often assumed, in, for example, studies of agriculture. Morris concludes that a wide swath of the literature simply fails to seriously interrogate the connection between environment and region. Instead, this work uncritically accepts or disavows the notion that environments impinge on southern history.[13]

Paul S. Sutter also eloquently identifies the constraints and difficulties of doing environmental history in and of the South. Environmental determinism, the notion that the South was the way it was because of nature alone, has held fast in southern historiographical traditions. The social and historiographical problems of race and environmental determinism have made southern historians leery of environmental analysis. Distancing from this tradition has, in Sutter's view, become the "burden" of southern environmental history. Writing the environmental history of the region forces historians to "reintroduce the environment as a causal force," while avoiding the facile "determinisms of the past."[14] Fortunately, newer generations of southern and environmental historians have walked this path with grace.

Southern environmental history has recently developed into a robust and dynamic subfield. The environment is by no means the linchpin of southern historical inquiry, but with a growing cohort of self-identified southern environmental historians and the institutional backing of a respected and growing book series, the efficacy of the subfield is no longer questioned. Practitioners have written explicitly environmental histories of the South.[15] In more recent years, they have even focused the environmental lens on the most fundamental aspects of southern history. Yet these studies largely remain bounded and constrained by the historical weight of the borders of the Confederate States of America, a teleology we aim to avoid.[16]

The Atlantic paradigm has largely failed to explicitly influence the coterie of southern environmental historians. Historically produced yet in many ways arbitrary intradisciplinary demarcations may explain why there are no self-conscious Atlantic environmental histories of the South, but the confluence of these fields promises rich scholarship, of which the symposium that spawned this anthology is but an entrée into a larger conversation and potentially a fruitful subfield.

The environment served as the connective tissue between the South and the Atlantic world. As we understand it, the South and the Atlantic are not two competing geographies. Instead, the Atlantic world operated as a series of processes that functioned in and on the specific environments of the South. Yet those ligaments have heretofore remained in large part uninterrogated. Environmental analysis, the central analytic tool of the field, has undergone revision as the field has developed over the past few decades. In an early appraisal of the emergent field, Richard White expressed trepidation for an environmental history based exclusively on intellectual and political frameworks.[17] If nature was something only made in the human mind, then, White observed that "thought about nature, in the end, only reflects other cultural values. The result, however, is often cultural solipsism since humans never see nature; all they see is themselves." In White's estimation Donald Worster's work represented a way forward in observing how such work showed how "nature was not just something being thought about; it was the sum of natural processes which altered and changed human lives."[18] Worster himself would soon offer a forceful proscription of conflating human culture and the seemingly natural world beyond.

Reflecting environmental history's growing legitimacy in the historical discipline, Donald Worster penned the central article in a roundtable on the subject published in the *Journal of American History* in 1990. In it Worster made the case that the field should work toward explicating the "autonomous, independent energies that do not derive from the drives and inventions of any culture." Reflecting the previous couple decades of nascent environmental history—what could be termed the field's first generation—Worster proclaimed that "most environmental historians would argue that the distinction [between the natural and cultural] is worth keeping, for it reminds us that not all the forces at work in the world emanate from humans."[19] Such a proclamation did not, however, shape the field's research agenda for the coming years. Instead, scholars became deeply invested in complicating and contextualizing nature as a cultural construction at the center of the developing historiography. William Cronon's words proved to be more prophetic in setting the research agenda with the simple observation that "'nature' is not nearly so natural as it seems," thus requiring studies to be more aware of cultural factors.[20]

The decades that succeeded Worster's and Cronon's grappling with the field's central analytical problems witnessed environmental history's impressive growth. But, as Paul Sutter outlined in the *Journal of American History*'s *re*appraisal in 2013, environmental history has deviated little from the goal of complicating nature as a unit of analysis. Hybridity has become a core concept as the accepted wisdom holds that environments encompass the natural and the cultural and that no landscapes are beyond the influence of human culture. Despite the vigor that hybridity introduced to the field, Sutter does relent that, if taken too far, the concept could become analytically dull since, with all environments being hybrid, useful distinctions are increasingly difficult to make. But despite Sutter's reasonable misgivings, or angst as he would later describe it, the hybrid turn irrevocably tied humans to their contexts—contexts that existed at points of overlap of multiple, and at times competing, cultures and ecologies. It is this lesson that makes environmental history so useful to Atlantic studies.[21]

Much of Atlantic history is partially environmental, but scholars need to adopt an explicitly environmental perspective. Despite Douglas R. Weiner's confident 2005 declaration that environmental history has become a "very big tent," much remains outside. Studies of early America and the Atlantic more broadly stand as the most glaring examples.[22] Environmental history's focus on "hybridity" serves the analytical needs of Atlantic history, too. In fact, Jorge Cañizares-Esguerra and Benjamin Breen used the very same term in their recent call for Atlanticists to go beyond narrowly defined national and imperial definitions of Atlantic systems. Working against teleological understandings of competing Atlantic entities, Cañizares-Esguerra and Breen persuasively suggest that the commercial, political, and cultural processes that defined the Atlantic were never guided by any single group, European, African, or American, nor were the consequences of these processes ever confined by imperial, national, or linguistic boundaries. Simply put, Cañizares-Esguerra and Breen observe that "differences in national imperial traditions appear increasingly insignificant relative to the contingencies of time and space. In lieu of a national Atlantic model, then, we suggest that future research considers each space as shot through with a multiplicity of entangled actors and agendas."[23] Environmental agents should be added to that list of actors. The field of environmental history has long recognized the ways environments disregard arbitrary boundaries. Stretching across borders—cultural, political, and economic—makes environments and their constructed natures indispensable to the hybridity that is becoming a central notion in Atlantic history. Fusing Atlantic topics and environmental approaches does more than merely fill a historiographical gap; it answers new questions and solves new problems.

The essays that follow came from a symposium we hosted at Rice University in the spring of 2016. We have structured the anthology into two parts: Slavery and Empire. While slavery and empire were not unique to the early modern period or the advent of the Atlantic system, when properly historicized these twin phenomena were central to the creation of Atlantic worlds and what would emerge as the American South. The setting of southeastern North America gives this collection a degree of geographic coherence, but it does not imply that the South was particular in bringing Atlantic forces to specific environments. Furthermore, the imperial lens and the employment of enslaved labor are optics uniquely suited to analyzing and understanding the environmental transformations that resulted from the increasingly close relationship of the lands that made up the Atlantic littoral. While the bifurcation of slavery and empire obscures their deeply shared historical contingency, if not their bald coconstitutive natures, they are appropriate themes to structure what might otherwise be a cacophonous mixing of actors, agendas, and contexts.

The first half of the anthology focuses on how the environments of the American South were uniquely influenced by the labor of enslaved African and Indigenous peoples. The specific environmental context of the South influenced not only the material realities of enslaved peoples but also how Euro-Americans understood how human bodies responded to this "new" part of the Atlantic world.

Part I traces ideas about slavery and climate in the Anglo-American Atlantic. Climate was a central aspect that related bondage and the environment in the South and the Atlantic-wide discourse surrounding the development of racialized slavery. The expansion of European empires in the hot climates of the Americas forced serious intellectual appraisals of how human bodies related to their environments. This intellectual discourse informed how both Europeans and Africans altered their New World environments and the resulting conditions both groups were forced to contend with, albeit unequally. Sean Morey Smith explores how understandings of specific climates in the British Atlantic during the seventeenth and eighteenth centuries were mediated by slavery and economic interest. Smith demonstrates that the colonies of South Carolina and Georgia were classified as "hot" in the minds of the British only when they joined their West Indian counterparts in embracing the enslavement of Africans, who they insisted were better equipped to contend with such heat. Elaine LaFay's contribution to section 1 brings the interplay of bondage and climate to the nineteenth century while rooting the experiences of both masters and the enslaved in the climatic realties of the American South. LaFay's analysis of ventilation on plantations in the antebellum South is not confined to an elite intellectual discourse. Instead, ideas about ventilation and air circulation became sites of contestation between planters seeking to create a modern, rationalized, and above all profitable plantation enterprise, and the enslaved who associated airflow and its control with resistance and freedom. This contest was seen in the physical ordering of the plantation as the siting and construction of slave dwellings was yet another struggle between slaver and enslaved, mastery and resistance.

Part II interrogates the intersection of colonial slavery and plantation landscapes. Landscapes, defined here as culturally mediated spaces, were changed in the process of European colonialism in drastic ways. Indeed, the conceptualization and curation of space was one of the signal battlegrounds over which Europeans fought for control over the inhabitants of Africa and the Americas. Europeans supplanted Native American agroecological landscapes in what Carolyn Merchant calls a "colonial ecological revolution." Historians such as Merchant, William Cronon, and Timothy Silver studied these processes in seminal works of environmental history. Continuing to follow the thread of climate, Matthew Mulcahy foregrounds drought in his discussion of the limits of landscape curation in the British Greater Caribbean. Colonists developed plantation landscapes based on sugar, to the detriment of sustenance, in many colonial outposts in the Caribbean, and paid dearly for it when drought showed the limits of human environmental control. Planters imagined themselves as part of a larger system whereby provisioning for many smaller Caribbean islands was produced in other locales, but as Mulcahy argues, drought and the isolation of warfare made the Greater Caribbean colonies even more susceptible to times of dearth than were the already-dangerous Lowcountry plantation regions. Mulcahy demonstrates that drought was a pervasive influence on the lives of enslaved peoples who were forced to toil away in these landscapes. Ironically, drought proved far more effective in sowing the seeds of unrest, even though British planters held a visceral, if unfounded, fear of hurricanes for that very reason.[24]

Hayley Negrin follows, taking English colonial conquest and adding an important new piece to these well-trodden scholarly debates concerning the conquest of Virginia and Carolina—namely, the domination of Native American women. In order for the English colonizers to justify dispossessing Native American peoples, they had to control those who controlled native landscapes: women. Therefore, taking and enslaving Native American women was central to the discourse justifying the creation of English-conceived landscapes. In the Greater Caribbean, the Chesapeake, and the Lowcountry, control and manipulation of landscape was central to how Europeans understood these environments.

The second half of the anthology turns to the analytic of empire. With an eye toward the pervasive influence of empires as institutions fostering the intermingling of nature and culture across the Atlantic, the concept and reality of infrastructure gives shape to part III. In recent years anthropologists have developed infrastructure as a concept, concluding that infrastructure is not just things—roads, bridges, water pipes, and IT networks—but also the relationship between things with the ability to influence, if not generate, those relations. As Ashley Carse observes, infrastructures "operate at material and poetic registers" while serving as important loci of interaction between the human and nonhuman worlds.[25] Imperial arrangements created and exploited infrastructure and its attendant political, economic, and cultural relations. Intriguingly, infrastructure is, and has been, deeply embedded in the environment and is vital in creating the distinction between nature and culture.[26] Shipping routes, rivers, and roads—at their base the core infrastructure of the early modern Atlantic—made possible the work of empires but were themselves incredibly fragile entities, prone to leakages, decay, and ruin.[27] Natural and manmade infrastructures were at best imperfect agents of empire. Contributions from Bradford Wood and Frances Kolb demonstrate how these inefficiencies influenced Atlantic and environmental interactions.

Bradford J. Wood's contribution explores the breakdown of infrastructure. Deploying the frame "ulterior Atlantic," Wood describes colonial North Carolina as a place near—and seemingly integrated with—the Atlantic yet distinct from it, as the colony was difficult to access because of an irregular coast and a lack of natural ports. This lack of effective infrastructure had important economic and political implications. Because early North Carolinians were unable to easily access far-flung markets, the colonial environment was not transformed into a plantation landscape. Instead, the economy of early North Carolina was marked by local consumption and the production of lumber and naval stores that could justify inflated transportation costs. The inability of colonial leaders to compensate for this infrastructural shortcoming limited the imperial landscape in which they could envision the colony participating.

In her essay, Frances Kolb explores how entrepreneurial individuals exploited natural infrastructures to facilitate commercial expansion. Beginning with the conclusion of the Seven Years' War, British traders in the Lower Mississippi Valley used the complex waterways of the region to infiltrate an area once controlled primarily by French merchants. Using knowledge of the environment and imperial asymmetries created by the Mississippi borderland, British merchants were successful in outmaneuvering their Spanish counterparts. In both North Carolina and the Lower Mississippi, the environments of southeastern North America were transformed or used in ways facilitated by the infrastructural arrangements imperial regimes attempted to control, or in some cases, overcome.

Euro-American empire building consisted of conquistadors armed with exotic animals, weapons, microbes, and coerced laborers from all over the globe. But building empires also required environmental knowledge. Firsthand knowledge of the southeastern environment guided colonialism on the ground. Some imperial agents, therefore, were people who professed environmental expertise in colonial lands, the topic of part IV. European colonial strategists needed environmental knowledge to support their imperial forays. This demand opened up an avenue for some colonial agents—whether in an official capacity or not—to claim environmental expertise on the basis of their lived experience. An epistemological shift toward empiricism meant that those who had been there, those who had seen exotic locales, and those who had experienced the colonial world could be deemed experts on colonial landscapes.

The three essays in the fourth part each involve Europeans vying for expertise on colonial environments, many times crossing both imperial and environmental borders. When English imperial agents began securing toeholds across the Caribbean and the Atlantic coast of North America, they came into environments that had not only been occupied and altered by Native peoples for millennia but had already been subjected to other European colonizing schemes. Both Melissa N. Morris and Keith Pluymers demonstrate the degree to which English colonial projects were built on information inherited or assumed from earlier Spanish endeavors. Morris's study of tobacco cultivation in early Virginia exposes how English colonial strategists sought to directly emulate Spain's early success, not just with attempts to find rich mineral deposits, but by aping the agricultural expertise necessary to grow tobacco in the Chesapeake. As Morris demonstrates, this was not a simple transfer of knowledge from Spanish to English imperial agents; it was the result of a complex series of interactions between Spanish and English partisans, and the Native American and African peoples they exploited in the process. Pluymers likewise focuses on the importance of Spanish exemplars in his study of Bermuda. English colonial agents assumed that the tiny island was in environment and in prospects similar to Spanish holdings in the Caribbean and looked to import the flora and enslaved labor that made the Iberian colonies so profitable. Anglo-Bermudians claimed expertise from their study of and experiences with Spain's colonies, using such knowledge to shape the environment of the island. Bermuda would itself serve as a model for future imperial enterprises, this time in Virginia. In all, Morris and Pluymers each demonstrate how environmental knowledge and expertise moved across the Atlantic, and like environmental contexts they were rarely confined by imperial borders.

The final essay in the section, that by Peter C. Messer, looks at the question of environmental expertise at a much smaller scale in a study of William Bartram. For Messer, Bartram's writing as represented in his 1791 *Travels* represented a careful balance of aesthetics and science. While moved by the beauty and sublimity of the southeastern landscape, Bartram tempered his writing with appeals to the ongoing transatlantic discourse of Linnaean taxonomies in an effort to avoid the decadence and vice of overwhelming beauty. Bartram sought to keep beauty within reason. Through his travels, Bartram assumed the mantle of expert on places in the Southeast soon to be incorporated into the new American imperium. Messer demonstrates that claims to experience and firsthand knowledge underwrote further claims to expertise and its potential for political influence. Messer shows that firsthand knowledge and the role of the expert are essential in understanding environments.

Atlantic and environmental historiographies have rarely participated in a self-conscious dialogue. So many Atlantic processes, from mineral extraction, to plantation agriculture, to transatlantic commerce, were deeply implicated in the human relationship with specific environments. Reaching beyond these relatively narrow disciplinary boundaries has the potential to invigorate all of these fields of study. As the essays in this collection show, exciting and innovative research is being done at this confluence and promises to be but the start of a dynamic conversation. These essays point the way forward by showing the distinctly environmental dimensions of the Atlantic world and illuminating the many ways in which the political, economic, and cultural elements of lived human experiences were in an all-too-often overlooked relationship with their environmental contexts. In a time of such dire environmental concerns, this connection cannot be so lightly ignored.

NOTES

1. Giovanni da Verrazzano, *The Voyages of Giovanni da Verrazzano, 1524–1528*, ed. Lawrence C. Wroth (New Haven, Conn.: Yale University Press, 1970), 134–35.

2. "Francis Yeardley's Narrative of Excursions into Carolina, 1654," in Alexander S. Salley Jr., *Narratives of Early Carolina, 1650–1708* (New York: C. Scribner's Sons, 1911), 25; Journal of Pierre Le Moyne d'Iberville, 1699, in *Iberville's Gulf Journals* (Tuscaloosa: University of Alabama Press, 1981), 39, 43. On the creation of the concept of the Atlantic as an ocean, see Joyce Chaplin, "The Atlantic Ocean and Its Contemporary Meanings, 1492–1808," in *Atlantic History: A Critical Appraisal*, ed. Jack P. Greene and Philip D. Morgan (New York: Oxford University Press, 2008).

3. J. H. Elliott, *Empires of the Atlantic World: Britain and Spain in America, 1492–1830* (New Haven, Conn.: Yale University Press, 2006); Ira Berlin, *Many Thousands Gone: The First Two Centuries of Slavery in North America* (Cambridge: Belknap Press of Harvard University Press, 1998); P. J. Marshall, *The Making and Unmaking of Empires: Britain, India, and America, c. 1750–1783* (New York: Oxford University Press, 2005); Robin Blackburn, *The American Crucible: Slavery, Emancipation, and Human Rights* (London: Verso, 2011); Laura Benton, *Law and Colonial Cultures: Legal Regimes in World History, 1400–1900* (New York: Cambridge University Press, 2002); David Brion Davis, *Inhuman Bondage: The Rise and Fall of Slavery in the New World* (New York: Oxford University Press, 2006).

4. David Hancock, *Citizens of the World: London Merchants and the Integration of the British Atlantic Community, 1735–1785* (New York: Cambridge University Press, 1995); W. Jeffrey Bolster, *Black Jacks: African American Seamen in the Age of Sail* (Cambridge, Mass.: Harvard University Press, 1997); Randy J. Sparks, *The Two Princes of Calabar: An Eighteenth-Century Atlantic Odyssey* (Cambridge, Mass.: Harvard University Press, 2004); James H. Sweet, *Domingos Alvares, African Healing, and the Intellectual History of the Atlantic World* (Chapel Hill: University of North Carolina Press, 2011); Martha Hodes, *The Sea Captain's Wife: A True Story of Love, Race, and War in the Nineteenth Century* (New York: W. W. Norton, 2006); Rebecca J. Scott and Jean M. Hebrard, *Freedom Papers: An*

Atlantic Odyssey in the Age of Emancipation (Cambridge, Mass.: Harvard University Press, 2012); Roquinaldo Ferreira, *Cross-Cultural Exchange in the Atlantic World: Angola and Brazil during the Era of the Slave Trade* (New York: Cambridge University Press, 2012).

5. But this is not to say that empires did not use, exploit, and alter ecological boundaries. See Alfred Crosby, *Ecological Imperialism: The Biological Expansion of Europe, 900–1900* (New York: Cambridge University Press, 1986).

6. Existing literature that exemplifies a nascent Atlantic environmental history include Warren Dean, *With Broadax and Firebrand: The Destruction of the Brazilian Atlantic Forest* (Berkeley: University of California Press, 1995); Judith Carney, *Black Rice: The African Origins of Rice Cultivation in the Americas* (Cambridge, Mass.: Harvard University Press, 2002); Virginia DeJohn Anderson, *Creatures of Empire: How Domestic Animals Transformed Early America* (New York: Oxford University Press, 2004); Matthew Mulcahy, *Hurricanes and Society in the British Great Caribbean, 1624–1783* (Baltimore: Johns Hopkins University Press, 2006); Edda Fields-Black, *Deep Roots: Rice Farmers in West Africa and the African Diaspora* (Bloomington: Indiana University Press, 2008); J. R. McNeill, *Mosquito Empires: Ecology and War in the Great Caribbean, 1620–1914* (New York: Cambridge University Press, 2010); Pekka Hämäläinen, "The Politics of Grass: European Expansion, Ecological Change, and Indigenous Power in the Southwest Borderlands," *William and Mary Quarterly* 67, no. 2 (2010): 173–208; Katherine A. Grandjean, "New World Tempests: Environment, Scarcity, and the Coming of the Pequot War," *William and Mary Quarterly* 68, no. 1 (2011): 75–100; Keith Pluymers, "Taming the Wilderness in Sixteenth- and Seventeenth-Century Ireland and Virginia," *Environmental History* 16, no. 4 (2011): 610–32; W. Jeffrey Bolster, *The Mortal Sea: Fishing the Atlantic in the Age of Sail* (Cambridge, Mass.: Harvard University Press, 2012); Marcy Norton, "The Chicken or the Iegue: Human-Animal Relationships and the Columbian Exchange," *American Historical Review* 120, no. 1 (February 2015): 28–60; Natale Zappia, "Revolutions in the Grass: Energy and Food Systems in Continental North America, 1763–1848," *Environmental History* 21, no. 1 (2016): 30–53; Keith Pluymers, "Atlantic Iron: Wood Scarcity and the Political Ecology of Early English Expansion," *William and Mary Quarterly* 73, no. 3 (2016): 389–426; Anya Zilberstein, *A Temperate Empire: Making Climate Change in Early America* (New York: Oxford University Press, 2016); Matthew Mulcahy and Stuart Schwartz, "Nature's Battalions: Insects as Agricultural Pests in the Early Modern Caribbean," *William and Mary Quarterly* 75, no. 3 (2018): 433–64; Molly A. Warsh, *American Baroque: Pearls and the Nature of Empire, 1492–1700* (Chapel Hill: Omohundro Institute of Early American History and Culture and University of North Carolina Press, 2018); Peter C. Mancall, *Nature and Culture in the Early Modern Atlantic* (Philadelphia: University of Pennsylvania Press, 2018).

A survey on the literature in the flagship journal, *Environmental History*, offers very few examples of articles we would consider to be a part of the Atlantic historiography. Atlantic environmental articles have been much more likely to appear—though still rare—in the *William and Mary Quarterly* or the *American Historical Review*. Recent field-defining compilations show just how little cross-field engagement there is. *The Princeton Companion to Atlantic History* shows little substantive engagement with environmental topics as articles pertaining to the environment represent less than 10 percent of the total, and those articles all rely on a relatively small number of monographs, including works by Judith Carney, William Cronon, Alfred Crosby, J. R. McNeill, and Marcy Norton. For a similar critique of early American history, see James D. Rice, "Early American Environmental Histories,"

William and Mary Quarterly 75, no. 3 (2018): 401–32. The environmental historiography seems even less inclined to include the Atlantic as the recent *Oxford Handbook of Environmental History* does not include a single entry on the Atlantic. See Joseph C. Miller, Vincent Brown, Jorge Cañizares-Esguerra, Laurent Dubois, and Karen Ordahl Kupperman, eds., *The Princeton Companion to Atlantic History* (Princeton, N.J.: Princeton University Press, 2015); Andrew C. Isenberg, ed., *The Oxford Handbook of Environmental History* (New York: Oxford University Press, 2014).

7. Sweet, *Domingos Alvares*; Ferreira, *Cross-Cultural Exchange*. Some of the best examples of commodities histories are Sidney W. Mintz, *Sweetness and Power: The Place of Sugar in Modern History* (New York: Penguin Books, 1986); Marcy Norton, *Sacred Gifts, Profane Pleasures: A History of Tobacco and Chocolate in the Atlantic World* (Ithaca, N.Y.: Cornell University Press, 2008); David Hancock, *Oceans of Wine: Madeira and the Organization of the Atlantic World, 1640–1815* (New Haven, Conn.: Yale University Press, 2009); Jennifer L. Anderson, *Mahogany: The Costs of Luxury in Early America* (Cambridge, Mass.: Harvard University Press, 2012).

Interestingly, David Armitage and Michael J. Braddock's collection on British Atlantic history is largely broken down along a cultural framework (race, gender, religion, science), eliding the environment, while Armitage and Alison Bashford's recent collection on the more recent subfield of Pacific histories does include a chapter on environments. See Armitage and Braddock, eds., *The British Atlantic World, 1500–1800* (New York: Palgrave Macmillan, 2002); Ryan Tucker Jones, "The Environment," in *Pacific Histories: Ocean, Land, People*, ed. David Armitage and Alison Bashford (New York: Palgrave Macmillan, 2014). Perhaps Pacific world histories have developed free of some of the intellectual baggage that accompanied the maturation of the Atlantic, thus allowing historians of the Pacific to embrace the environmental angle, which was itself, as a field, better developed as the Pacific has come about as a topic of historical inquiry. See David Igler, *The Great Ocean: Pacific Worlds from Captain Cook to the Gold Rush* (New York: Oxford University Press, 2013); Gregory T. Cushman, *Guano and the Opening of the Pacific World: A Global Ecological History* (New York: Cambridge University Press, 2013); Matt K. Matsuda, *Pacific Worlds: A History of Seas, Peoples, and Cultures* (New York: Cambridge University Press, 2012).

8. Warsh, *American Baroque*; Molly Warsh, "A Political Ecology in the Early Spanish Caribbean," *William and Mary Quarterly* 71, no. 4 (2014): 517–48. On Atlantic fisheries, see Bolster, *Mortal Sea*. In a recent forum titled "History Meets Biology," the authors argue that just as biologists became more aware of thinking historically, especially after the publication of E. O. Wilson's *Sociobiology* in 1975, historians were growing more wary of biological—read as essential—modes of inquiry: "the impact of the sociobiology controversy was amplified by the fact that historians, anthropologists, and literary scholars were moving in the opposite direction [from sociobiologists]. Gender and sexuality were being denaturalized, and Geertzian hermeneutics was reshaping the analysis of social action. Culture was ascendant, and its power to reshape human thought, action, and emotions became a rallying cry, a way to resist the unwelcome encroachments of biology." Biology and history, it seems, were ships passing in the night. See the forum "History Meets Biology" in *American Historical Review* 119, no. 5 (December 2014): 1492–1629.

9. Fernand Braudel, *The Mediterranean and the Mediterranean World in the Age of Philip II* (New York: Harper & Row, 1972–73), 20–21, 25–355; Braudel, *Civilization and Capitalism, 15th–18th Century* (New York: Harper & Row, 1982); Braudel, "History of the Social

Sciences: The *Longue Durée*," in *On History* (Chicago: University of Chicago Press, 1980), 25–54; Donald Worster, *Dust Bowl: The Southern Plains in the 1930s* (New York: Oxford University Press, 1979); Worster, *Rivers of Empire: Water, Aridity, and the Growth of the American West* (New York: Oxford University Press, 1985); Alfred W. Crosby, "Virgin Soil Epidemics as a Factor in the Aboriginal Depopulation in America," *William and Mary Quarterly* 33, no. 2 (1976): 289–99; Crosby, *The Columbian Exchange: Biological and Cultural Consequences of 1492* (Westport, Conn.: Greenwood, 1973); Crosby, *Ecological Imperialism: The Biological Expansion of Europe, 900–1900* (New York: Cambridge University Press, 1986); Nicholas Canny, "Writing Atlantic History; Or, Reconfiguring the History of Colonial British America," *Journal of American History* 86, no. 3 (1999): 1108.

10. Some examples of southern Atlantic history include James Sidbury, *Ploughshares into Swords: Race, Rebellion, and Identity in Gabriel's Virginia, 1730–1810* (New York: Cambridge University Press, 1997); Philip D. Morgan, *Slave Counterpoint: Black Culture in the Eighteenth-Century Chesapeake and Lowcountry* (Chapel Hill: University of North Carolina Press, 1998); Michael A. Gomez, *Exchanging Our Country Marks: The Transformation of African Identities in the Colonial and Antebellum South* (Chapel Hill: University of North Carolina Press, 1998); Jennifer L. Morgan, *Laboring Women: Reproduction and Gender in New World Slavery* (Philadelphia: University of Pennsylvania Press, 2004); April Lee Hatfield, *Atlantic Virginia: Intercolonial Relations in the Seventeenth Century* (Philadelphia: University of Pennsylvania Press, 2007); Stephanie E. Smallwood, *Saltwater Slavery: A Middle Passage from Africa to American Diaspora* (Cambridge, Mass.: Harvard University Press, 2008); Emma Hart, *Building Charleston: Town and Society in the Eighteenth-Century British Atlantic World* (Charlottesville: University of Virginia Press, 2009); Ras Michael Brown, *African-Atlantic Cultures and the South Carolina Lowcountry* (New York: Cambridge University Press, 2012); Sophie White, *Wild Frenchmen and Frenchified Indians: Material Culture and Race in Colonial Louisiana* (Philadelphia: University of Pennsylvania Press, 2012); Richard S. Dunn, *A Tale of Two Plantations: Slave Life and Labor in Jamaica and Virginia* (Cambridge, Mass.: Harvard University Press, 2014); Alejandra Dubcovsky, *Informed Power: Communication in the Early American South* (Cambridge, Mass.: Harvard University Press, 2016).

11. These early southern environmental histories still loom large in the field. See Albert E. Cowdrey, *This Land, This South: An Environmental History* (Lexington: University Press of Kentucky, 1983); Timothy Silver, *A New Face on the Countryside: Indian, Colonists, and Slaves in South Atlantic Forests, 1500–1800* (New York: Cambridge University Press, 1990); Jack Temple Kirby, *Poquosin: A Study of Rural Landscape and Society* (Chapel Hill: University of North Carolina Press, 1995); Mart A. Stewart, *"What Nature Suffers to Groe": Life, Labor, and Landscape on the Georgia Coast, 1680–1920* (Athens: University of Georgia Press, 1996).

12. In fact, the first major work concerning environmental politics in the South was not written by a historian. See Robert D. Bullard, *Dumping in Dixie: Race, Class and Environmental Quality* (Boulder, Colo.: Westview, 1990).

13. Christopher Morris, "A More Southern Environmental History," *Journal of Southern History* 75 (August 2009): 586–87. Classic works of southern agricultural history include Avery Odelle Craven, *Soil Exhaustion as a Factor in the Agricultural History of Virginia and Maryland, 1606–1860* (Urbana: University of Illinois Press, 1926); Ulrich Bonnell Phillips, *Life and Labor in the Old South* (Boston: Little, Brown, 1929); L. C. Gray and Esther Katherine Thompson, *History of Agriculture in the Southern United States to 1860* (Gloucester, Mass.: Peter Smith, 1958).

14. Paul S. Sutter, *Let Us Now Praise Famous Gullies: Providence Canyon and the Soils of the South* (Athens: University of Georgia Press, 2015), 9; Sutter, "No More the Backward Region: Southern Environmental History Comes of Age," in *Environmental History and the American South: A Reader*, ed. Paul S. Sutter and Christopher J. Manganiello (Athens: University of Georgia Press, 2009), 2–3.

15. Kathryn Newfont, *Blue Ridge Commons: Environmental Activism and Forest History in Western North Carolina* (Athens: University of Georgia Press, 2012); Steven Stoll, *Larding the Lean Earth: Soil and Society in Nineteenth-Century America* (New York: Hill & Wang, 2002); Mikko Saikku, *This Delta, This Land: An Environmental History of the Yazoo-Mississippi Floodplain* (Athens: University of Georgia Press, 2005); Megan Kate Nelson, *Trembling Earth: A Cultural History of the Okefenokee Swamp* (Athens: University of Georgia Press, 2005); Mark Hersey, *My Work Is That of Conservation: An Environmental Biography of George Washington Carver* (Athens: University of Georgia Press, 2011); Christopher Morris, *The Big Muddy: An Environmental History of the Mississippi and Its Peoples, from Hernando de Soto to Hurricane Katrina* (New York: Oxford University Press, 2012); Randal L. Hall, *Mountains on the Market: Industry, the Environment, and the South* (Lexington: University Press of Kentucky, 2012); Claire Strom, *Making Catfish Bait Out of Government Boys: The Fight against Cattle Ticks and the Transformation of the Yeoman South* (Athens: University of Georgia Press, 2005); Christine Keiner, *The Oyster Question: Scientists, Watermen, and the Maryland Chesapeake Bay since 1880* (Athens: University of Georgia Press, 2009).

16. Lisa Brady, *War upon the Land: Military Strategy and the Transformation of Southern Landscapes during the American Civil War* (Athens: University of Georgia Press, 2012); James C. Giesen, *Boll Weevil Blues: Cotton, Myth, and Power in the American South* (Chicago: University of Chicago Press, 2011); Mark Fiege, "King Cotton: The Cotton Plantation and Southern Slavery" and "The Nature of Gettysburg: Environmental History and the Civil War," in Fiege, *The Republic of Nature: An Environmental History of the United States* (Seattle: University of Washington Press, 2013); Lynn Nelson, *Pharsalia: An Environmental Biography of a Southern Plantation, 1780–1880* (Athens: University of Georgia Press, 2007); Ellen Griffith Spears, *Baptized in PCBs: Race, Pollution, and Justice in an All-American Town* (Chapel Hill: University of North Carolina Press, 2014).

17. Two touchstones of the developing field that White singled out as embodying the intellectual and political frameworks included those by Roderick Nash and Samuel P. Hays. See Nash, *Wilderness and the American Mind* (New Haven, Conn.: Yale University Press, 1967); Hays, *Conservation and the Gospel of Efficiency: The Progressive Conservation Movement, 1890–1920* (Cambridge, Mass.: Harvard University Press, 1959).

18. Richard White, "American Environmental History: The Development of a New Historical Field," *Pacific Historical Review* 54 (August 1985): 316–17. Also see Donald Worster, *Nature's Economy: A History of Ecological Ideas* (New York: Cambridge University Press, 1977).

19. Donald Worster, "Transformations of the Earth: Toward an Agroecological Perspective in History," *Journal of American History* 76 (March 1990): 1089–90.

20. See William Cronon, "Introduction: In Search of Nature," in *Uncommon Ground: Rethinking the Human Place in Nature*, ed. William Cronon (New York: W. W. Norton, 1996), 23–56. For reappraisals of the field's historiography, see Richard White, "Environmental History: Watching a Historical Field Mature," *Pacific Historical Review* 70

(February 2001): 103–11; J. R. McNeill, "Observations on the Nature and Culture of Environmental History," *History and Theory* 42 (December 2003): 5–43; Douglas Cazaux Sackman, ed., *A Companion to American Environmental History* (Malden, Mass.: Wiley-Blackwell, 2010); Sarah T. Phillips, "Environmental History," in *American History Now*, ed. Eric Foner and Lisa McGirr (Philadelphia: Temple University Press, 2011), 285–313.

21. Paul S. Sutter, "The World with Us: The State of the American Environmental History," *Journal of American History* 100, no. 1 (June 2013): 95–96, and "Nature Is History," *Journal of American History* 100, no. 1 (June 2013): 145–48. Also see Richard White, "From Wilderness to Hybrid Landscape: The Cultural Turn in Environmental History," *Historian* 66 (Fall 2004): 557–64.

22. Douglas R. Weiner, "A Death-Defying Attempt to Articulate a Coherent Definition of Environmental History," *Environmental History* 10 (July 2005): 415. For early America and its environmental history, see Peter Mancall, "Pigs for Historians: Changes in the Land and Beyond," *William and Mary Quarterly* 67 (April 2010): 347–75.

23. Jorge Cañizares-Esguerra and Benjamin Breen, "Hybrid Atlantics: Future Directions for the History of the Atlantic World," *History Compass* 11 (August 2013): 602. They go on to note that "future scholarship integrating climate, ecology, and environment with fine-grained attention to local contexts and archival sources has the potential to become one of the richest subfields of early modern history" (603). Also see the forum on Atlantic cultural change where James Sidbury and Jorge Cañizares-Esguerra call for similar perspectives: "Mapping Ethnogenesis in the Early Modern Atlantic," *William and Mary Quarterly* 68, no. 2 (2011): 181–208. Jo Guldi and David Armitage have recently called out to historians to bring back the analytical framework of Braudel's *longue durée* in order to engage more directly with the public in *The History Manifesto* (New York: Cambridge University Press, 2014). Atlantic environmental historiographies could also potentially be a way of discussing other salient questions such as climate change. See the forum "Climate and Early American History," *William and Mary Quarterly* 72, no. 1 (2015): 25–158, and Joyce E. Chaplin, "The Other Revolution," *Early American Studies* 13, no. 2 (Spring 2015): 285–308.

24. Carolyn Merchant, *Ecological Revolutions: Nature, Gender, and Science in New England* (Chapel Hill: University of North Carolina Press, 1989); William Cronon, *Changes in the Land: Indians, Colonists, and the Ecology of New England* (New York: Hill & Wang, 1983); Silver, *New Face on the Countryside*; Andrew Sluyter, *Colonialism and Landscape: Postcolonial Theory and Applications* (Lanham, Md.: Rowman & Littlefield, 2002); Craig E. Colten and Geoffrey L. Buckley, *North American Odyssey: Historical Geographies for the Twenty-First Century* (Lanham, Md.: Rowman & Littlefield, 2014); W. J. T. Mitchell, *Landscape and Power* (Chicago: University of Chicago Press, 1994).

25. Ashley Carse, *Beyond the Big Ditch: Politics, Ecology, and Infrastructure at the Panama Canal* (Cambridge, Mass.: MIT Press, 2014), 13.

26. Casper Bruun Jensen and Atsuro Morita, "Infrastructures as Ontological Experiments," *Engaging Science, Technology, and Society* 1 (2015): 81–87.

27. Cymene Howe, Jessica Lockrem, Hannah Appel, Edward Hackett, Dominic Boyer, Randal Hall, Matthew Schneider-Mayerson, et al., "Paradoxical Infrastructures: Ruins, Retrofit, and Risk," *Science, Technology, and Human Values* (2015), https://doi.org/10.1177/0162243915620017.

PART I *Slavery and Climate*

Differentiating Hot Climates in the Anglo-American Colonial Experience

SEAN MOREY SMITH

"English people contemplating transplantation to the southern parts of North America and to the West Indies in the sixteenth and seventeenth centuries expressed profound anxiety over the effect hot climates would have on them," began Karen Ordahl Kupperman's seminal 1984 article "Fear of Hot Climates in the Anglo-American Colonial Experience." The article went on to explain that Britons worried that hot climates would sicken them but that they still colonized hot regions because of the perceived potential for gaining material wealth. Heat made a place insalubrious for Europeans as well as agriculturally productive and minerally rich. Specifically, Kupperman argued, "settlers' health fared badly in both the southern mainland colonies and the West Indies. This fact confirmed their expectations and contributed important evidence that hardened generalized anxieties into medical dogma by the eighteenth century. The link between weather and disease then became axiomatic."[1] Yet, while contemporaries did describe the climatic similarities between "hot" colonies in the Caribbean and in North America, they also differentiated them. Especially in the seventeenth century, colonial promoters were more likely to discriminate between mainland and West Indian colonies than lump them together. Such promoters used competing scientific theories strategically to stress the benefits of their subjects implicitly, and often explicitly, in comparison with other "hot" colonies. Through such comparisons, the common categorization of southern mainland and archipelagic colonies as "hot" emerged as Carolina and later Georgia followed the example of their Caribbean forebears and turned to large-scale plantation slavery. This turn to plantation slavery, as much as the areas' climates, led contemporaries to understand the Caribbean and southern continental colonies as similar.

In this reading of promotional literature focused on Jamaica, Barbados, Carolina, and, to a much lesser extent, Georgia, pamphleteers actively chose between different theoretical representations of climates to make the colonies they described appear more salubrious and productive to potential colonies and investors. Historians have long used these kinds of writings to understand what arguments authors used to attract colonists and to explain what the English thought about the American climate. Though these tracts' writers did cling to old ideas of latitudinal climate zones even as they encountered contradictory evidence much as Kupperman has described, they purposively and creatively made use of competing explanations of health's relationship to climate.[2] Colonial promoters of Jamaica and Barbados actively countered latitudinal zone theories of climate nearly from the beginning, but Carolina's promoters purposefully revivified and applied these theories in order to differentiate themselves from the Caribbean colonies. Ultimately, descriptions of the climate of the coast of southern North America changed to acknowledge its heat and insalubrity not simply because of better evidence that it did not match the Mediterranean climate as predicted by the assumption of latitudinal climate zones. Instead, the expansion of chattel slavery and the rise of plantation agriculture in the region changed not only the disease environment but also what promoters and potential colonists wanted to believe about the climate. Planters introduced new and more virulent diseases and made the environment more hospitable to certain transmission vectors such as mosquitoes at the same time they declared those regions too insalubrious for European bodies and demanded enslaved African labor.[3]

In the last two decades, a handful of historians have followed Kupperman's lead in considering southern parts of the American continent as extensions of the "hot" Caribbean. As a result, historians have studied mainland sites from the Virginia Tidewater to the Brazilian sugar fields, including the coastal regions of the Gulf of Mexico and the Caribbean Sea in between, as part of an analytical "Greater Caribbean."[4] For example, Matthew Mulcahy includes the Lowcountry of the Carolinas and Georgia alongside islands such as Barbados and Jamaica as part of a "British Greater Caribbean." Like most writers using the Greater Caribbean framework, Mulcahy explains that the region, like any other, is a human construction built as much on cultural similarities as environmental ones: "Although physical geography—climate, terrain, land use patterns, and the like—plays a key role in defining regions, regions are as much cultural creations as they are physical ones. Shared history and experiences, common customs, practices, and mentalities, similar social and economic systems also can delineate regional boundaries." Specifically, these colonies shared "a number of similar socioeconomic characteristics. The size and scale of plantation operations, including the average size of landholdings and slaveholdings, dwarfed those of the other major plantation zone in British America, the Chesapeake tobacco colonies." Mulcahy also includes the region's urbanism, its enslaved majority, and the prevalence of natural disasters such as hurricanes and earthquakes, as well as its disease environment, especially the pervasiveness of yellow fever and malaria, to differentiate it from other areas.[5]

Though the rise of plantation slavery in the Carolina-Georgia Lowcountry undoubtedly made these places economically and socially similar, it is doubtful that the promoters and early colonists of the "hot" mainland colonies saw this space as a climatic extension of the Caribbean until that transformation to plantation agriculture occurred. Seventeenth- and eighteenth-century Englanders and Anglo-Americans understood the climates of the southern American colonies and those of the Caribbean islands to be warmer than England but still differentiated them by other factors such as their continental or archipelagic situation and their location in the temperate or torrid zones. The eventual association of insalubrity with Carolina and Georgia arose as much from the increasing use of enslaved African labor there as from increasing evidence of disease in the region. Thus, the inclusion of the southern North American colonies in the Greater Caribbean can best be understood not solely as a product of the natural environment but also of the development of plantation monoculture based on enslaved labor.

During the colonial period, classical theories of climate and bodies dominated how Europeans thought about the world and health. Aristotelian climate zone theory and Hippocratic medical theory related health and even the viability of human life to different climatic conditions. Aristotle's theory of climate divided the world into three zones: the frigid zone was north of the Arctic Circle; the equatorial tropics constituted the torrid zone; and the temperate zone was in between. Aristotle believed that only the temperate zone could support human life while the other zones were too hot or too cold to be habitable. This body of thought also contributed to the belief that places at a given latitude shared a climate.[6] The Hippocratic corpus also stated that human health was climate dependent, but in a less bifurcated way. It stressed that Europeans (and, as interpreted by Anglophone doctors, especially British Islanders) were acclimated to cool, temperate climates. Because of this acclimation, Hippocratic theory argued that dislocation to more extreme climates could unbalance a body's humors, causing disease. However, Hippocratic tradition also stressed that diet and behavior affected individuals' constitutions and that they as much as the climate determined overall health.[7] Present in both of these discourses was the idea that hot climates were inherently unhealthy. However, Hippocratic tradition acknowledged the influence of other health factors, and its Roman propagator, Galen, enumerated the six "nonnaturals" (food and drink, sleep, physical exertion, bodily waste, mental state, and the heat of the air) that affected a body's humoral balance.[8] This amalgamated Hippocratic and Galenic system, then, allowed for personal health factors to combat climatic ones. Colonial promoters used these related but ultimately different systems strategically to differentiate their colony from others that historians have commonly described as "hot" or as part of the "Greater Caribbean." Only in the second quarter of the eighteenth century did descriptions of the continental and archipelagic plantation colonies truly converge into a common discourse of "hot" climates.

☙

Hot locales attracted colonists despite the perceived risks of disease because the potentially dangerous heat also provided the opportunity for great riches.[9] Nevertheless, seventeenth-century works describing England's Caribbean possessions downplayed their health hazards. In particular, they attempted to refute the Aristotelian understanding of the torrid zone as uninhabitable.

An early pamphlet on Jamaica written in 1657 just two years after its conquest by Oliver Cromwell's Protectorate forces ignored any potential ill effects on Britons' health.[10] Instead, the author repeatedly stressed a different property attributed to hot places: the island's extreme fertility. To that end, its author explained that "whatever fruits God and Nature have planted from the beginning, or have by the industry and diligence of man been transplanted thither from any other part, do thrive in this Land wonderfully." Only in making his larger point about the island's extreme fruitfulness did the author include human health: "I need not inform you of the great variety of Fish, and Fowl, nor the healthfulness of the place, when a man hath some little time been acquainted with the Ayr." Though purposefully understated, the author implied that English bodies would only be healthy in Jamaica after a short adjustment period.[11]

While the pamphlet on Jamaica largely avoided discussing the potential insalubriousness of the island, another work published the same year, concerning Barbados, explored the unhealthiness of the smaller island in detail. In *A True & Exact History of the Island of Barbados*, Richard Ligon explained that "with this great heat, there is such a moysture, as must of necessity cause the ayer to be very unwholesome. . . . Besides, our bodyes having bin used to colder Clymates, finde a debility, and a great fayling in the vigour, and sprightliness we have in colder Climats." According to this understanding of climate, Barbados's greater heat and humidity debilitated English bodies. However, Ligon attributed the natural productivity of the island's flora to "this great heat and moysture together," again reinforcing the connection between hot places as both sickly and fertile and suggesting that the climate's potential gains outweighed its risks.[12]

Though Ligon dwelt on the unhealthiness of the Barbadian climate, he also suggested ways that colonists could and did mitigate the ill effects of the heat. Allowing that Barbados lay in the torrid zone, Ligon invoked the Galenic non-naturals to stress that colonists would have to change factors such as behavior, food, and drink to stay healthy on the island. The effects of the torrid zone, for instance, would force a colonist "to change the pleasures which he enjoyed in a Temperate [Zone]." He blamed ill health on those "who by the ill dyet they keep, and drinking strong waters, bring diseases upon themselves," arguing that disease was a product of poor (though alterable) behavior. Just as proper food and water were necessary to good health in Barbados, its inhabitants needed to carefully regulate their alcohol intake: "Though some of these [spirits] be needfull if they be used with temper; yet the immoderate use of them, over-heats the body, which causes Costivenesse, and Tortions in the bowels . . . but certainely, strong drinks are very requisit, where so much heat is." According to traditional humoral ideas, alcohol added heat to the body. Following humoral thought, Ligon argued that colonists needed "spirits" because they could help restore some of the heat sapped by the climate. However, he further stressed the need for temperance in drink to prevent overheating. In terms of the Galenic non-naturals, the careful regulation of drink could help colonists mitigate the effects of the climate. This emphasis gave hope to potential colonists that careful action would keep them healthy and that the stories of illness on the island described the effects of the climate only on the imprudent.[13]

Though some promotional literature largely ignored the unhealthy aspects of the colonies they discussed, most works on Jamaica and Barbados from the 1660s specifically countered Aristotelian climate zone theory and stressed the importance of empirical experimental knowledge in the form of firsthand experience. Not only did this rhetorical move allow writers to establish themselves as credible sources of information about the colonies, it also fit with the era's politics. As Steven Shapin and Simon Schaffer have explained, the Restoration political settlement in England was created hand in hand (or coproduced) with a new scientific settlement that favored experimental knowledge while leaving room for disagreement about experiments' interpretations.[14]

Coming on the heels of the Restoration, Edmund Hickeringill explained that Jamaica's "climate is placed betwixt the Tropicks . . . whence it borrowed the style of Torrid Zone; a name which did so bugbear and affright the credulity of our Ancestors, that they unjustly exil'd and raz'd it out from the habitable part of the world, (then monopoliz'd in the Temperate Zones) till the more daring spirits of Columbus, and others, convoy'd us to an *experimental* confidence in the contrary."[15] By directly attacking climate zone theory, Hickeringill implied that knowledge of the theory scared potential colonists from moving to Jamaica. Accordingly, he contradicted them and explicitly argued that new experimental data proved those old theories incorrect. Furthermore, he explained that any problem with heat was mitigated by breezes: "the fresh Breezes that rise always with the Sun, doe fanne the sweltering and sultry Climes within the Tropicks: so that the dayes are usually as cold as the nights, except towards the morning."[16] According to Hickeringill, experience discredited Aristotelian climate theory, and even though the tropics were hot, breezes cooled the islands and kept them healthy for colonists. Much like Ligon used humoral medical ideas to explain how careful behavior could keep colonists healthy in Barbados, Hickeringill's invocation of "fresh Breezes" pointed to a less latitudinal approach to determining a place's salubrity.

Writing a few years after Hickeringill, Richard Blome reiterated that Jamaica had been experimentally deemed as healthy as anywhere: "It hath been *experimentally* found, that there is no such Antipathy betwixt the constitutions of the English, and this clime, for the occasioning Sickness to be Mortal or Contageous, more than in other parts."[17] He, too, described the parts of the island that mitigated the potential heat of the tropics. Preferring Hippocratic notions of air, water, and places to Aristotelian climate zones, he explained that "the Air is here more temperate then [*sic*] in any of the Caribbee Isles, as seated more Northerly, and of as mild a temperature (as to Heate) as any place between the Tropicks, being always cooled with fresh Breezes . . . and refreshed with frequent Showers of Rain . . . that it may truly be called temperate and healthful."[18] While the tropics were hot, breezes and rains cooled Jamaica, leaving its overall climate temperate.

Having no other factor than the climate to blame for instances of bad health, pamphleteers scrambled to attribute whatever illnesses or other misfortunes colonists experienced in Jamaica to a variety of other factors. Hickeringill suggested that problems encountered by the English after conquering the island might have been due to "want of timely recruits, always found necessary for such Infant-settlements: or, through some fatal Conjunction of the superiour Luminaties." Returning to the topic later, Hickeringill explained that the colony's newness had led to troubles that had now been overcome: "though Infant-Settlements, like Infant-years, are usually most fatal; yet their Blossomes once Set, are not so easily Blasted. Happily experimented in Iamaica, whose Blooming hopes now thrive so well."[19] Similarly, Blome claimed "the reason of the great Mortality of the Army, at their first arrival, was their want of Provisions, together with an unwillingness to labour or excercise, joyned with discontent." Blome also argued that any current unhealthiness was "occasioned often by ill diet, drunkeness, and slothfulness" leaving colonists to "enjoy a competent measure of Health" assuming they kept "a good Dyet, and moderate Exercises are used."[20] In short, reports of Caribbean insalubrity circulating in metropolitan Britain were due to the problems of starting a colony or individuals' poor behavior, not the islands' climates.

Ultimately, all of these descriptions of Barbados and Jamaica mentioned the *potential* health problems that settlement in the torrid zone could induce but stressed that cooling sea breezes and temperate personal behavior could ameliorate such threats. Authors called on personal expertise using the language of experimentation to counter the wisdom of the ancients and refute the classical notion that the torrid zone would not support human life. However, their denial of latitudinal climate zones did not necessitate a rejection of all traditional knowledge. Instead, they often privileged Hippocratic and Galenic humoral understandings of health as an established alternative to explain the islands' impact on English bodies. Though supporters of Jamaica and Barbados rejected climate zone theories because it fit their goals, pamphleteers for Carolina would flip this trend, preferring to differentiate their continental colony from its archipelagic forebears in climatic-zonal terms.

⟳

With migration to Carolina coming chronologically later than the colonization of its Caribbean cousins, Carolina's supporters quickly turned to comparisons with other colonies in hopes of gaining European migrants. They hoped to convince potential colonizers to come to their nascent colony through claims of greater salubrity, especially in comparison with Jamaica and Barbados. To make these claims, pamphleteers revivified climate zone theory and stressed Carolina's position in the temperate zone versus the islands' positions in the torrid zone.

In contrast to attempts to downplay the effects of the tropical climate on the Caribbean islands, early descriptions of Carolina promised its perfect situation in the temperate zone but in a part of the Americas with fewer weather fluctuations. One pamphlet printed in 1666, after Charles II had granted the colony to its Lords Proprietors but before its settlement had officially begun, argued that Carolina had "the most temperate Clime" being near Virginia but with less "inconstancy of the Weather, which is a great cause of the unhealthfulness thereof." Its author, Robert Horne, also used latitudinal climate band theory to buttress the nascent colony's claim to salubriousness. He explained that Carolina, "being in the latitude of the Barmoodoes may expect the like healthfulness which it hath hitherto enjoy'd, and doubtless there is no Plantation that ever the English went upon, in all respects so good as this."[21] Blome similarly pronounced Carolina "a Countrey blest with a Temperate, and Wholesome Air, the heat in Summer, nor the Cold in Winter . . . being no wayes offensive to the Inhabitants. Neither is the Air thus Temperate, and Agreeable, to the Natives only, but it is as Favourable to the English."[22] By repeatedly stressing the temperateness of Carolina's climate, these works implied its difference from the torrid islands.

As Carolina became more established, writers not only increasingly accentuated its temperateness but explicitly invoked its location in the temperate zone. In 1682 Thomas Ashe described it as being "in the Northern temperate

Zone."[23] In that same year, another writer explained that Carolina benefited from its location in the warmer reaches of the temperate zone. The warm climate made "all sorts of English Grane" grow naturally but was never "so predominant whereby to suffocate the air with intemperance."[24] According to this work, Carolina was located in a temperate climate that protected its inhabitants from the debilitating effects of excessive heat and cold yet remained warm enough that plants grew prolifically with minimal effort. In this model, Carolina bettered the Caribbean in its healthiness and its northern continental neighbors in its bounty.[25]

One inventive pamphleteer writing in support of Carolina cleverly turned the logic of the West Indian devotees to his own advantage. Accepting their contention that the torrid zone was habitable, John Archdale, a former governor of the colony, argued that realignment of the earth's habitable zones located Carolina even more perfectly: "Now Carolina . . . is indeed the very Center of the habitable Part of the Northern hemisphere . . . and may be called the Temperate Zone comparatively, as not being pestered with the violent Heats of the more Southern Colonies, or the extream and violent Colds of the more Northern Settlements."[26] Again, a writer represented Carolina as the happy medium between the sweltering Caribbean and the less plentiful northern continental colonies. Archdale also explicitly invoked Carolina's location in the temperate zone and its latitudinal equivalency with the eastern edge of the Mediterranean. Via these latitudinal comparisons, he described Carolina as healthy but also a bit exotic and thus capable of producing unique commodities.

Writers supportive of colonizing Carolina occasionally found the opportunity to attack its archipelagic counterparts by other means as well. For instance, amid a description of the useful commodities and medicines found in Carolina (a staple element in all of these works), Ashe took the opportunity to insult the islands subtly. He explained that the "three sorts of the Rattle-Snake Root" found in Carolina "are all Sovereign against the Mortal Bites of that Snake, too frequent in the West Indies."[27] According to this description, Carolina not only contained helpful medicines as part of its natural bounty, but its products could help alleviate a negative aspect of the Caribbean that its author just happened to mention. Implicitly, rattlesnakes were a greater threat in the West Indies than on the North American mainland.

Despite the positive portrayal of the Carolina climate in promotional literature, reports of ill health in the area encouraged writers to add progressively more arguments for Carolina's salubriousness to their works. Ashe described the colony as having "Air of so serene and excellent a temper, that the Indian Natives prolong their days to the Extremity of Old Age. And where the English hitherto have found no Distempers either Epidemical or Mortal, but what have had their Rise from Excess or Origine from Intemperance."[28] While Ashe focused on the inherent healthiness of the Carolinian climate, he followed the Caribbean example of blaming any illness found there on the habits of the colonists.

Writers supporting Carolina also made use of climate band theory in order to encourage the idea that exotic crops could be grown there. As early as 1666, Horne described the "many sorts of fruit Trees, as Vines, Medlars, Peach, Wild Cherries, Mulburry-Trees, and the Silk-worm breeding naturally on them" to be found in Carolina.[29] A decade and a half later, Ashe specifically linked silk production to the climate: "A Manufactory of Silk well encouraged might soon be accomplisht, considering the numerousness of the Leaf for Provision, the clemency and moderateness of the Climate to indulge and nourish the Silk-worm."[30] Though historians often mention the Lords Proprietors' dreams of growing silk in the colony to demonstrate the grandiose and ultimately false hopes of Carolina's founders, their belief that the necessary mulberry trees and silkworms as well as various citrus fruit trees would grow in the area reflected their assumptions about climate bands and Carolina's location latitudinally even with the Mediterranean Sea. These hopes may have proven false, but the writers describing Carolina and later Georgia wrote from an established scientific perspective that buttressed their hopes at the same time that it encouraged their ignorance of what could be grown there.[31]

Even after a generation of settlement in Carolina, colonists and their promoters continued to stress the potential benefits of their latitude because it neatly made their point for them: great benefits would spring from the latitude's natural environment. For instance, Thomas Nairne argued in 1710 that "between the same Parallels with *South Carolina*, lie some of the most fertile Countries in the World, as some Parts of the Coast of *Barbary*, all the middle Part of *China*, from the middle to the South Parts of *Japan*, those Countries of *India* about *Lahore*, the best part of *Persia, Egypt* and *Syria*."[32] English culture's emphasis on gaining material wealth from the natural world as well as established scientific theory encouraged them to disregard a growing body of evidence that goods such as silk could not be produced along the southern coast of North America.

The greatest changes in descriptions of Carolina occurred as the colony turned into a full-fledged slave society. As colonists increasingly invested in staple rice production toward the end of the seventeenth century, imports of enslaved Africans increased dramatically from 1695, and from around 1710 enslaved Africans outnumbered Europeans in the colony. Though there were roughly three thousand "Negro slaves" in the colony by 1703, promoters resisted mentioning slavery and made only passing references to it in tracts published before 1710.[33] Horne's 1666 pamphlet mentioned slavery only to promise that the Lords Proprietors would grant "Free-men" fifty acres for every enslaved person that they "transport[ed]" to the colony.[34] Similarly, tracts published in the 1680s mentioned the existence of slavery only once or twice and failed to explore the institution or the enslaved in any detail.[35]

Pamphleteers only began describing slavery after rice had become a proven export commodity and as advice literature replaced earlier descriptive tracts. Nairne, for instance, specified how many enslaved people a planter would need to develop estates of different sizes and generating different amounts of revenue. He further specified that half the land should be planted with rice, accentuating the coupling of rice and slavery.[36] In another pamphlet, John Norris similarly presented his own calculations concerning the relationship of enslaved people to potential plantation revenues. He also described chattel slavery and emphasized the "Necessity for these Slaves, because very few Servants are there to be procured to perform the Business of the Country."[37] These descriptions emphasized the colony's move toward monoculture produced through enslaved labor.

The same works that began discussing Carolina's chattel enslaved labor regime in detail also directly dealt with the colony's increasing insalubrity. Gradually, descriptions of health and behavior in Carolina aped those of Jamaica and Barbados: proper temperate behavior could mitigate the effects of a potentially insalubrious climate. Nairne warned his readers that "the Heats of Carolina are indeed troublesome to Strangers in *June, July,* and *August*" and suggested that "the best Time for Europeans to arrive here, in respect to Health, is September; for then they have eight Months of Moderate Weather, before the Heat comes, in which Time the Climate will become agreeable."[38] Similarly, Norris admitted that "in the Spring of the Year, a Feaver and Ague seizes many that are settled on the lowest Marsh Land, especially when they are new Comers to the Country, which is commonly call'd a Seasoning to them; after which, if their Habitations is on dry healthy Land, they are, generally, very healthful, if temperate."[39] As Carolina became a plantation society based on enslaved labor, it also became a more sickly place as colonists imported African people carrying the malaria plasmodia and as rice culture increased breeding grounds for the disease's mosquito transmission vector.[40] Following the example of its Caribbean forebears, Carolina's promoters shifted to describing factors that could mitigate the Lowcountry's risk to personal health using humoral medical ideas that focused on specific places in the colonies and allowed for healthy acclimatization.

Though both Nairne and Norris admitted the Carolina climate contained dangers to personal health, they also strove to explain how those dangers could be mitigated. As illustrated above, both writers explained that the climate was only dangerous to new arrivals.[41] They also stressed the importance of behavior. Norris explained that the climate "is generally Healthful to most People that live Temperate, and not drink Immoderately, or use immoderate Exercises, thereby destroying their Health, and too often their Life also." Similarly, even the summer heat could be mitigated by "shady Groves, open Air, Arbours, Summer-Houses, and frequent cool Bathings."[42] Increasingly, then, the climate of Carolina was portrayed like that of Jamaica and Barbados: potentially dangerous but healthy to those who lived temperately. Significantly, this shift toward describing Carolina as less than perfectly temperate accompanied its transition to enslaved labor.

The clearest example of the pairing of insalubrious environment and slavery comes from Georgia. Initially established as a colony without slavery, colonists eventually contested this prohibition publicly, arguing that they needed enslaved people to labor if they were to become as prosperous as neighboring Carolina. In making their argument, some campaigners specifically recast the climate of the southern North American coast as unhealthy for Europeans. For instance, Patrick Tailfer and his cowriters lamented the inability of whites to work in such a hot climate, explaining that their constitutions were "very unequal" to cutting timber and hoeing fields due "to the sultry Heat of the Sun." However, the coauthors added, "the Negroes' . . . Constitutions are much stronger than white People, and the Heat no Way disagreeable nor hurtful to them." They continued on to complain in a quoted letter to Georgia's preeminent founder James Oglethorpe that "'all the neighboring Colonies, by Reason of their Negroes, prosecute all Branches of it [trade] as a sixth Part of the Expense we can; they would forever preclude us of any Benefit therefrom'" and that "'it were simply impossible to manufacture the Rice by white Men; the Exercise being so severe, that no Negro can be employed in any other Work or Labour comparable to it.'" These maneuvers continued the process of alienating white Europeans from the climate of the southern North American coast and inadvertently made it appear more Caribbean. However, these eighteenth-century writers did not encourage this alienation for its own sake. Instead, their arguments arose from desires to justify slavery and argue for its expansion. In this way, Carolina and Georgia became more Caribbean through the process of becoming territories where commodity production depended on enslaved labor.[43]

&

Despite Carolinian efforts to differentiate it climatically from the Caribbean colonies, writers for Jamaica and Barbados countered by stressing the differences between their islands and the mainland. Climatic justifications for slavery and the continued incidences of disease and mortality made continuing claims to true salubriousness difficult to support for any of the Greater Caribbean colonies. However, eighteenth-century writers avoided this problem by increasingly describing specific areas in these colonies as having relatively salubrious microclimates.[44] They also increasingly stressed the importance of temperate behavior in mitigating the effects of climate, claiming that drinking too much alcohol and consuming too much meat in hot places were the true source of morbidity. Though these claims had been around since the earliest accounts of the colonies, descriptions of other factors intended to make the colonies seem more salubrious, such as the direct contradiction of climate zones, faded in the eighteenth century.

In the closing decades of the seventeenth century and for much of the eighteenth century, works on Jamaica emphasized the variety of climates found on the island. Also, writers trying to differentiate the islands from Carolina increasingly stressed the cool ocean breezes already introduced by Hickeringill and Blome. As early as 1683, Thomas Malthus introduced two themes to differentiate Jamaica from temperate zone colonies: seasoning and climatic variation. First, Malthus contended that Jamaica's "climate subjects no body inevitably to Diseases, here being no such thing as Seasoning, which is common in Ireland and Virginia, &c." Taking the opportunity to defame two other popular colonial destinations, Malthus argued that his Jamaica did not have the inherent illnesses found elsewhere. Second, he stressed the variety of climates found on the island, building on his observation that "this Island differs one part from another as much in the temper of the Climate, as nature of the Soyl." Therefore, any disease was due to "ill chosen Seats when they Plant in low Valleys, and have no Air, or by Rivers, and have too much moisture, or by Mountains or Morossos, and have too much Rain, or by the Sea-side and on Bays, where they are Sandy, want good Water, and have the Reflection of the Sun too violent." Building on writers who proclaimed illness to be the product of intemperate behavior, eating, or drinking, Malthus contended that a poor choice in picking where to live made people ill rather than the climate of the island itself.[45]

Over the next century, other writers also claimed that judging the whole of a colony as having the same climate overlooked the variation among its parts. The infamous Edward Long repeatedly argued for a more nuanced approach to Jamaica's climate, stressing the salubrity of the cooler north side and of the island's Blue Mountain ridges.[46] This localized approach followed Hippocratic theory and allowed him to argue that Jamaica itself was not unhealthy, though perhaps some of its parts were. It also contradicted climate zone theory, though not by name, by suggesting that areas within a zone could have radically different climates. Additionally, by describing nearby locations as more healthful,

Long suggested that Europeans could simply move to those cooler areas during hotter parts of the year to maintain their health.[47]

Additionally, authors regularly described ocean breezes as keeping Jamaica and Barbados cool despite their tropical location. Writers such as Malthus continued earlier arguments that winds "which they call Breeses" kept Jamaica cool during the summer.[48] One later account of Barbados attacked its continental competitors directly: "The climate, though warm, is by no means unhealthful. The heat is much alleviated by a constant cool sea-breeze . . . [and] will appear moderate, compared to some parts of the continent of America."[49] By arguing that a cooling breeze could ameliorate the heat of an island, this account implicitly suggested ignoring climate zone theory in favor of a more experimental approach to determining the effective heat of a colony. Furthermore, it indicted continental colonies as perhaps feeling hotter and thus being less healthy. While the author named no particular continental colony, South Carolina may have been his target, considering that despite its location in the temperate zone, it had developed a reputation for being hot and unhealthy by the middle of the eighteenth century. Significantly, writers focused on island breezes in order to continue a long tradition of differentiating colonies understood to be "hot."

Ultimately, no colony's pamphleteers gained a monopoly on interpreting climate. The varying goals of writers describing the archipelagic and continental plantations led them to different representations of climate. Especially in the seventeenth century, works on Jamaica and Barbados rejected Aristotelian climate zone theories, preferring Hippocratic readings of specific places and their airs and waters. Descriptions of Carolina, which was colonized permanently starting in 1670, revivified climate zone theories in order for their authors to argue for its more salubrious situation in the temperate zone. However, as African slavery and the rice monoculture it supported gained prominence around the turn of the eighteenth century, the colony's pamphleteers conceded, at least partially, the unhealthiness of the climate and began stressing the need for enslaved Africans who they believed would be better able to work in hot climates. Political arguments to allow slavery in Georgia furthered this trend of admitting the unhealthiness of the climate of coastal southern North America for white bodies in order to advocate for enslaved black labor there. In due course, writers described both the Caribbean and mainland colonies for the bulk of the eighteenth century as unhealthy for whites but stressed a myriad of ways Europeans could survive there.

The connection of slavery to climates unhealthy for Europeans illustrates that cultural factors made Carolina and Georgia part of the Greater Caribbean, not environmental ones alone. The dominance of slavery and plantation monoculture made Carolina like Jamaica as much as the prevalence of yellow fever and hurricanes did. After all, the colonies shared neither a predominant crop (rice vs. sugar) nor a common enslaved labor system (task vs. gang). Neither does weather alone define the boundary of the Greater Caribbean as hurricanes have struck much farther north along the Atlantic seaboard (if with less frequency). Therefore, historians must cautiously consider exactly what the Greater Caribbean is and whether it applies each time they invoke it. Furthermore, colonial promoters repeatedly differentiated the continental and archipelagic colonies, suggesting that contemporaries only came to see these colonies as similar as they developed similar economic and social structures. The discursive nature of promotional literature highlights the strategic use of competing systems of natural knowledge and the development of the Lowcountry's climatic connection to the Caribbean.

NOTES

1. Karen Ordahl Kupperman, "Fear of Hot Climates in the Anglo-American Colonial Experience," *William and Mary Quarterly* 41, no. 2 (April 1984): 213. Kupperman generally included Virginia among "the southern mainland colonies"; however, this paper will concentrate on colonies to the south of Virginia.

2. Karen Ordahl Kupperman, "The Puzzle of the American Climate in the Early Colonial Period," *American Historical Review* 87, no. 5 (December 1982): 1262–89.

3. This alteration of the disease environment is the consensus of a variety of historians, but this essay attempts to explore their implications for contemporary conceptions of climate. See Mart A. Stewart, *"What Nature Suffers to Groe": Life, Labor, and Landscape on the Georgia Coast, 1680–1920* (Athens: University of Georgia Press, 1996); J. R. McNeill, *Mosquito Empires: Ecology and War in the Greater Caribbean, 1620–1914* (New York: Cambridge University Press, 2010); Peter McCandless, *Slavery, Disease, and Suffering in the Southern Lowcountry* (Cambridge: Cambridge University Press, 2011).

4. The term "Greater Caribbean" came to prominence with the publication of David Barry Gaspar and David Patrick Geggus, eds., *A Turbulent Time: The French Revolution and the Greater Caribbean* (Bloomington: Indiana University Press, 1997). More recently, other works have continued to use the term. See Matthew Mulcahy, *Hurricanes and Society in the British Greater Caribbean, 1624–1783* (Baltimore: Johns Hopkins University Press, 2006); Mulcahy, *Hubs of Empire: The Southeastern Lowcountry and British Caribbean* (Baltimore: Johns Hopkins University Press, 2014); and McNeill, *Mosquito Empires*. In *Hurricanes and Society*, Mulcahy attributes the original concept to Immanuel Wallerstein as the "extended Caribbean." Immanuel Maurice Wallerstein, *The Modern World-System II: Mercantilism and the Consolidation of the European World-Economy, 1600–1750* (New York: Academic Press, 1980), 103.

5. Mulcahy, *Hubs of Empire*, 2, 4–6.

6. Kupperman, "Puzzle of the American Climate," 1278; Joyce E. Chaplin, *Subject Matter: Technology, the Body, and Science on the Anglo-American Frontier, 1500–1676* (Cambridge, Mass.: Harvard University Press, 2001), 43–44.

7. Kupperman, "Fear of Hot Climates," 213–14; Chaplin, *Subject Matter*, 116–21.

8. Lawrence I. Conrad, Michael Neve, Vivian Nutton, Roy Porter, and Andrew Wear, *The Western Medical Tradition: 800 BC to AD 1800* (New York: Cambridge University Press, 1995), 141.

9. Kupperman, "Fear of Hot Climates," 217.

10. Carla Gardina Pestana has recently argued that the English did not truly have control of the entire island for years after the "conquest." See Pestana, *The English Conquest of Jamaica: Oliver Cromwell's Bid for Empire* (Cambridge, Mass.: Belknap Press of Harvard University Press, 2017).

11. *A True Description of Jamaica with the Fertility, Commodities, and Healthfulness of the Place* (London: J. M., 1657), 2, 4.

12. Richard Ligon, *A True & Exact History of the Island of Barbados Illustrated with a Mapp of the Island, as Also the Principall Trees and Plants There, Set Forth in Their Due Proportions and Shapes, Drawne out by Their Severall and Respective Scales* (London: Humphrey Moseley, 1657), 27–28.

13. Ibid., 104, 21, 27.

14. Steven Shapin and Simon Schaffer, *Leviathan and the Air-Pump: Hobbes, Boyle, and the Experimental Life*, reprint ed. (Princeton, N.J.: Princeton University Press, 2011).

15. Edmund Hickeringill, *Jamaica Viewed with All the Ports, Harbours, and Their Several Soundings, Towns, and Settlements Thereunto Belonging Together, with the Nature of It's Climate, Fruitfulnesse of the Soile, and Its Suitableness to English Complexions. With Several Other Collateral Observations and Reflexions upon the Island*, 2nd ed. (London: John Williams, 1661), 2–4, emphasis added.

16. Ibid., 6.

17. Richard Blome, *A Description of the Island of Jamaica with the Other Isles and Territories in America, to Which the English Are Related . . . : Taken from the Notes of Sr. Thomas Linch, Knight, Governour of Jamaica, and Other Experienced Persons in the Said Places : Illustrated with Maps* (London: Richard Blome, 1672), 26, emphasis added.

18. Ibid., 5.

19. Hickeringill, *Jamaica Viewed*, 1, 80.

20. Blome, *Description of the Island of Jamaica*, 26–27.

21. Robert Horne, "A Brief Description of the Province of Carolina, by Robert Horne (?), 1666," in *Narratives of Early Carolina, 1650–1708*, ed. Alexander S. Salley Jr. (New York: Barnes & Noble, 1911), 66–67, 70.

22. Blome, *Description of the Island of Jamaica*, 126.

23. Thomas Ashe, "Carolina, or a Description of the Present State of That Country, by Thomas Ashe, 1682," in Salley, *Narratives of Early Carolina*, 141.

24. R. F., *The Present State of Carolina with Advice to the Setlers by R.F.* (London: John Bringhurst, 1682), 8–9.

25. S. Max Edelson has argued that in its early decades Carolina held both the promise of English-style agriculture and the possibility of producing exotic crops that could not be grown in England. This tension undoubtedly diffuses throughout the promotional literature, but this essay stresses that that representation differentiated Carolina from both Caribbean and continental colonies. See S. Max Edelson, *Plantation Enterprise in Colonial South Carolina* (Cambridge, Mass.: Harvard University Press, 2006), chap. 1.

26. John Archdale, "A New Description of That Fertile and Pleasant Province of Carolina, by John Archdale, 1707," in Salley, *Narratives of Early Carolina*, 288.

27. Ashe, "Carolina," 145.

28. Ibid., 141.

29. Horne, "Brief Description," 68.

30. Ashe, "Carolina," 143.

31. Kupperman explained this hope as well as its failed implementation in "Puzzle of the American Climate," 1267–69. Mart A. Stewart argued that the Trustees of Georgia likely suspected the climate of the area was not as perfect as described but remained hopeful because such an image fit with their knowledge of climate as well as their hopes for their endeavor. I echo Stewart that hope and need rather than ignorance motivated overly optimistic descriptions of, as well as policy for, the lower North American seaboard. See "*What Nature Suffers to Groe,*" 34–38. More recently, Ben Marsh has recognized the persistence of attempts at sericulture in the region: "Silk Hopes in Colonial South Carolina," *Journal of Southern History* 78, no. 4 (November 2012): 807–54.

32. Thomas Nairne, "A Letter from South Carolina (London, 1710)," in *Selling a New World: Two Colonial South Carolina Promotional Pamphlets,* ed. Jack P. Greene (Columbia: University of South Carolina Press, 1989), 37.

33. Peter H. Wood, *Black Majority: Negroes in Colonial South Carolina from 1670 through the Stono Rebellion* (New York: W. W. Norton, 1974), 131, 144. On "slave society," see Ira Berlin, *Many Thousands Gone: The First Two Centuries of Slavery in North America* (Cambridge, Mass.: Belknap Press of Harvard University Press, 1998).

34. Horne, "Brief Description," 7.

35. For instance, see R. F., *Present State of Carolina,* 5, 20. An example of a work not mentioning slaves or "negroes" at all is Ashe, "Carolina."

36. Nairne, "Letter from South Carolina," 63–65.

37. John Norris, "Profitable Advice for Rich and Poor (London, 1712)," in Greene, *Selling a New World,* 86–87, 127–30.

38. Nairne, "Letter from South Carolina," 42, 66.

39. Norris, "Profitable Advice," 92.

40. McCandless, *Slavery, Disease, and Suffering,* 12–14, 43–45. The case for slavery and rice production transforming the disease environment is even stronger for Georgia, where historians have discerned that the delayed introduction of slavery and plantation agriculture postponed the introduction of malaria to the colony. See Gerald L. Cates, "'The Seasoning': Disease and Death among the First Colonists of Georgia," *Georgia Historical Quarterly* 64 (1980): 146–58.

41. Joyce E. Chaplin has argued that white southerners came to see their ability to survive the dangers of the climate as a mark of belonging and ingenuity by the turn of the nineteenth century. *An Anxious Pursuit: Agricultural Innovation and Modernity in the Lower South, 1730–1815* (Chapel Hill: University of North Carolina Press, 1993).

42. Norris, "Profitable Advice," 89.

43. Patrick Tailfer, Hugh Anderson, and David Douglas, *A True and Historical Narrative of the Colony of Georgia, in America, from the First Settlement Thereof until This Present Period* (Charles-Town, S.C.: P. Timothy, 1741), 50, 104, 154.

44. Katherine Johnston, "The Constitution of Empire: Place and Bodily Health in the Eighteenth-Century Atlantic," *Atlantic Studies* 10, no. 4 (2013): 443–66.

45. Thomas Malthus, *The Present State of Jamaica with the Life of the Great Columbus the First Discoverer: To Which Is Added an Exact Account of Sir Hen. Morgan's Voyage to, and Famous Siege and Taking of Panama from the Spaniards* (London: Fr. Clark, 1683), 5–7. This

Thomas Malthus is not the famous demographer and social theorist, who would be born more than eighty years later.

46. Edward Long, *The History of Jamaica: Reflections on Its Situation, Settlements, Inhabitants, Climate, Products, Commerce, Laws, and Government* (Montreal: McGill–Queen's University Press, 1774), 1:359, 366; 2:124–29.

47. In the nineteenth century this approach became common in British India, where hill forts were used to garrison troops, and in South Carolina, where planters moved between their plantations and Charleston as the seasons changed. See Mark Harrison, "'The Tender Frame of Man': Disease, Climate and Racial Difference in India and the West Indies, 1760–1860," *Bulletin of the History of Medicine* 70, no. 1 (1996): 81; McCandless, *Slavery, Disease, and Suffering*, 249–50.

48. Malthus, *Present State of Jamaica*, 8.

49. George Frere, *A Short History of Barbados, from Its First Discovery and Settlement to the Present Time*, corrected and enlarged ed. (London: J. Dodsley, 1768), 128.

"The Wind Can Blow Through and Through"

Ventilation, Public Health, and the Regulation of Fresh Air on Antebellum Southern Plantations

ELAINE LAFAY

When planter Thomas Affleck moved from Louisiana to East Texas in 1859, he wrestled with how to pleasingly accommodate slave rooms in the construction of his family's new home. As he wrote to his wife, he was torn between considerations for ventilation and aesthetics. "If I place them so as to have a breeze through them, they will sit awkwardly" relative to the rest of the house, he wrote. "And if I place them to look well, they will have no air! I am pondering it!"[1] At roughly the same time, also in Texas, John White lived as a slave in an attachment to the planters' house similar to the one Affleck planned. Although the slave room was attached to the main house, it was not built as sturdily. White recalled constantly shivering when the winter winds would "go through the cracks between the logs" as if the walls did not exist.[2] These two examples of experiences with ventilation by a slaveholder and an enslaved man had profoundly different consequences. A question born of luxury for a plantation owner—should his estate look attractive—could become a matter of pain and suffering for the men, women, and children who were forced to live with this decision. But enslavers were paying attention to more than aesthetics in their appraisals of ventilation and airflow. Drawing on recent theories in race science, proponents of new plantation management techniques claimed that manipulating airflow could enhance the physical strength and obedience of enslaved people. In practice, many slaves resisted these totalizing theories and sought to ventilate their dwellings on their own terms.

Nearly everyone in the nineteenth century craved fresh air. Health reformers were campaigning for legislation on the ventilation of buildings and homes; slaveholders wrote about the need for fresh air and occasionally built their plantations accordingly; and enslaved men and women modified their homes to regulate it. For enslaved people and planters, the pursuit of ventilation was in the service of positions on health that were fundamentally in conflict and became a site of contest between oppressors and the oppressed.

For physicians and slaveholders, ventilation was important for its material realization of a particular vision of black physiology and its significance to capitalist ideals of plantation management. As part of planters' fixation on increasing profit, they regularly experimented with new methods to accelerate labor productivity. Recent scholarship has identified new management and accounting technologies that enslavers deployed to surveil the enslaved and maximize their labor.[3] In that vein, they also focused on the built environment, claiming that ventilation was key to healthy laborers, thereby displacing blame for illness from the backbreaking demands of labor they themselves demanded. The related claim that ventilation could only be effective with impeccable personal hygiene invoked long-standing arguments about individual responsibility for health.[4] At the same time, planters drew on racist assumptions about the inherent uncleanliness of black men and women to justify their regulation of chimneys, construction materials, and spaces between logs. While enslaved men and women lived in a diverse array of structures, with some often living or sleeping intermittently in the main house, concerns over ventilation were often a matter of degree, not of kind.

But for enslaved individuals, ventilation meant something very different. Many enslaved people craved access to fresh air and actively pursued the ventilation of their quarters. They drew on principles similar to those of slaveholders—that fresh air was healthful and revitalizing—but saw their efforts as part of the need to control their environments and to exert agency over their physical surroundings and bodily comfort. At the same time, access to air became a powerful symbol for freedom in published narratives written by formerly enslaved men and women. In other words, rhetorically, fresh air was a symbol for being free, but practically, "ventilation" as enslavers practiced it could indicate neglect, freezing wind, discomfort, and more evidence of enslavers' callousness shrouded by an appeal to enslaved health care. In how enslaved people responded to the latter efforts, their attempts to ventilate their houses on their terms became a subtle form of resistance.[5] Disregarding planters' attention to ventilation as a means of maximizing the production from their human capital, enslaved people often exercised some influence over the ventilation of their homes by sealing cracks and holes in the walls. Debates over the extent to which ventilation could shape slaves' bodies thus became imbricated in tensions over the degree of power the enslaved had over their bodies at home. Ventilation was therefore both a matter of personal lived experience and deeply symbolic.

This chapter is about the pursuit of ventilation. It brings together histories of medicine and antebellum architecture to show how ventilation reflected mid-nineteenth-century concerns about the constitution of black bodies, the relationships between planters and the enslaved, and the efficiency and health of slave laborers. While historians of medicine and slavery have explored the contours of plantation medicine, they have devoted little attention to the medical implications of plantation dwellings designed to facilitate airflow.[6]

Architectural historians, while exploring the inscription of authority and power in plantation architecture, have neglected to consider the role of medicine and management in shaping these structures.[7] Exploring these themes thus sharpens our understandings of the tensions between planters who sought to modernize their plantations along the latest physiological theories promoted in slave management literature and the enslaved men and women who bore the brunt of these efforts.

To elucidate the multiple meanings of ventilation, I explore the imperative to dictate spatial, economic, and bodily management, all of which inevitably exceeded planters' control. First, I examine the relationships that antebellum physicians observed between airs and bodies, and black bodies in particular. Ventilation emerged as a prominent public health concern for crowded, urban spaces, raising questions about individual versus collective responsibility toward the cleanliness of airs. Next, I discuss how theories of ventilation informed plantations in particular and affected daily life for enslaved peoples. Slaveholders who invoked poor ventilation as a cause for concern were influenced by a combination of medical theories about blackness, popular perceptions of black bodies, and management literature that coalesced in a vision of absolute control over environments, bodies, and property. I conclude by exploring sources by enslaved people, who directly discussed how conceptions of airs shaped their lives and the built environment on plantations. People who were formerly enslaved commented extensively on their dwellings both in published contemporary literature as well as in the Works Progress Administration (WPA) Ex-Slave Interviews conducted in the 1930s. They frequently modified their homes, sealing cracks in the woodwork, and in many cases they exercised a degree of control over the construction of cabins. In doing so, enslaved people refuted the claim that slave dwellings were little more than plantation technologies that manufactured soundness and challenged the erasure of black suffering and personhood that cut across physicians' and planters' discourse on ventilation. Instead, they viewed access to fresh air as central to domestic comfort as well as a profoundly symbolic element of their lives in bondage.

☙

Common knowledge in the nineteenth century held that disease spread by means of miasma, the noxious result of decomposed organic matter in the air.[8] Antebellum Americans associated miasma with an array of sources, including bad smells, night air, poor hygienic conditions, and rotting animal or vegetable products. Physicians agreed that moving air, in whatever form, was superior to air that stood still as both a preventive measure against miasmatic conditions and a means of ridding the air of miasma that was already there. In 1851 New

Orleans physician Edward Barton declared, "Stagnation in air or water, nay, in any form of vegetable or animal life, seems to be against the laws and will of Providence."[9] Movement—air circulating on winds, water flowing through the rivers and tides, clouds and stars drifting across the sky—defined their world: stillness was suspect. Barton elaborated, writing that stagnant air allowed "the exhalations from foul localities to accumulate in the atmosphere . . . but all winds operate to disperse and dilute them with purer air."[10] The objective of nineteenth-century methods of ventilation was to keep domestic air moving, to mimic the health-giving properties of the natural world.[11] In the context of nineteenth-century public health, "fresh air" meant outside air. But too much outside air, or poorly managed air, could be as deadly as too little. Ill-ventilated dwellings could be alternately too drafty or too stuffy, and the consequences could be quite dire and could include chills, aches, fevers, and a range of other ailments. The science of ventilation was therefore about striking a balance, being always attentive to the quality and quantity of airs, the mixing of indoor and outdoor airs, the cadence of the wind, the construction of flues and windows, and, not least, the architecture and spatial arrangement of homes. It was a local, domestic means of harnessing the built environment to shape interactions between bodies and the tumultuous airflow outside.

The domestic circulation of air was part of everyday prevention of disease and maintenance of health and was the subject of dozens of treatises devoted wholly to the proper ventilation of homes, hospitals, and schools, and so on up to the ventilation of entire cities.[12] Theories of ventilation were based on etiology that traced its origins to classical Hippocratic medicine but was undergoing a revival as a centerpiece of mid-nineteenth-century reform movements. Nineteenth-century medical and conventional wisdom argued that public health began in the domestic environment, and that without the introduction of fresh air to dilute and disperse the toxic exhalations that arose from the earth, human bodies, and decaying organic matter, disease would surely set in. Reformers also emphasized that good ventilation was a basic element of civilized homes, linking proper ventilation with the general improvement of hygiene and morality. On a broader scale, the theory was that good ventilation would prevent the city-wide spread of epidemic disease, flushing out the sickly effects of overcrowding and poor sanitation with clean air before illness could spread.

Nearly everyone worried about the circulation of healthy or unhealthy air, and white citizens were anxious about airflow and crowding in their own homes as well as in public venues.[13] Domestic health manuals devoted whole chapters to the proper circulation of air in the home.[14] In 1835 one popular medical manual declared that "no consideration of economy should prevent the most constant attention being paid to proper ventilation, so essential is the latter to health and comfort."[15] In Catherine Beecher's *Treatise on Domestic Economy*, ventilation was central to the domestic science she touted for young ladies. "Every pair of lungs," she wrote, "is constantly withdrawing from the surrounding atmosphere its healthful principle, and returning one, which is injurious to human life."[16] The work provided detailed floor plans and discussions of the best locations for various rooms, windows, flues, boilers, and anything else affecting the quality or movement of air inside. Ventilation operated on two planes: horizontally, through windows and doors, and vertically, through chimneys and flues. Many practitioners particularly valued vertical ventilation for its ability to suck miasmatic air upward, away from human inhalation. For Beecher, good aeration of domestic spaces was an issue of not only public health but also individual mental sharpness. She claimed that poor ventilation and relatedly, overcrowding, could produce "languor, restlessness, and inability to exercise the intellect and feelings," until a person "can never enjoy that elasticity and vigor of the mind."[17]

Ventilation was a topic of keen interest for reformers from a variety of causes. For example, on the front page of the 1838 issue of the *Graham Journal of Health and Longevity*—the health and hygiene periodical espousing physician and reformer Sylvester Graham's adherence to vegetarianism and temperance—the editors declared that "the subject of ventilation is very little thought of, and its importance very little felt, or understood." Ventilation was necessary, they claimed, "to secure the purification of the blood."[18] More specifically, the editors cited what they held to be common knowledge, which was that "the blood enters the lungs thick and dark and . . . leaves them thin and light-colored; and that in the accomplishment of this change the air has some agency." But the editors cautioned that relying on the usual telltale signs of unhealthy air—bad smells, heavy humidity, and "fainting or convulsions"—offered false comfort against a more insidious problem, the constant pollution of indoor air by the exhalations of human beings.[19]

Southern physicians agreed. In the southern states, the hot, humid climate, which had a long-standing reputation as being exceptionally sickly, exacerbated concerns about ventilation in particular as fundamental to the containment of epidemic diseases. New Orleans physician Edward Barton highlighted the necessity of ventilation in a specifically southern climate when he wrote, "From the peculiarity of our climate and position the sanitary condition is so much influenced by the *structure of our dwellings*, that no building should be erected without due surveillance by the authorities. . . . Moisture and crowding are the great enemies we have to guard against. These are corrected by ventilation and space."[20] While unhealthy air and crowding were concerns with which public health authorities grappled across the country, Barton framed his arguments with the "peculiarity" of the southern climate, insistent that it warranted more emphatic attention to domestic airflow.

Planters' fixation on the ventilation of their buildings was therefore part of much broader impulses in public health in the United States and Europe, where ventilation had become increasingly central to health reformers' ambitions. Ventilation was ideologically significant and also had immediate physical consequences. European and northern United States reformers' attention to ventilation, while not in the service of enslaved labor maximization, was in the service of a moralizing health crusade that sharply denounced filthy habits and concentrated its efforts on the working class and peasantry. This discourse blended Enlightenment-era faith in individual rights and a conviction that ill health was the result of a mixture of innate susceptibility, morality, and environmental conditions.[21] A focus on ventilation appealed not only for its ability to harness the spread of disease but also for its centrality to bourgeois hygienic sensibilities.

Planters considered ventilation for these reasons, but their interest in ventilation was shaped by two additional factors: first, ventilation seemed a relatively straightforward means of keeping enslaved people healthy and so protecting planters' investments; but second, ventilation ultimately became a fixture of systematized plantation management, driven by the pursuit of profit, that rose to prominence in the middle decades of the nineteenth century.

એ

The role of ventilation in preserving the health and labor of enslaved people cut across plantation societies in the Atlantic world in the middle decades of the nineteenth century. Flows of knowledge about black physiology, theories of labor and hot climates, and slave management connected planters across the circum-Caribbean world as fears about slave revolt and emerging principles of scientific efficiency further prompted efforts among planters to instill absolute control over the world around them.[22] A tropical or partially tropical climate amplified the conviction that with the right permutation of environmental and bodily oversight, enslavers could extract a higher profit from their labor force. Most colonial-era slave owners were not concerned with the healthful construction of slave quarters, but by the middle decades of the nineteenth century, slaveholders wanted to both maximize their profits and morally justify their ownership of human beings. Ventilation promised both.

Along with the perceived demands of the southern climate that informed medical decision making, ventilation straddled the tension between an imagined benevolent paternalism and the ruthless extraction of labor, and it presented an alluring false promise to further both ends. Worth noting is that physicians who brought a critical eye to living conditions of the enslaved did not, as a matter of course, offer the same attention to the inherently debilitating effects of slavery itself, neglecting to consider the effects of overwork, fatigue, or enslavers' violence on the health of the enslaved.[23] Instead, physicians and planters devoted attention to ventilation as it related to the amount and types of airs enslaved people needed in order to survive but also to work longer and more efficiently.[24] At the heart of this imperative was the concept of "soundness," which informed slave owners' and physicians' health care toward the enslaved. For slaveholders, an enslaved person's health was defined inextricably in relation to her or his ability to work. "Soundness" stripped away the many intricate dimensions of a person's health and determined it according to a single metric of performing physical and reproductive labor. "The great objective is to prevent disease and prolong the useful laboring period of the negro's life," wrote one Mississippi planter in 1847. Ventilation seemed to offer a solution by which, the same planter concluded, economic "interest point[s] out the humane course."[25]

Planters increasingly saw ventilation as a part of highly sophisticated management systems including the latest agricultural technologies that were designed to extract labor from enslaved people at higher and higher rates.[26] Plantations became laboratories for experimenting with new ways of monitoring and analyzing labor. They were sites for planters to not only compare new breeds of cotton but also to experiment with intimate aspects of enslaved people's lives to increase physical and reproductive labor.[27] Planters considered diet, lodging, medicine, and climate in their assessments of how to expedite labor among the enslaved. The rise of new management techniques—characterized by systematization, uniformity, a reliance on technological interventions, and bureaucratic control—allowed planters to incorporate new ideals of a relentless churn of production into their visions of laboring black bodies. The desire to instill order, regimentation, and control over the circulation of airs in the homes and bodies of the enslaved was a manifestation of these new managerial innovations.

Many planters saw properly ventilated buildings as hallmarks of progress. "As there seems to be quite a progressive spirit of improvement pervading the whole Southern country in every branch of agriculture, plantation economy and improvement," wrote one planter in 1852, "I should be gratified indeed, to see more attention manifested in the comfort and durability of negro houses." The planter, going by the pseudonym "Arator," continued to link ventilation with plantation management explicitly, arguing that a plantation could not be truly improved without attentiveness to airflow in slave quarters. For this planter and others, ventilation was part of a broader vision of efficient, stream-lined plantations, part of the same exhilarating impulse by which "cities and towns are rapidly growing; steamboats plow our grand and beautiful rivers; and steam-cars glide gracefully through our valleys and hills, conveying to distant markets the products of our industry and skill." "Every thing bears the impress of progress," he concluded, "save plantation buildings, which continue to wear in the face of neglect and decay."[28] This was more than merely a matter of aesthetics, though that was part of it. Ventilation became a catchall aspect of plantation administration, correcting issues ranging from worker efficiency to responses during epidemics.

It also appealed to enslavers' ideals of paternalistic obligations toward enslaved people. In 1860 the *Hygienic and Literary Magazine*'s inaugural issue opened with an article on the "Physical Treatment of Negroes." In it, one of physician J. Hickson Smith's first orders of business was to address the construction of slave quarters: "As guardians," he declared, "we are to provide comfortable and healthful quarters for our negroes. They *are* provided with houses, it is true . . . yet many of these houses are not constructed upon that plan most favorable for the health of the occupants." Ventilation, he pointed out, was the key to this issue in the form of chimneys, large doors and windows, elevation from the ground, and so on. "In this way," he concluded, "noxious effluvia, in and about the house, will be prevented, and the occupants will have pure, fresh air to breathe; they will sleep comfortably and awake in the morning duly refreshed and qualified for labor."[29] Increasingly captivated by a system of plantation management that guaranteed stronger and more efficient laborers, planters saw ventilation as a humane aspect of disease prevention that was also fundamentally in their own economic self-interest.

Arguments about ventilation on plantations stressed its importance on the enduring medical conviction that black lung capacity was diminished vis-à-vis whites, making black men and women especially susceptible to lung diseases. For instance, physicians and planters often discussed whether hot or cold air was better for maintaining the health of the enslaved. This question hinged on the conviction that black men and women were physiologically suited for labor under the hot sun, which was a popular and long-standing element of the medicolegal justification for slavery. This conviction rested on a diverse assortment of texts, treatises, and personal observations that crisscrossed the Atlantic and stretched from the ancient world to the recent past.[30] In particular, lung function emerged as a central marker of difference. Physician John Stainback Wilson noted, "It is said, and we believe truly, that the chest of the negro is less expanded than that of the white man, and consequently that his breathing capacity is less."[31] Though he was quick to add that lung capacity had nothing to do with muscular development (and so would not hinder physical labor), the broader conviction that black men and women were uniquely susceptible to lung problems remained. In this light, the question of airflow took on new meaning: not only was ventilation a promising means of ensuring that enslaved people remained healthy and productive laborers, but it also demanded particular modifications for dwellings in which enslaved men and women lived based on their biological differences.

Even skeptics of the argument about black susceptibility acknowledged some value in ensuring proper ventilation. For example, one anonymous contributor to the *Southern Cultivator*, writing on slave cabins from Mississippi in 1855, argued that the enslaved were less susceptible to illness from poor ventilation because "owing to certain constitutional peculiarities," they did not "consume as much oxygen as the white man."[32] But "less susceptible" did not mean immune, and despite his overall argument the author acknowledged that some ventilation "ought not to be overlooked."[33] Even when authors were less convinced by the value added from thorough ventilation, it had become such a staple in reformers' assessments of their plantations that it was almost always suggested.

Ventilation was a means for slaveholders to fulfill their sense of paternalistic obligation, and to do so in a way that both reflected and reinforced understandings of black physiology and its relation to air and labor. New Orleans physician Samuel Cartwright highlighted the importance of avoiding heavy, warm airs in slave cabins because such airs would stimulate an innate slothfulness: "a warm atmosphere," he argued, "loaded with carbonic acid and aqueous vapor, was the most congenial to his [an enslaved person's] lungs during sleep, as it is to the infant; that, to insure the respiration of such an atmosphere, he invariably, as if moved by instinct, shrouds his head and face in a blanket."[34] For reasons related to the interaction between warm air and the blood, he claimed that this kept the enslaved in a "natural" state of laziness due to "imperfect atmospherization or vitalization of the blood in the lungs, as occurs in infancy [of whites]." Citing the purportedly lazy and unclean habits of free blacks, Cartwright explained that this natural predilection could be remedied by hard work "in the open air and sunshine," which had the effect of "expand[ing] the lungs . . . thereby to vitalize the impure circulating blood."[35] Cartwright underscored a physiological vision of slavery by which blood, lungs, and airs were the machinery that kept the enslaved at work.

The idea that airs and airflow could affect brain function among the enslaved was prevalent across the Atlantic, as well. Robert Chambers, the natural historian who wrote the widely read *Vestiges of the Natural History of Creation* in 1844, authored a review of scientific management practices among enslavers in the U.S. South in his general-interest publication, *Chambers's Journal*.

"Contrary to the received opinion," he wrote, "a northern climate, though not so favorable to the physical health, is the most favourable to the intellectual development of the negroes; those of Missouri, Kentucky, and the colder parts of Virginia and Maryland, having much more mental energy, being more bold and ungovernable than in the southern lowlands; a dense atmosphere causing better ventilation of their blood." While Chambers himself was an abolitionist, his review of the southern literature on the "improved dwellings" of slaves was positive and even admiring at points.[36] Chambers agreed with physicians such as Cartwright who were convinced that the local climate and the domestic manipulation of airs were a means by which planters could exert tremendous control over the enslaved. Ventilation seemed to offer a means of disciplining enslaved people according to the inner machinery of the human body, linking reforms of living conditions with other management ideals that encouraged the adoption of new agricultural technologies and accounting practices that allowed planters to calculate and control productivity on their plantations.

Fantasies about plantations—and enslaved people—that planters could manage with the silent aid of airs and winds drew on a long-standing investigation into what was "natural" for enslaved men and women. Many plantation owners were convinced that with a replication of an imagined "natural" environment would come health, longevity, endurance, and stamina. The discussion of what constituted "natural" included queries over air and lung function, and particularly the question of whether hot or cold air would be more fortifying for the enslaved. Some planters and doctors fixated on the observed tendency for some enslaved people to cover their heads with a blanket while they slept, convinced that this was a telling detail that shed light on the kinds of airs that would best preserve their health. "The disposition of the negro to cover his head and sleep with it to the fire is well known," wrote Wilson.[37] Chambers agreed, claiming that "the negro's lungs are very sensitive to the impressions of cold air. . . . [They] seem to take a positive pleasure in breathing heated air and warm smoke. If they sleep beside a fire, they turn their heads to it."[38] Wilson and Chambers displayed a conviction that sleeping bodies, which seemed to reveal inner truths of physiology and constitution, could not lie. Planters and physicians could thus use the subconscious actions of the enslaved to tailor the local environment with an eye toward the systematic maintenance of health and the improved capacity to labor.

Like much of the medical literature about enslaved people, the discourse on ventilation—whether writers promoted it or not—therefore became an avenue for observers to express their profound disgust at black bodies. The discourse on ventilation should be considered in a context of enslavers' personal revulsion to dirt and filth, which they attributed to moral deficiencies in enslaved people rather than deficient living conditions. According to prevailing medical thought, airs influenced and were influenced by local building materials, bodies, and vegetation, but this seemingly neutral etiological fact that drove reformers' hygienic imperatives was deeply infused with revulsion. "It must be apparent," one anonymous planter from Mississippi wrote, "that the noxious exhalations emenating [*sic*] from the half-burried and decaying timbers, and from the abundant collections of every description of putrifying trash, usually to be found underneath and about these old, dirty habitations, together with other numerous deleterious influences inseparably connected therewith, are well calculated to generate disease."[39] For physicians and planters, describing and moralizing on the filth of enslaved people's dwellings was a means of both explaining its pathological import as well as displacing blame for their physical well-being entirely on enslaved people themselves.

This language paralleled that of sanitary reformers in the northern United States and western Europe, directed mainly at members of the working class and immigrants.[40] These reformers' obsessions with ventilation were partly a practical matter of disease prevention but were also laced with the politics of disgust, filth, and above all the aesthetic threat of the working class.[41] Similarly, it was not uncommon for physicians and planters to class the bodies of enslaved men and women as a source of rot in the air.[42] In his article about the construction of slave cabins, Wilson emphasized keeping cabins both warm *and* ventilated, thereby keeping the enslaved from exposure to "all the evils arising from breathing an impure air impregnated with the reeking exhalations of [the enslaved person's] filthy body."[43] One writer, under the initials R. W. N. N., laid bare his disgust for enslaved men and women, promoting ventilation as a remedy for what he believed to be unforgivable filthiness of their living quarters. Describing the "excrements and emanations from the human body" that could gather beneath a slave quarter, this Virginia planter reached the limits of language, writing that the reader "must excuse an unrefined word now and then, for, to tell the truth, I can't find a synonym for the word which would at all convey the idea I intend."[44] The politics of disgust, marshalled for a moralizing and hygienic mission, also served to rationalize the poverty, squalor, and hardships of life under the slave regime.

The emphasis on cleanliness, and the consequent directive for regular surveillance by slaveholders or overseers, revealed another set of reasons behind the concern for ventilation in slave quarters. While planters and physicians advocated for ventilation ostensibly for health reasons, some of their recommendations served to increase surveillance and eliminate contraband. Physicians and slaveholders advocated the lifting of slave cabins off the ground to facilitate ventilation, but this also guaranteed that slaves would no longer be able to conceal supplies or stolen goods in underground cellars or "hidey-holes."[45] It also gave planters another reason to surveil enslaved people when they were not working. R. W. N. N., for instance, was explicit: the aims of slave cabins were, he wrote, "First, the health and comfort of the occupants; Secondly, the convenience of nursing, surveillance, discipline, and the supply of wood and water; and thirdly, the economy of construction."[46] Planters marshalled the need for medical supervision in support of a broader surveillance, as well. For example, Robert J. Draughon, an Alabama physician, claimed that "small, low, tight and filthy" houses were so poorly ventilated that enslaved people napped outside in the evenings, leading, he contended, to chills and illness. To see for themselves, Draughon wrote, "Let planters go at this hour around their quarters, and feel the hands and feet" of enslaved people sleeping outside.[47]

The attention planters gave to slave quarters in terms of actual construction was contingent on local circumstance and above all motivated by a desire for surveillance and control.[48] There were accounts by proslavery writers of planters who had torn down and reconstructed slave quarters to rectify unhealthy quarters. Boston clergyman Nehemiah Adams, whose 1854 travelogue *A South-Side View of Slavery* argued that slavery was beneficial for black peoples' religious instruction, overheard one such story about a physician-planter who tore down the brick cabins in the slave quarter and replaced them with log houses after enslaved people "grew sick in them." "A great fire, and at the same time thorough ventilation, are essential," Adams elaborated. "Both of these are obtained together in the cabins better than in framed or brick dwellings."[49]

Ventilation is fascinating because it is a window into the fraught world of a cultivated sense of disgust, moral crusading and justification, distorted pictures of health as labor efficiency, techniques of disciplinary control, and the frank material reality of logs and winds that made architectural questions anything but benign or straightforward. As part of the impulse to make their plantations more efficient, nineteenth-century slaveholders latched onto ventilation for its perceived effects on black bodies' capacity for labor. In this discourse, they drew on a long history of disgust to reinforce slaveholders' claims that poor hygienic habits among enslaved people rendered ventilation both necessary and insufficient. This reveals a tension between planters' visions and a sense that they could exert control over the environment to suit their aims. Their arguments— that the conditions in which enslaved people lived determined the likelihood of contracting disease or becoming otherwise "unsound"—grated against the reality of the enslaved who cooked, slept, and tried to maintain households in woefully deficient environments. Abolitionists such as Robert Chambers, as well, admired and lauded ventilation for its perceived public health effects. At the same time, planters took up the cause of ventilation in part because it offered a thinly veiled means to offset the blame for the realities of the slave system—its hours, fatigue, and violence—and drew on a ready-made discourse for the essentialization of enslaved bodies and behaviors.

છે

Enslaved men and women spent a lot of time considering the quality of air in their dwellings. But their perceptions of ventilation, and the reasons they craved it, were markedly different from those of the planters and physicians who sought to surveil and manage their domestic lives. Moreover, while ventilation was a practical matter of construction, the movement of air—and the restriction of it—was central to the discourse on the institution of slavery and held profound metaphorical meaning that went beyond the details of construction. The living conditions under slavery were overwhelmingly poor. Enslaved men and women regularly described suffering from exposure, overcrowding, and a lack of light in their dwellings.[50] Many sought to ameliorate these conditions as best they could, and these efforts, specifically the daubing of walls, attracted the attention and sometimes ire of enslavers. While some enslaved people had a degree of latitude over the construction and maintenance of slave quarters, others were forced to endure impoverished quarters with little recourse for improvement. This section considers both slave narratives about lived experience on plantations and the efforts to rhetorically mobilize airflow for its metaphorical meaning. These were not the same, and in fact were often at odds with each other, but they were also sharply conflicting with planters' formulations of efficiency and labor.

The lived experience of the enslaved reveals how people experienced airflow in an enclosed space.[51] As physicians debated the best building material for keeping enslaved people sound—brick, log, or weatherboards—Clara Brim, who was enslaved on a plantation in Branch, Louisiana, remembered in the 1930s that there was no discernible difference between log and plank houses (especially, she noted, since they all had brick chimneys) on the plantation where she was raised. Describing both log and plank homes, she said, "Dey houses what de wind didn't blow in."[52] But for others, cracks between logs and drafts of air were a regular feature of slave quarters. Many enslaved people modified the cabins in this regard as a matter of course, using a combination of mud and dirt to seal the openings. George Eason, who had been enslaved on Jack Ormond's plantation in Georgia, remembered that residents would use mud to close the openings between logs and prevent "the weather," as the WPA interviewer paraphrased, from entering.[53] Henry Bland, another former slave from Georgia, said the same.[54] Enslaved men and women largely did the work of construction and made use of the materials they had at their disposal. Henry

Kirk Miller, for example, recalled the pragmatism of constructing the log quarters on the plantation where he was enslaved, saying matter-of-factly that "they'd just go out in the woods and get logs and put up a log house. Put dirt and mud or clay in the cracks to seal it. Notch the logs in the end to hitch them at corners. Nailed planks at the end of the logs to make a door frame."[55] The modification of cabin construction was a way for enslaved men and women to exert an element of control over their environment. Daubing walls and cracks was a means of manipulating building materials for warmth or comfort, but it was also a method for determining precisely what kinds of airs would circulate in both homes and veins.

But on other plantations, dwellings offered no such solace, and meanings ascribed to the entry of winds were much different. Former slave Josiah Henson explicitly invoked the "system of management" of the plantation on which he grew up that relegated enslaved people to dwellings that were beyond their abilities to reform. In the 1849 narrative of his life, Henson described slave quarters that consisted of "log huts, of a single small room, with no other floor than the trodden earth, in which ten or a dozen persons—men, women, and children—might sleep, but which could not protect them from the dampness and cold, nor permit the existence of the common decencies of life."[56] When Jourden Banks arrived at the Alabama plantation where he had been sold, he was horrified at the conditions of the cabin that he was to share with five others. "Here you have it," he wrote bitterly, "a log cabin with the cracks wide open. No chinking or daubing. The wind can blow through and through. . . . Here you can lie on your board and count the stars between the boards that are over your head as a mockery for a roof." Driven past the point of exhaustion each day, under the watch of an overseer who was miserly with rations, Banks ended each day "miserable even when I thus lay me down."[57] Often, ventilation as experienced by the enslaved was not healthful but rather a testament to dismal construction of walls that did not keep the elements out, and as a result the problem was more often a failure to keep warm.

Enslaved peoples' houses occupied a tenuous, seemingly paradoxical position. Dwellings were key sites of surveillance and exploitation within a regime whose only priority was the extraction of labor; at the same time, they were enslaved peoples' permanent dwellings replete with expectations of comfort, familial belonging, and safety.[58] The question of ventilation brings the inherent tensions of this duality into stark contrast. In a narrative of his childhood spent enslaved on a South Carolina plantation, Thomas Jones remembers his parents' efforts to make their house "a happy place for their dear children." To do this, he went on, they built furniture and "spent many hours of willing toil to stop up the chinks between the logs of their poor hut, that they and their children might be protected from the storm and cold."[59] Breathing clean air was only one part of modifying dwellings; another was producing a domestic space that provided some element of comfort and reprieve. In doing so, enslaved people transformed their living spaces, valuing things like comfort and survival rather than efficiency. The drive with which enslaved men and women sought to exert influence over their homes was a means of resisting a system that understood the flow of air as abstracted from bodily feeling. For both enslavers and the enslaved, the flow of air was charged with meaning, but the logics in which it operated led to markedly different priorities.

Some planters, moreover, eyed the willful alteration of quarters with something close to disdain and even fury. They sought to restrict attempts to modify the buildings. One anonymous planter in 1852 wrote in *The Soil of the South* that he was "opposed to daubing the cracks with mud as it renders the house disagreeably warm during the spring and summer months and does not allow of the ready escape of the unwholesome exhalations pervading negro houses generally."[60] Other planters would go out of their way to prevent enslaved people from altering their dwellings, and the physician John Stainback Wilson suggested that "ventilation should be secured by having openings *near the top of the house*, where impurities naturally tend to escape, and where the negroes are not so likely to interfere by chinking up with old rags, &c."[61] Domestic architecture thus became a site of struggle for enslaved people who wanted to ameliorate their exposure to the elements and planters who wanted to exert control over everything within their domains of mastery, including the airflow in and out of enslaved peoples' homes and bodies. This reflected, on one side, expectations about what constituted cozy or drafty and the experience of appropriate indoor temperatures, versus the medical understanding of physiologically small lungs.

Access to air held particular relevance in Harriet Jacobs's *Incidents in the Life of a Slave Girl*, published in 1861. The protagonist, under the pseudonym Linda Brent, is unwilling to leave her children behind, so she hides in her grandmother's attic to be near them. Jacobs's descriptions of her arrival and early weeks in the attic, which she called the loophole, illustrated the link between her physical debilitation and severance from her family. Her description alternated between the repressive atmosphere and her repressed access to her children, underscoring the connection between access to fresh air and her humanity: "The air was stifling; the darkness total," she wrote of her hiding place. "I suffered for air even more than for light."[62] The language illustrated a cultural shift in the meanings of ventilation. For planters and physicians, ventilation was about filth and control; for Harriet Jacobs, lack of ventilation was about the erasure of her personhood. This rhetoric was not only opposed to enslavers' accounts of ventilation; it also operated on a different axis from most of the foregoing slave narratives, which mainly emphasized reducing drafts. Jacobs's oppressive lack of air forces her readers to contend with the depravity of the slave regime as she struggles to breathe, all the while affirming the sanctity of her motherhood in her refusal to leave her children behind. Cognizant of medical and popular ideas of black men and women that characterized them as possessing blunted emotional and physical sensibilities, antislavery writers and former slaves such as Jacobs used ventilation to underscore the depths of suffering experienced on both counts.

Jacobs then brings in a therapeutic element to provide at least partial emotional and physical relief. As she carved a small hole in the roof of her loophole, she consoled herself with the thought that "now I will have some light. Now I will see my children." The fresh air through her one-square-inch opening provided relief on two planes: social, in her still restricted but improved access to her children; and physical, from the relief, however slight, that she felt from "the little whiff of air that floated in."[63] She tried to engage in traditional domestic pastimes of reading, sewing, and watching her children, but the extent to which her dwelling restricted her access to air and light was so severe that her attempts became almost absurd. Though she is escaped and supposedly free, the shackles of slavery in this rendering extended beyond direct life on the plantation to control her life even when she was supposedly beyond its reach. In the condition of supposed or attempted freedom, she continued to suffer from the "heat of [her] den," still lacking for air.[64]

Access to air was a prominent theme in antislavery writing, and formerly enslaved men and women often highlighted struggles with ventilation to communicate to their northern audience the extent to which the slave regime dehumanized and tortured them. These writers drew on the embedded nature of ventilation in a series of reform movements and its place as a central feature of civilized life to emphasize the tragic outcome of efforts to control airflow on plantations. But the power of air—inhaling "free air," or "breathing free"— went beyond the metaphorical and carried a literal component that bolstered its literary effect. The correlation between breath and life, between airs and freedoms, is not notable by itself, but this connection gains new meaning against the backdrop of the physical construction of homes and the regulation of airs and lungs on plantations.

Abolitionists contrasted the polluted air of the slave regime with the pure, free air of the northern states. Elias Smith's "Flight of the Bondman," which appeared in the 1849 publication of William Wells Brown's account of Brown's escape from slavery, promised that for enslaved people who sought freedom in the North, "There is room 'mong our hills for the true and the brave / Let his lungs breathe our free northern air!" He returned to the air again in the last stanza, closing the song with "May a free northern soil soon give freedom to *all* / Who shall breathe in its pure mountain air."[65] Mountains had a long-standing reputation as sites of exceptionally clean air in both medical and popular literature, but Smith's insistence on air that is "free" gestured to the encompassing nature of slavery as well as the centrality of breath and air to abolitionist conceptions of freedom.

Living conditions and ventilation specifically were topics of note for enslaved men and women in their contemporary accounts of life under slavery as well as in the WPA interviews with the formerly enslaved in the 1930s. These accounts clearly did not agree with the view put forward by planters and physicians. The flow of air in and out of slave quarters was not only a reality enslaved people experienced; it was at times an element of domestic life over which they could have some influence. Their perspective was informed by the desire to make impoverished conditions as comfortable as possible, not efforts to optimize their efficiency as laborers. In other words, they wanted reprieve from the demands of the day, not preparation to meet them more optimally. The modification of dwellings—filling cracks in the architecture in the winter, opening them up in the summer—was for many enslaved people a regular feature of life on plantations, though some slave owners tried to keep them from doing so.

The regulation of air became a point of reference for much broader conversations about slavery and human rights, and access to fresh air was a common motif in national debates over slavery. In the 1830s, the time of the upswing in ventilation concerns, there was a sharp change in abolitionist and antislavery rhetoric. The antislavery rhetoric from the Enlightenment that was rooted in cool logic and reason was replaced by deeply emotional, sensationalist accounts of slavery that were mediated by the exposé genre and focused on sadism, torture, depravity, and suffering as the defining aspects of life for the enslaved.[66] These sources drew on the emotional resonance of slavery to extol the universal right to act as a free moral agent. Ventilation, and lack thereof, became a telling detail of living conditions under slavery and ultimately a commentary on the inherent contradictions in planters' efforts to improve a slave society.

Part of the reason that enslaved people had such different views from enslavers was that enslaved people found the conditions in which they were forced to survive almost uninhabitable. Ventilation in slave quarters was not, in this metric, the rationally enacted, hygienically fit apotheosis of southern plantation science; rather, slave quarters were emblematic of shoddy construction and were barely fit for human habitation based on the resources enslavers invested. In the abstract, however, when taken out of the context of gaping log holes that did not keep the weather out, access to air still had a lot of value in abolitionist debates about access to freedom and the stifling conditions that extended to reach even those who were supposedly free. Debates over ventilation in many ways illustrate the extent to which slaveholders sought to control the bodies of the enslaved, and how antislavery writers drew on a rich metaphorical tradition of linking freedom with fresh air to illuminate the extent of suffering under slavery. At the same time, the experience of ventilation on plantations could also be a site of resistance as enslaved men and women undertook extensive efforts to modify their dwellings from the initial construction to the maintenance of seals in cracks and holes in spite of slaveholders' attempts to regulate their abilities to do so. This was contingent on the availability of resources, however, and for many enslaved people, ventilation, or lack thereof, remained a source of suffering. As former slave Mary Ella Grandberry recalled of the cabins on a plantation in Colbert County, Alabama, "Dey wasn't fitten for nobody to lib in. We jes' had to put up wid 'em."[67]

‌ ℰℐ

The contours of how planters, physicians, and the enslaved imagined and experienced ventilation reveal diverse perspectives on a core aspect of plantation life. The rise of ventilation as a public health issue came to prominence in the middle decades of the nineteenth century as part of sweeping new reforms that highlighted open, airy dwellings as hallmarks of the sanitary age. Antebellum Americans framed their approach to ventilation as central to disease prevention and a concrete element of public health reform.

Looking at medical views about airflow broadens our understanding of control on the plantation. In the southern states, this discourse reveals how doctors and planters pursued a vision of plantation architecture that directed air for health but also in pursuit of ideals of plantation management. The depths of paternalism and the new managerial science collided with slave resistance in the domestic architecture of slave quarters. For enslavers, pursuing ventilation designs that catered to the particular respiratory needs of their slaves was a means of upholding ideals of efficiency, vigor, and compliance within a broader managerial system of production. Medical and scientific knowledge was a core component of this vision. Physicians published in agricultural journals and general interest publications about the physiological demands of black lungs, blacks' natural inclinations, and the particularities that shaped black bodies' interactions with the outside world.

For the enslaved, however, over- and underventilation were conditions to be endured, and the regulated access to air a powerful symbol of their enslavement. When they could, enslaved people drew on resources they had at their disposal to modify their dwellings to survive but also to wrench back an element of bodily integrity in domestic space. The ventilation of slave quarters was a site of resistance not only in the literal structures on plantations but also in antislavery rhetoric that highlighted poorly ventilated dwellings as a devastating and dehumanizing aspect of plantation life. Just like the mechanistic control of slavery could never be totalizing, the desire for environmental management also confounds and rejects complete control.

NOTES

The author would like to acknowledge Eram Alam, David Barnes, Rachel Elder, Beth Linker, Alexis Rider, J. Maxwell Rogoski, and Jesse Smith for their incisive comments on prior versions of this essay. I am also grateful to Rana Hogarth and Stephen Kenny for their commentary and encouragement on this paper's earliest form at the Southern Historical Association annual meeting. Thanks to D. Andrew Johnson and Thomas Blake Earle for their patience, organizational efforts, and valuable feedback.

1. Thomas Affleck to Alice Affleck, April 27, 1859, Thomas Affleck Papers, box 9, folder 6, Louisiana and Lower Mississippi Valley Collections, LSU Libraries, Baton Rouge, La. Thomas Affleck fostered a long-standing interest in plantation management and efficiency. See Caitlin Rosenthal, "Slavery's Scientific Management: Masters and Managers," in *Slavery's Capitalism: A New History of American Economic Development*, ed. Sven Beckert and Seth Rockman (Philadelphia: University of Pennsylvania Press, 2016).

2. T. Lindsay Baker and Julie P. Baker, eds., *The WPA Oklahoma Slave Narratives* (Norman: University of Oklahoma Press, 1996), 468, 323.

3. This literature is extensive. See Caitlin Rosenthal, *Accounting for Slavery: Masters and Management* (Cambridge, Mass.: Harvard University Press, 2018); Edward E. Baptist, *The Half That Has Never Been Told: Slavery and the Making of American Capitalism* (New York: Basic Books, 2014); Walter Johnson, *River of Dark Dreams: Slavery and Empire in the Cotton Kingdom* (Cambridge, Mass.: Harvard University Press, 2013); Daniel B. Rood, *The Reinvention of Atlantic Slavery: Technology, Labor, Race, and Capitalism in the Greater Caribbean* (New York: Oxford University Press, 2017); Sven Beckert, *Empire of Cotton: A Global History* (New York: Alfred A. Knopf, 2014).

4. Kathleen M. Brown, *Foul Bodies: Cleanliness in Early America* (New Haven, Conn.: Yale University Press, 2009). See also Suellen Hoy, *Chasing Dirt: The American Pursuit of Cleanliness* (New York: Oxford University Press, 1995).

5. This builds on work that has argued for taking seriously "small" acts of resistance by subjugated peoples. For this argument generally, see James Scott, *Weapons of the Weak: Everyday Forms of Peasant Resistance* (New Haven, Conn.: Yale University Press, 1985), and Scott, *Domination and the Arts of Resistance: Hidden Transcripts* (New Haven, Conn.: Yale University Press, 1990). On the dimensions of everyday forms of slave resistance, see Stephanie M. H. Camp, *Closer to Freedom: Enslaved Women and Everyday Resistance in the Plantation South* (Chapel Hill: University of North Carolina Press, 2004); Dea Boster, *African American Slavery and Disability: Bodies, Property, and Power in the Antebellum South, 1800–1860* (New York: Routledge, 2013); Deborah Gray White, *Ar'n't I a Woman? Female Slaves in the Plantation South* (New York: W. W. Norton, 1985); Stephanie Shaw, "Mothering under Slavery in the Antebellum South," in *Mothers and Motherhood: Readings in*

American History, ed. Rima D. Apple and Janet Golden (Columbus: Ohio State University Press, 1997).

6. See especially Sharla M. Fett, *Working Cures: Healing, Health, and Power on Southern Slave Plantations* (Chapel Hill: University of North Carolina Press, 2002); Todd Savitt, *Medicine and Slavery: The Diseases and Health Care of Blacks in Antebellum Virginia* (Urbana: University of Illinois Press, 1978); Steven Stowe, *Doctoring the South: Southern Physicians and Everyday Medicine in the Mid-Nineteenth Century* (Chapel Hill: University of North Carolina Press, 2004); Marli F. Weiner with Mazie Hough, *Sex, Sickness, and Slavery: Illness in the Antebellum South* (Urbana: University of Illinois Press, 2012); Peter McCandless, *Slavery, Disease, and Suffering in the South Carolina Lowcountry* (New York: Cambridge University Press, 2011). Historians of medicine have explored ventilation in many other settings, however, including tenements, children's hospitals, and prisons. On ventilation and other sanitary reforms as part of a broader class conflict over how to redirect public health during the Industrial Revolution, see David S. Barnes, *The Great Stink of Paris and the Nineteenth-Century Struggle against Filth and Germs* (Baltimore: Johns Hopkins University Press, 2006), and Christopher Hamlin, *Public Health and Social Justice in the Age of Chadwick: Britain, 1800–1854* (New York: Cambridge University Press, 1998).

7. Dell Upton, "White and Black Landscapes in Eighteenth-Century Virginia," in *Material life in America, 1600–1860*, ed. Robert Blair St. George (Boston: Northeastern University Press, 1988), 357–69; John Michael Vlach, *Back of the Big House: The Architecture of Plantation Slavery* (Chapel Hill: University of North Carolina Press, 1993); Vlach, "'Snug Li'l House with Flue and Oven': Nineteenth-Century Reforms in Plantation Slave Housing," in *Gender, Class, and Shelter: Perspectives in Vernacular Architecture*, vol. 5, ed. Elizabeth Collins Cromley and Carter L. Hudgins (Knoxville: University of Tennessee Press, 1995), 118–29; Gwendolyn Wright, "The 'Big House' and the Slave Quarters," in Wright, *Building the Dream: A Social History of Housing in America* (New York: Pantheon, 1981); Theresa A. Singleton, *The Archaeology of Slavery and Plantation Life* (Orlando: Academic Press, 1985); Clifton Ellis and Rebecca Ginsburg, *Cabin, Quarter, Plantation: Architecture and Landscapes of North American Slavery* (New Haven, Conn.: Yale University Press, 2010); Whitney Battle-Baptiste, "'In This Here Place': Interpreting Enslaved Homeplaces," in *Archaeology of Atlantic Africa and the African Diaspora*, ed. Akinwumi Ogundiran and Toyin Falola (Bloomington: Indiana University Press, 2007), 233–48. See also Lauren LaFauci, "Taking the (Southern) Waters: Science, Slavery, and Nationalism at the Virginia Springs," *Anthropology and Medicine* 18 (April 2011): 7–22.

8. On miasma more generally, see Melanie Kiechle, *Smell Detectives: An Olfactory History of Nineteenth-Century Urban America* (Seattle: University of Washington Press, 2017); Caroline Hannaway, "Environment and Miasmata," in *Companion Encyclopedia of the History of Medicine*, ed. W. F. Bynum and Roy Porter (New York: Routledge, 1993), 1:292–308; Conevery Bolton Valencius, *The Health of the Country: How American Settlers Understood Themselves and Their Land* (New York: Basic Books, 2002).

9. E. H. Barton, *Report to the Louisiana State Medical Society, on the Meteorology, Vital Statistics and Hygiene of the State of Louisiana* (New Orleans: Davies, Son & Co., 1851), 17.

10. E. H. Barton, "Report upon the Sanitary Condition of New Orleans," *Report of the Sanitary Commission of New Orleans on the Epidemic Yellow Fever of 1853* (New Orleans: Picayune Office, 1854), 305.

11. In his 1846 treatise on ventilation, physician Morrill Wyman described the circulation of winds around the earth as the *"ventilation of the globe"* (emphasis in original). Morrill Wyman, *A Practical Treatise on Ventilation* (Boston: Monroe, 1846), 8.

12. See Kiechle, *Smell Detectives*. The literature on hospital and asylum construction was heavily influential on the construction of healthful homes. Florence Nightingale, for instance, famously maintained that the "very first canon of nursing" was "TO KEEP THE AIR [THE PATIENT] BREATHES AS PURE AS THE EXTERNAL AIR, WITHOUT CHILLING HIM." See *Notes on Nursing: What It Is, and What It Is Not* (New York: D. Appleton, 1860), 12. Nightingale devoted the first two sections of her work to the pursuit of pure air and sound ventilation. Advocates for better ventilation in schoolhouses, especially William Alcott, also claimed that sound ventilation and regular exposure to fresh air would facilitate mental sharpness. See William Andrus Alcott, *Essay on the Construction of Schoolhouses: To Which Was Awarded the Prize Offered by the American School of Instruction, August, 1831* (Boston: Hilliard, Gray, Little and Wilkins, and Richardson, Lord and Holbrook, 1832).

13. Ventilation was of widespread concern among factory owners who wanted to facilitate efficiency and skill in their workforce. This discourse mirrored that among slave owners and physicians who wished to use the built environment to stimulate efficiency on plantations in an earlier context. See Gail Cooper, *Air Conditioning America: Engineers and the Controlled Environment, 1900–1960* (Baltimore: Johns Hopkins University Press, 1998).

14. For a discussion of domestic advice manuals and ventilation, see Kiechle, *Smell Detectives*, esp. "Smells Like Home: Odors in the Domestic Environment," 78–105. For a post–bacteriological revolution discussion of ventilation and the pursuit of germ-free airs, see Nancy Tomes, *Gospel of Germs: Men, Women, and the Microbe in American Life* (Cambridge, Mass.: Harvard University Press, 1998).

15. "A physician in Philadelphia," *The Home Book of Health and Medicine: A Popular Treatise on the Means of Avoiding and Curing Diseases, and of Preserving the Health and Vigour of the Body* (Philadelphia: Key & Biddle, 1835), 102.

16. Catherine Beecher, *A Treatise on Domestic Economy for the Use of Young Ladies at Home and at School* (Boston: T. H. Webb, 1841), 196.

17. Ibid.

18. "Ventilation of Apartments," *Graham Journal of Health and Longevity* 2, no. 16 (1838): 241. The centrality of fresh air to the purification of the blood had roots in the fifteenth-century anatomical investigations of William Harvey and subsequent scientific theories about circulation from chemists including Joseph Priestley and Antoine Lavoisier. See Kiechle, 25–27.

19. "Ventilation of Apartments," 241. The potential offenses of human bodies, especially unclean ones, were vast. See Brown, *Foul Bodies*.

20. Edward H. Barton, *The Cause and Prevention of Yellow Fever at New Orleans and Other Cities in America* (New York: H. Bailliere, 1857), 218–19. A fixation on the particularity of the southern climate was long-standing, if not unique in medical climatology. For an excellent analysis of the history of this concept, see Jason Hauser, "Scarce Fit for Anything but Slaves and Brutes: Climate in the Old Southwest, 1798–1855," *Alabama Review* 70 (April 2017): 112–25. See also Jason Hauser, "By Degree: A History of Heat in the Subtropical American South" (PhD diss., Mississippi State University, 2017).

21. In practice, moral management offered a strictly controlled environment within which physicians enforced Protestant, middle-class social values. Eventually, as asylums

and prisons became overcrowded, moral management changed into another brand of authoritarian control, and evolved alongside older methods of physical restraint, isolation, and punishment instead of replacing them entirely. On the rise of moral management, see Nancy Tomes, *A Generous Confidence: Thomas Story Kirkbride and the Art of Asylum Keeping, 1840–1883* (New York: Cambridge University Press, 1984).

22. Recent scholarship has situated circum-Caribbean theories of blackness and labor in imperial and transnational contexts. See Ikuko Asaka, *Tropical Freedom: Climate, Settler Colonialism, and Black Exclusion in the Age of Emancipation* (Durham, N.C.: Duke University Press, 2017); Rana Hogarth, *Medicalizing Blackness: Making Racial Difference in the Atlantic World, 1780–1840* (Chapel Hill: University of North Carolina Press, 2017); Pablo F. Gomez, *The Experiential Caribbean: Creating Knowledge and Healing in the Early Modern Atlantic* (Chapel Hill: University of North Carolina Press, 2017); Suman Seth, *Difference and Disease: Medicine, Race, and Locality in the Eighteenth-Century British Empire* (New York: Cambridge University Press, 2018).

23. For southern physicians' roles on plantations, see Stowe, *Doctoring the South*, and Deirdre Cooper Owens, *Medical Bondage: Race, Gender, and the Origins of American Gynecology* (Athens: University of Georgia Press, 2017).

24. This was related to the discourse on "soundness," or fitness for labor. For extended discussions of soundness as well as the complex systems of health care enslaved people developed among themselves, see Fett, *Working Cures*; Marie Jenkins Schwartz, *Birthing a Slave: Motherhood and Medicine in the Antebellum South* (Cambridge, Mass.: Harvard University Press, 2006); Boster, *African American Slavery and Disability*, 34–51.

25. A Citizen of Mississippi, "The Negro," *De Bow's Review*, May 1847, 420.

26. On reforms and plantation management in the American South, see Steven Collins, "System, Organization, and Agricultural Reform in the Antebellum South, 1840–1860," *Agricultural History* 75 (Winter 2001): 1–17; Drew Gilpin Faust, *James Henry Hammond and the Old South: A Design for Mastery* (Baton Rouge: Louisiana State University Press, 1982); Eugene D. Genovese, *The Political Economy of Slavery: Studies in the Economy and Society of the Slave South* (New York: Pantheon, 1965); Anthony E. Kaye, "The Second Slavery: Modernity in the Nineteenth-Century South and the Atlantic World," *Journal of Southern History* 75 (August 2009): 627–50; Mark M. Smith, *Mastered by the Clock: Time, Slavery, and Freedom in the American South* (Chapel Hill: University of North Carolina Press, 1997).

27. Historians used to believe that southern planters borrowed management techniques from textile mills and factories in northern cities. Recent scholarship suggests, however, that enslavers were refining such techniques much earlier. See Rosenthal, "Slavery's Scientific Management."

28. Arator, "Negro Houses," *Soil of the South*, March 1852, 229.

29. J. Hickson Smith, "Physical Treatment of Negroes," *Hygienic and Literary Magazine*, January 1860, 1–10, quotations on 5, 9.

30. On the long history of proslavery ideology and climate in the Atlantic world, see David Brion Davis, *Inhuman Bondage: The Rise and Fall of Slavery* (New York: Oxford University Press, 2006); Valencius, *Health of the Country*, esp. "Racial Anxieties," 229–58; Katherine Johnston, "The Constitution of Empire: Place and Bodily Health in the Eighteenth-Century Atlantic," *Atlantic Studies* 10 (December 2013): 443–66.

31. John Stainback Wilson, "The Peculiarities and Diseases of Negroes," *American Cotton Planter and Soil of the South* 4, no. 1 (1860): 46.

32. Omo., "Negro Houses—Plantation Hospitals," *Southern Cultivator* 14 (January 1856): 18. Racial difference in lung capacity was a prevalent concern into the twentieth century. Cartwright drew on a long history of speculation about the difference between white and black lungs, including by Thomas Jefferson. See Lundy Braun, *Breathing Race into the Machine: The Surprising Career of the Spirometer from Plantation to Genetics* (Minneapolis: University of Minnesota Press, 2014).

33. Arator, "Negro Houses," 17. The author placed slightly greater emphasis on the ventilation of slave hospitals, which would, he added, ensure a protection "from atmospheric vicissitudes," ensuring that "convalescence will not only be hastened, but rendered doubly sure" (17). On slave hospitals specifically, see Rana Hogarth, "Charity and Terror in Eighteenth-Century Jamaica: The Kingston Hospital and Asylum for Deserted 'Negroes,'" *African and Black Diaspora: An International Journal* (March 2016): 281–98; Stephen C. Kenny, "'A Dictate of Both Interest and Mercy?' Slave Hospitals in the Antebellum South," *Journal of the History of Medicine and Allied Sciences* 65 (January 2010): 1–47.

34. Samuel Cartwright, "Diseases and Peculiarities of the Negro Race," in *The Industrial Resources, Etc., of the Southern and Western States . . . by J. D. B. De Bow*, vol. 2 (New Orleans, 1852), 333–34. See also Cartwright, "The Diseases of Negroes—Pulmonary Congestions, Pneumonia, &c.," *De Bow's Review of the Southern and Western States* 11, no. 4 (1851): 209–13.

35. Cartwright, "Diseases and Peculiarities," 334.

36. "A Few Statistics of American Slavery," *Chambers's Edinburgh Journal*, March 1853, 185.

37. Wilson, "Peculiarities and Diseases of Negroes," 93.

38. "Few Statistics of American Slavery," 185.

39. Omo., "Negro Houses," 18.

40. Barnes, *Great Stink*, 78–100.

41. On the politics of disgust and class, see Alain Corbin, *The Foul and the Fragrant: Odor and the French Social Imagination*, trans. Miriam L. Kochan (Cambridge, Mass.: Harvard University Press, 1986); Barnes, *Great Stink*; Connie Y. Chiang, "Monterey-by-the-Smell: Odors and Social Conflict on the California Coast," *Pacific Historical Review* 73 (May 2004): 183–214; Karen Halttunen, "Humanitarianism and the Pornography of Pain in Anglo-American Culture," *American Historical Review* 100 (April 1995): 303–34. For the context of race and slavery, see Elizabeth B. Clark, "The Sacred Rights of the Weak: Pain, Sympathy, and the Culture of Individual Rights in Antebellum America," *Journal of American History* 82 (September 1995): 463–93; Mark M. Smith, *How Race Is Made: Slavery, Segregation and the Senses* (Chapel Hill: University of North Carolina Press, 2006).

42. There were fears that the miasma from slave quarters would affect enslavers in the "Big House," and by the nineteenth century it was common for planters to have slave quarters built "downwind" from their own homes. See Wright, *Building the Dream*, 43.

43. Wilson, "Peculiarities and Diseases of Negroes," 79. See also J. F. Marshall, "The Domestic Treatment of Slaves," *De Bow's Review and Industrial Resources, Statistics, Etc. . . . ,* 24 (1858): 63–64.

44. R. W. N. N., "Negro Cabins," *Southern Planter* 16 (April 1856): 121–22.

45. Vlach, *Back of the Big House*; Fett, *Working Cures*, 96, 173.

46. R. W. N. N., "Negro Cabins," 122.

47. Robert J. Draughon, "Houses of Negroes—Habits, Modes of Living, &c.," *Southern Cultivator* 8 (May 1850): 66, 67.

48. See Vlach, *Back of the Big House*, and Singleton, *Archaeology of Slavery*. See also Teresa A. Singleton, "Nineteenth-Century Built Landscape of Plantation Slavery in Comparative Perspectives," in *The Archaeology of Slavery: A Comparative Approach to Captivity and Coercion*, ed. Lydia Wilson Marshall (Carbondale: Southern Illinois University Press, 2014), 96–110.

49. Nehemiah Adams, *A South-Side View of Slavery; Or, Three Months at the South in 1854* (Boston: T. R. Marvin, and Sanborn, Carter, and Bazin, 1855), 37.

50. See, for example, Ira Berlin, *Generations of Captivity: A History of African-American Slaves* (Cambridge, Mass.: Harvard University Press, 2003). Darkness went hand in hand with poor ventilation. Sanitarians believed that a lack of light, like a lack of air, could breed a wealth of human depravity and debasement in addition to ill health. On the importance of sunshine and light in the nineteenth century, and specifically with regard to health and reform movements, see Daniel Freund, *American Sunshine: Diseases of Darkness and the Quest for Natural Light* (Chicago: University of Chicago Press, 2012).

51. For an examination of slave housing through data gleaned from former slave interviews, see Vlach, "'Snug Li'l House."

52. Clara Brim, "WPA Slave Narrative Project," vol. 16, 1936. Texas Narratives, part 1, Federal Writers Project, Manuscript Division, Library of Congress (hereafter FWP), 147.

53. George Eason, "WPA Slave Narrative Project," vol. 4, 1936. Georgia Narratives, part 1, FWP, 302.

54. Henry Bland, "WPA Slave Narrative Project," vol. 4, 1936. Georgia Narratives, part 1, FWP, 82.

55. Henry Kirk Miller, "WPA Slave Narrative Project," vol. 2, 1936. Arkansas Narratives, part 5, FWP, 88.

56. Josiah Henson, *The Life of Josiah Henson, Formerly a Slave, Now an Inhabitant of Canada, as Narrated by Himself* (Boston: Arthur D. Phelps, 1849), 7, 8.

57. Jourden H. Banks, *A Narrative of Events of the Life of J. H. Banks, an Escaped Slave, from the Cotton State, Alabama, in America* (Liverpool: M. Rourke, 1861), 50–51, 54.

58. On domestic life on plantations, see Camp, *Closer to Freedom*; White, *Ar'n't I a Woman?*; Fett, *Working Cures*; Anthony E. Kaye, *Joining Place: Slave Neighborhood in the Old South* (Chapel Hill: University of North Carolina Press, 2007); Thavolia Glymph, *Out of the House of Bondage: The Transformation of the Plantation Household* (Cambridge: Cambridge University Press, 2008).

59. Thomas Jones, *The Experience of Thomas Jones, Who Was a Slave for Forty-Three Years. Written by a Friend, as Given to Him by Brother Jones* (Springfield, Mass.: H. S. Taylor, 1854), 5.

60. Arator, "Negro Houses," 229.

61. John Stainback Wilson, "The Negro—His Mental and Moral Peculiarities," *American Cotton Planter and Soil of the South* 3 (March 1859): 93.

62. Harriet Jacobs, *Incidents in the Life of a Slave Girl* (Boston: Thayer and Eldridge, 1861), 173.

63. Ibid., 175. This builds on the work of literary scholar Mary Titus, who explores the representations of sickness in enslaved bodies and the body politic in *Incidents*. See Mary Titus, "'This Poisonous System': Social Ills, Bodily Ills, and *Incidents in the Life of a Slave*

Girl," in *Harriet Jacobs and Incidents in the Life of a Slave Girl*, ed. Deborah M. Garfield and Rafia Zafar (New York: Cambridge University Press, 1996), 199–216.

64. Jacobs, *Incidents*, 176.

65. William W. Brown, *Narrative of William W. Brown, an American Slave, Written by Himself* (London: Charles Gilpin, 1849), 130.

66. On the intellectual evolution of abolitionist discourse, see Manisha Sinha, *The Slave's Cause: A History of Abolition* (New Haven, Conn.: Yale University Press, 2016).

67. Mary Ella Grandberry, "WPA Slave Narrative Project," vol. 1, p. 157, 1936. Alabama Narratives, part 1, FWP.

PART II *Slavery and Landscape*

"Miserably Scorched"

Drought in the Plantation Colonies of the British Greater Caribbean

MATTHEW MULCAHY

In a 1732 pamphlet that outlined various challenges faced by sugar planters in Britain's Leeward Islands, Rev. Robert Robertson, an Anglican minister on Nevis, called particular attention to the issue of drought. Having
catalogued the dangers associated with hurricanes and fires, both of which
routinely caused significant damage to plantations across the four islands, Robertson concluded that "the surest and severest of all" calamities was the extreme
"dry Weather, which in every Island affects some Plantations every Year, and
in many Years every Plantation throughout the Leward [sic] Islands." Drought
produced a chain of distress for colonists: "A Scarcity of Indian Provisions, and
a proportionate Dearth of those from England, Ireland, and the North Continent; then a most dreadful Mortality among the Negroes and Live-Stock,
Crops next to nothing, and ships returning with dead Freight." In sum, Robertson observed, extended periods of dry weather produced nothing but "Debt,
Anguish, and Distress."[1]

Seventeenth- and eighteenth-century colonists—and later historians—often point to hurricanes as the greatest natural threat to colonial societies in the
British Greater Caribbean (defined here as the island colonies and the Lowcountry of southeastern North America), and with good reason: the powerful
storms caused physical and economic devastation on a scale far beyond anything Europeans had known. Their fury symbolized all that was new and dangerous about life in the Greater Caribbean. But as one leading environmental
historian of the Caribbean has written, "Often more insidious than hurricanes
are the effects of drought in the regional climatic cycles." Unfolding slowly
over time and without the tremendous physical destruction that accompanied
hurricanes, earthquakes, and large-scale fires, drought—and famine conditions
that often followed—nonetheless exacted a heavy human and economic toll.
Indeed, drought likely caused more deaths and, in some colonies, had a greater
economic impact over time than any of these other major calamities. Modern
studies of the United States indicate that although drought formed 17 percent
of weather-related disasters between 1980 and 2003, they accounted for more
than 40 percent of the total economic losses.[2]

Early American historians have documented some of the challenges posed by drought to the colonization of British America, particularly in the southern colonies. Dendrochronological work, for example, has revealed the extent of a drought during the late 1580s and early 1600s, which in turn has reshaped our understanding of events at Roanoke and Jamestown.[3] Likewise, scholars such as S. Max Edelson, Bradford J. Wood, Justin Roberts, Richard B. Sheridan, and David Barry Gaspar, among others, have discussed the impact of drought on plantation agriculture in various parts of the southern mainland and Caribbean islands.[4] The most complete work has been done by Alexander Jorge Berland, whose research has focused on drought in Antigua in the late eighteenth and nineteenth centuries. Nevertheless, as Berland observes, few historians have systematically investigated the impact of drought on the plantation societies of the British Greater Caribbean during the early modern period.[5]

Drought, of course, was not unique to the Greater Caribbean, but it did create some shared and significant challenges throughout the region. Drought, for example, threatened the production and profitability of plantation economies in both the Lowcountry and the islands and often resulted in significant privation for enslaved Africans and African Americans who formed the majority of the region's population. That said, it is also clear that extended dry weather posed greater and more frequent challenges to the islands for environmental, economic, and cultural reasons. Building from the work of Berland and others, this chapter outlines some of those challenges in various parts of the Greater Caribbean, although much of the analysis focuses on the island colonies, and particular attention is paid to the impact of drought on enslaved peoples of African descent in those colonies. Drought created particularly difficult working conditions for the enslaved. More importantly, drought-related shortages of food and water resulted in the death of hundreds and at times thousands of enslaved people. Island planters specifically complained about metropolitan legislation that limited the trade in provisions during dry periods, but their own actions—namely, a dedication to monoculture and overarching concern about profits—played a central role in exacerbating the distress. Indeed, the impact of drought generally worsened over the course of the seventeenth and eighteenth centuries, as the plantation complex took hold and the enslaved population soared. Increasingly dry weather threatened famine and economic damage on a much greater scale than had been the case in the initial decades of colonization. Finally, drought and the privation that accompanied it resulted in greater resistance and rebellion by the enslaved compared to other kinds of disasters. Planters feared the breakdown of social order following hurricanes and earthquakes, but little major resistance occurred in the wake of those calamities. This was not the case with drought.

&

Drought is a complex phenomenon and differs from events such as hurricanes, earthquakes, and fires in several ways. First, the beginning and ending of a drought is often difficult to determine. It is only over time that a drought reveals itself, and short-term relief (in the form of rainfall) may not signal the end of a drought. Drought conditions can linger for months, even years. Second, there are multiple ways to define a drought. Scientists often distinguish between four different kinds of drought: meteorological, hydrological, agricultural, and socioeconomic. Lack of rainfall is a central feature in all, but the definitions reveal myriad forces at work. For example, because different plant species have different moisture requirements, what constitutes a drought for one species might not for another. Moreover, while human activity shapes the impact of all "natural" disasters, human activity can actually cause a drought. Erosion from overfarming, deforestation, and excessive use of existing water sources can all contribute to a drought event. Socioeconomic drought occurs when the available water supply cannot meet the demand for water. Lack of precipitation is a major factor in socioeconomic drought, but the demand for water and the ability of soil to hold water also contribute, and both are linked to human activity (the 1930s dust bowl in the western United States is a classic example). Finally, unlike hurricanes and earthquakes, drought does not usually affect structural elements of a society. Houses, mills, and other infrastructure are not affected by drought. There is no need to rebuild in the wake of a drought. Nevertheless, the impact on humans and the economy can be immense.[6]

Drought should also be distinguished from aridity. Both involve levels of precipitation, but the latter is a permanent feature of a particular place while the former is an occasional or intermittent occurrence. The amount of precipitation in the Greater Caribbean varies considerably from year to year; some places are more arid than others. All of the islands in the region experience a dry season that runs from roughly December through May and a wet season between June and November, although recent research has highlighted a midsummer dry period between peak rainy periods in May–June and September–November. Most precipitation falls during the rainy season. In Antigua, for example, 70–80 percent of the total annual rainfall occurs during those months. The Carolina Lowcountry also has something of a rainy season. Roughly 57 percent of total precipitation falls between May and September, with the highest rain levels in July, August, and September (those three months account for 40 percent of annual precipitation).[7]

A number of climatic factors influence weather and rainfall in the Caribbean basin. One is the El Niño/La Niña sequence in the Pacific, which generally results in higher frequency of drought in the Caribbean during warmer El Niño events and greater rainfall (and more frequent hurricanes) during the cooler periods of La Niña. In addition, the seasonal movement of the North Atlantic High (NAH) affects rainfall in the region. Stronger trade winds and drier weather emerge as the NAH moves south and decreases in size during the winter months. Conversely, weaker trade winds and wetter weather develop as the NAH shifts northward and expands in the summer. This also brings more warm, moist air to the Lowcountry coast. Drought or excessive rains can emerge at any time during years when persistently strong or weak trade winds persist, thereby inhibiting or promoting the development of clouds, rain, and storms. Other factors also influence precipitation in the region, such as southward-moving cold fronts from North America, which can produce significant rains on the northern coasts of the Greater Antilles during winter months.[8]

The end result is that a great deal of variation exists across the Greater Caribbean as a whole, and averages for rainfall can obscure wild swings from periods of drought to abundance. Rainfall, moreover, varies from colony to colony, and even within colonies, in any given year. This is especially true for the islands. On islands with significant mountains, for example, the orographic effect influences rainfall patterns. Locations to the windward and in higher elevations on these islands generally receive significantly more precipitation than those to the leeward side, often called a rain shadow. Port Antonio on Jamaica's north coast, for example, receives 125 inches of rain a year. Twenty miles inland, but higher up, the Blue Mountains receive more than two hundred inches. Kingston, by contrast, on Jamaica's southern, leeward coast, receives less than thirty inches a year. Even on small islands such as Nevis, significant variation exists. Almost ninety inches of rain fall on average at higher elevations on the island, while only forty inches fall in the lowlands. Despite Nevis being only seven miles across, drought conditions can differ from windward to leeward.[9]

The existence of such microclimates meant that drought was often a localized experience for colonists. Simon Taylor, a resident planter and attorney in Jamaica, wrote to the absentee planter Chaloner Arcedeckne in April 1769, for example, that the weather at his estate had been very fine, "but plays the Devill every where else being so dry." Thomas Thistlewood suggested that while abundant rains fell within three or four miles of the estate in southwestern Jamaica where he was employed as a penkeeper in July 1750, "we can get none;

has been excessive dry many months." One estate manager in Antigua reported that while plantations in the southwest corner of Antigua experienced good rains in the summer of 1780, the rains were "by no means general, & all the rest of the island . . . never made so bad a crop." Such regional variation appeared at times in South Carolina as well. While the Lowcountry experienced a long dry spell in August and September 1755, Henry Laurens reported, "In the [interior] back Settlements the Drought was of a much longer continuance" and had worse consequences.[10]

English colonists in Barbados first complained of drought in the late 1640s. Some reports suggested as much as one-fifth of the island's population perished from the combination of drought and disease between 1647 and 1650. The island suffered drought conditions again in 1668, 1670, and 1700–1702, and then periodically across the 1730s and the rest of the eighteenth century. The face of the island, one colonist stated in the mid-1730s, "appeared, as it were, a dry crust, burnt up and gaping." Reports at the time suggested that a number of colonists died from a want of food, and local clergy preached charity sermons to raise money to purchase food for the poor. Drought conditions returned during the Revolutionary era.[11]

Accounts of drought began to appear from the Leeward Islands during the second half of the seventeenth century, although drought was likely an issue in earlier decades, especially in Antigua, which lacked any significant rivers. Governor William Byam reported that a "great drought" in 1670 "has rendered the crops backward and bad, and brought the planters into debt." He feared worsening conditions might result in a "general desertion of the land." That same fear concerned officials in Nevis in 1688 when the governor worried that "the drought has been so severe as much to distress the poorer classes," many of whom "wished to go to a better furnished island." Planters in Antigua reportedly were "forced to send off numbers of their negroes to be sold for want of food," and some colonists emigrated to northern colonies during a drought in 1718. Severe drought struck the Leeward Islands again in the following two decades. Indeed, this period of extended drought ranks among the worst of the past ten thousand years.[12]

Jamaica likewise experienced frequent droughts. Officials delayed the opening of the general court in 1672 "owing to the great suffering under the long and present drought." An extended drought that followed a hurricane in 1726 was "dreadfull in its consequences." Extended and severe dry periods occurred again in the first half of 1754, and again between October 1768 and May 1770. Writing in 1774, Edward Long noted "the longest and severest drought ever remembered in this island." One overseer wrote of the "amazing devastation occasioned by the expanded drought." Large numbers of cattle perished. So, too, did many enslaved Africans, who "perished as well by famine as by thirst."[13]

Drought also caused considerable trouble for Lowcountry colonists. Drought conditions plagued the initial year of colonization, drying out provision crops as well as indigo and ginger. Colonists did take some comfort from Native reports that "such droughts [are] not usual." Droughts, however, did occur, and they challenged early efforts to cultivate rice, the crop that would come to dominate the Lowcountry economy. Colonists began to grow rice for export in the late seventeenth century, and they depended on regular rains to water their fields. Periods of dry weather and accompanying economic losses from rain-watered rice fields pushed many colonists to find a more reliable source of water for their fields. Indeed, according to historian S. Max Edelson, "the dual threat of drought and flooding was the driving force behind technological innovation in planting." Lowcountry colonists gradually learned to take advantage of the region's swamplands. Enslaved people were forced by colonists to build reservoirs to hold water and constructed series of ditches and embankments around their rice fields, which allowed them to control the flow of water and offset the danger of drought. When drought hit in the mid-1750s, Henry Laurens informed one correspondent that while many planters' rice crops withered, "we hope as Multitudes have reserves of Water, the Crop upon the whole will be a middling one." Likewise, when dry weather scorched the region in the summer of 1762, "those who have not great resources of Water damm'd in" suffered significant losses.[14]

The water from reservoirs and swamps lessened, but did not eliminate, the danger of drought (or flooding), pushing many planters to innovate further and to gradually adopt tidal irrigation beginning in the middle decades of the eighteenth century. Planters and their slaves constructed floodgates that allowed fresh water to cover the fields when pushed upriver during high tides. Advertisements for tidal plantations emphasized that the land was "over flow'd with fresh Water, every high Tide, and of Consequence not subject to the Droughts." Tidal rivers reduced much of the uncertainty in production and made rice plantations "the most certain in the world," in the words of one early nineteenth-century commentator. Nevertheless, extended periods of dry weather could—and did—have an impact on rice fields if they occurred at the wrong time of year. Henry Laurens wrote to several correspondents in September 1762, for example, that notwithstanding early indications of a "vast Crop of Rice . . . an uncommon spell of dry weather in the time of Earing" (when the head of the grain emerges) generated fears that output would fall short of expectations. A few years later he observed during a summer dry spell that while "rice will endure much more hardship . . . the produce of it must be stinted by this Iron burning Weather that we have had for some Weeks past."[15]

Even as planters' command of water lessened the impact of drought on rice production, sustained dry weather remained a problem for the colony's secondary crop, indigo. The plant required an immense amount of water, not only for cultivation but also for processing. Laurens recorded in October 1755 that no rain had fallen for two months and that many planters "lost fine Fields of Indigo for want of Water to work it." Drought returned the following summer. The dry weather had relatively little impact on rice production, but a "large part" of Carolina's indigo crop was "destroy'd" by the extended dry weather. Exports of the blue dye dropped considerably in 1756 before rebounding the following year. Drought again reduced indigo crops in 1762 and 1777, the latter compounded by wartime disruptions. As with rice, planters took steps to reduce the challenges posed by drought by constructing dams to control the flow of water to indigo vats, a fact they advertised when selling properties.[16]

Drought had major consequences for sugar plantations as well, as the lack of rainfall had a significant impact on crop yields and thus planter profits. Plantation accounts, letters from local officials, and other sources all highlight economic losses from drought. Sugarcane in the fields withered for lack of rain, and what canes survived often produced little juice. As a result, output often fell dramatically in drought years. Walter Tullideph, a planter in Antigua, reported in April 1738 that the "extream drie" weather meant "many plantations can't make tolerable Sugar, & att Barbadoes we are told they won't exceed half a Crope it is so very drie." Although planters took "all Imaginable pains" to secure their canes, such efforts often brought little result when the ground was "soe miserably scorched." One planter in Jamaica wrote that young canes appeared "burnt as if they had been in an oven." Another wrote that "the canes have been burning so fast" he was forced to cut them earlier than he wished. But even those that survived "were so much tainted that the quality of the sugar has been much injured." Estates that relied on water mills to crush their canes faced the additional issue of not having enough water to power mills to extract what juice remained in the withered canes.[17]

No scholars have systematically studied the economic impact of drought, but limited evidence suggests significant disruptions. David Barry Gaspar's work on Antigua reveals the shifting level of sugar production during the tumultuous 1730s when regular drought and a major hurricane considerably reduced sugar exports. Strong exports in 1728 and 1729 were followed by an almost 40 percent drop in 1731 as drought and "the blast" (an infestation of insects) ruined cane fields. Production remained low in 1732 and 1734 (a hurricane in 1733 contributed to a weak harvest the following year) before reaching its nadir in 1737 at only 1,732 tons. According to the governor, 90 percent of the island's crop was lost to drought. During the extended drought in Jamaica during the late 1760s and early 1770s, one overseer reported that because of dry conditions in 1770–71, he anticipated only seven hogsheads of sugar from 50 acres of new canes and 150 acres of ratoons. Moreover, he continued, the lack of rain meant that other estates on the island that had produced 1,500 hogsheads a few years before would struggle to ship a hundred hogsheads.[18]

The lack of rain also had an impact on rum production on many island estates. Water was an important component in the process of distilling rum. Indeed, when possible, planters sometimes situated distilleries near rivers or streams. Water was important both as an element of the "wash" (a combination of scum skimmed off boiling sugar, molasses, dunder—waste from earlier distillations—and water) used to make rum, as well as for cooling the stills wherein alcohol vapor was condensed into liquid. The former required less water, but it needed to be clean water, while the latter required water in larger quantities regardless of its quality.[19]

In addition to parched fields, drought often combined with other hazards to threaten plantation operations. Most obviously, drought increased the likelihood and danger of fires. An account from Saint Croix in 1768 reported that "some of their cane pieces have taken fire by mere accident" during an "excessive drought" and that "very few of them which were standing [were] like to produce any thing." A visitor to Barbados in 1749 witnessed a "Cane-Field taking Fire, which, it seems, sometimes happens, when the Blades are dry, and does much Damage." Fires scorched thousands of acres of woodlands, plantations, and provision grounds in Jamaica during a dry year in 1754.[20]

Insect infestations in sugar fields were also linked to drought. Planters in Barbados and the Leeward Islands routinely complained that crops that survived extended dry weather were often "miserably destroyed by caterpillars, locusts [grasshoppers], and other vermin." During the 1720s and 1730s Leeward Island planters faced simultaneous assaults from drought and the "blast," an infestation of insects and ants that destroyed sugarcane and plagued colonists during these years. One observer noted that "it is difficult to distinguish the Blast in its infancy, from the Effects of dry Weather," and that "the Blast is observed to be most frequent in very dry Years."[21]

Colonists' focus on monocropping for export throughout the plantation zone of the Greater Caribbean exacerbated the impact of extended periods of dry weather. Because just a few crops dominated the economic landscape of the colonies, any shortfalls in production had major financial consequences for individual planters and for the colony's economy more broadly. As Edelson observes, this characteristic distinguished colonial plantations from agricultural enterprises in Britain: "Whatever damage storms and droughts might inflict on the diversified English countryside, they did so region by region and crop by crop; catastrophic losses to any one of South Carolina's three dominant eighteenth-century crops (rice, maize, and indigo) had the potential to plunge the province as a whole into crisis." This was perhaps even more true for the sugar islands.[22]

The loss of valuable export crops was the most pressing issue for most colonists whose raison d'être was profit, but drought created additional problems as well. Drought devastated provision crops and caused the price of food and fresh water to soar. The governor of Barbados wrote during a drought in 1690 that corn which had sold for twelve pence a bushel was now selling for fifteen to twenty shillings a bushel, while the price of a barrel of beef had tripled. This rise in prices caused one observer to remark that "unless speedily relieved from Old or New England, the commoner sort of people and slaves must starve." Water brought from Guadeloupe and Martinique to the English Leeward Islands during the 1720s sold at the inflated price of fifteen shillings a hogshead. Poorer colonists in the Danish islands collected what groundwater they could find and boiled it with white cinnamon to alleviate their thirst, skimming off the cloudy residue before drinking it. The combination of high prices and limited supplies of food and water, in turn, often forced poor and marginal colonists to migrate to other colonies in hopes of bettering their prospects.[23]

Extended drought periodically put pressure on the available food supply in the Lowcountry as well. Henry Laurens noted in 1756 and again in 1757 that dry weather withered much of the colony's corn crop and other provisions and that colonists sought to import supplies from neighboring colonies. "Negro provisions" in particular remained "scarce and dear." In August 1756 Laurens suggested that provision fields yielded 50 percent less than normal, which must have occasioned significant privation and suffering. He complained that few planters were interested in purchasing enslaved Africans because they did not know if they could feed them. As drought lingered into the fall of that year the governor issued a proclamation halting all exports of food from the colony (with the exception of rice to Europe). Drought affected the availability of food in other ways as well. Residents of Charleston struggled to procure adequate provisions in the summer of 1773 when dry weather lowered water levels in Lowcountry rivers so much that it interfered with the transport of corn and flour from the interior to the city.[24]

Animals also suffered from the dry weather. Horses, cattle, and mules were essential to plantation operations on most islands, even after use of windmills expanded in the eighteenth century. "The Loss of Horses, Mules, and Cattle, in Dry-weather Years especially, is very considerable," reported one Leeward

Island planter. Planters in Barbados worried that they had neither water nor feed for cattle in 1687. An extended drought in the early summer of 1752 in the Lowcountry resulted in the death of many animals, and cattle in particular "perished for want both of pasturage and water," a situation that repeated itself in the summer of 1759 and again in 1773. Desperate colonists posted guards around animal water holes that year to protect what water they had. Large numbers of cattle were likewise lost in Jamaica during the 1763–64 drought and again in 1769–70. Some five thousand cattle were estimated to have perished in Antigua during a drought in 1789, and more likely did so in the following two drought-plagued years, although no specific numbers were given.[25]

While all colonists felt the impact of drought, the effects were especially severe for enslaved Africans. Even in its early stages drought created difficult working conditions for enslaved laborers. On sugar plantations, enslaved people were forced to spend more time weeding to get the best results from surviving canes. Moreover, that task became more difficult as the dry ground became harder to break with a hoe. One planter in Jamaica noted that during dry weather, the ground had the "hardness of a brick." An observer of slavery in the Leeward Islands emphasized that picking grass for animal feed during periods of drought was particularly difficult work, and "the most frequent cause of [enslaved people] running away, or absenting himself from [their] work." In addition, many enslaved Africans found themselves working to supply plantations with water. The governor of the English Leeward Islands reported in April 1689 that "it cost the daily labour of near twenty slaves to supply me and my family with water from ponds eight miles distant." Water was transported in animal-drawn carts, but enslaved Africans also carried water, weighing eight pounds per gallon, by hand or on their heads. Samuel Martin worried that such grueling work weakened the enslaved and left them more vulnerable to disease.[26]

As drought conditions lingered, hunger became a bigger issue as crops that enslaved people had planted in their provision grounds failed. Although many islands relied on food imported from Europe or North America, enslaved Africans on all of the islands produced some of their own food. Drought rendered those fields barren. Plantains, another staple of enslaved people's diets in some colonies, also suffered from drought conditions. Moreover, the loss of profits from diminished sugar yields combined with high prices meant that planters often were unwilling to purchase enough food to make up for any shortfall. The governor of Antigua reported that the high cost of water brought in from Guadeloupe and Montserrat limited its use and "has occasioned the loss of many of the Cattle and Negroes." One absentee planter was particularly blunt on this issue. Rachel Tudway wrote to her manager in Antigua that she hoped to send out more food from London to ease the impact of drought in 1717–18, "but returns being so small and sugars so low hinders me from following my inclination." Another absentee, in response to reports of drought-related shortages on her Jamaica plantation in 1754, wrote that she was "contended about it, knowing we must submit to God's will; whether it be drought, rains or hurricanes." Such parsimony and inhumanity exacerbated the impact of drought and increased the suffering among enslaved peoples throughout the region.[27]

Such conditions, in turn, exacted a horrific toll in human lives. Accounts from the Stapleton plantation on Nevis reveal some of the particular misery that accompanied drought. The attorney, Joseph Herbert, reported to William Stapleton in October 1725 that the "Negroes [were] likely to suffer" from the dry conditions. Eight months later, in June 1726, he wrote that "many Negroes and stock lost for want of provisions and water" on the island, a bland accounting of what must have been terrible suffering. Such conditions became so routine that when Herbert wrote later to Stapleton he did not feel the need to offer any details on the ongoing dry weather and its effects, as he assumed Stapleton had "heard so much of it already."[28]

Continuing dry conditions in the 1730s meant ongoing shortages. A new overseer wrote in December 1736 that "our famine still continues, or rather Increases . . . [and] swept off a great many people." One contemporary observer suggested that mortality rates among enslaved people in Nevis doubled during periods of drought: one in seven perished during drought years, compared to one in fifteen during other, already deadly, periods. At least some Leeward Island planters sought enslaved Africans from the Gold Coast because they believed that the heat and "Scarcity of Provisions" in that region rendered individuals better able to survive similar conditions in the Caribbean. By contrast, enslaved peoples from Kongo and Angola were less valued because planters argued that "the Plenty of Provisions in their own, more temperate, and cool Countries, renders them lazy, and consequently, not so able to endure Work and Fatigue."[29]

Drought became particularly deadly at times when supplies of outside food were disrupted. This often occurred during wars, when ships sailing in and out of the region became vulnerable to attack. Barbados suffered such shortages in 1746 and 1747 when drought, the blast, and the War of Austrian Succession combined to produce shortages. Planters in Antigua likewise found "our North American trade is intirely cut off by ye great numbers of Privateers." In some cases, embargoes on trade intended to hurt the enemy had equally painful consequences for loyal colonists. "God knows what will become of our poor slaves for we have no salt provision of any sort to be brought here," wrote one Saint Christopher planter in 1757. Embargoes intended to "starve our enemies," he continued, "hath had a quite contrary affect, for his majesty's subjects have only suffered by them."[30]

The worst situation developed during the 1770s and 1780s when the combination of dry weather and the American Revolution resulted in a catastrophe for enslaved peoples throughout large sections of the Caribbean. The Leeward Islands, heavily dependent on imported food from North America, were hit especially hard. The governor of the Leeward Islands wrote in 1778 that "the Island of Antigua has lost above a thousand Negroes, Montserrat near twelve Hundred, and some whites—Nevis three to four Hundred, and This Island as many from the Want of Provisions." The drought continued the following year. Reports from Antigua "paint nothing but ruin, and its face the deserts of Arabia." An overseer on the Tudway plantation on the island wrote in April 1779 that they were experiencing "the severest Drought that was ever known in this Island & . . . yt if we are [not] soon relieved by plentiful showers, the consequences must be very shocking." The consequences were shocking. One-tenth of the enslaved people on the Tudway plantation in Antigua died between the fall of 1779 and the summer of 1780. Lack of food was not the only issue. The lack of potable water led to dysentery among enslaved Africans. Overall, one-fifth of Antigua's enslaved population of thirty-eight thousand perished from drought, famine, and diseases linked to such shortages during the war years.[31]

Jamaica also experienced drought and famine during the 1770s and 1780s, with devastating consequences for enslaved peoples. Reports from the island throughout the second half of the 1770s were filled with "melancholy detail[s] of dry weather, which continues still with great severity." Despite a hurricane in October 1780, observers reported that "since the hurricane we have been burned up with dry weather all over the island," and that "Negroes are every where complaining of a want of victuals and there is no place now where we can get supplies." Without rain "we must inevitably have a famine all over the country." The Jamaican planter and attorney Simon Taylor highlighted the overlapping calamities of hurricanes, drought, and trade restrictions that plagued the island in 1781, writing to one correspondent, "If we do not very soon gett rain, we shall certainly have a famine every where, the mountains are as much burned up as the low lands and sea coast, and our prospect is really horrid as there is but little flour or any other but salt provisions in the country and no place to gett them from but England or Ireland."[32]

Hurricanes continued to batter Jamaica throughout the 1780s, and despite the rains that accompanied major storms, so, too, did drought. The "uncommonly hot" and dry summer of 1786 scorched sugar and provision fields. Colonists reported that the enslaved were dying by the hundreds and it was "not uncommon . . . in many places to find two or three of them lying dead upon the common roads." Simon Taylor stated that "very great numbers of negroes especially in Trelawney St. James's Hanover & Westmoreland perished for real want they are very dry there now & if they do not get rains soon there will be another famine there." A committee of the Jamaican Assembly reported that the combined impact of "repeated Calamities" of hurricanes and droughts between 1780 and 1786 and "the unfortunate Measure of interdicting foreign Supplies" meant that as many as fifteen thousand enslaved people had perished from "famine, or of Diseases contracted by scanty and unwholesome diet."[33]

Colonists were quick to blame the horrific loss of life during these droughts on forces beyond their control. The lack of rain, of course, was one factor, but late eighteenth-century planters and officials in many islands also blamed imperial policies that limited trade as a major reason for the loss of life. Few, however, considered the extent to which the plantation system itself was a key factor in the shift from drought to famine, especially in the islands. The steady expansion of sugar production in the islands at the expense of provisions placed colonists, and, more accurately, enslaved Africans, in positions of heightened vulnerability over time. When the rains ceased, none were prepared for the shortages that ensued. Even then, some planters or their agents appeared unwilling to sacrifice space in the fields for provisions, preferring to plant sugar and hope that outside provisions would arrive. In the early years of the Seven Years' War, one overseer on Saint Christopher wrote that a "severe spell of dry weather" left the plantation "greatly distressed for provisions for slaves." Yet he hesitated to shift too many fields to provision crops. Only "if war continues" would he "need to plant a piece in yams and potatoes." The lack of rain created difficult conditions on the islands, but weather was never the only, and often not even the primary, cause of shortages and famine. Famine was a social crisis as much as an environmental one.[34]

The severe shortages that accompanied droughts contributed to increased resistance (or what planters at times perceived as resistance) among enslaved peoples. Thomas Thistlewood reported that hungry enslaved people took to eating canes, which resulted in brutal retaliation by planters. In other cases, colonists worried that the enslaved would flee the plantation if they could not provide them with food. During the 1757 dearth on Saint Kitts, one colonist wrote he was concerned that "most of them will run away from us to the mountains before the year is out for as we have it not in our power to feed them."[35]

An even greater fear was that starving enslaved people would turn to more violent measures, which it appears many did. Reports of rebellions or planned rebellions during periods of drought emerged from several islands in the region, especially during the eighteenth century as the plantation complex intensified across the region. Rumors circulated on Nevis in 1725 that the enslaved, hungry and desperate, were plotting to "cut off all the whites and take the Island for themselves." No solid evidence of a plot existed and no one confessed, but officials nevertheless jailed ten purported conspirators and executed two. Several years later, provision shortages caused by drought, a hurricane, and an insect infestation appeared to have pushed enslaved Africans on the Danish island of Saint Johns to rebel in 1733. Similar factors may have spurred enslaved people in Antigua to plot to take over the island in 1736. The plot was uncovered, dozens of slaves were executed, and hundreds more banished. Drought and the accompanying food shortages likewise preceded an alleged plot of enslaved people in Hanover Parish, Jamaica, that was uncovered in 1776. An overseer on Antigua wrote at roughly the same time that "famine (the worst of all Evils) approaches fast, which may, & probably will bring on a rebellion of our slaves." Throughout the war years in the 1770s and 1780s, planters on various islands expressed fears that the lack of food would result in starving enslaved people rising up in general rebellion.[36]

Interestingly, accounts of slave conspiracies during these periods of dearth often included lengthy descriptions of the enslaved engaging in elaborate feasts. The purported plot in Nevis in the mid-1720s involved feasts, as did the 1736 conspiracy on Antigua. Testimony in the Antigua trials described multicourse meals among the enslaved that included "Fresh Porke, Goat, Mutton, Fowles, Salt Beefe, Salt Porke, Chees, Wine Beer and Punch." How enslaved people managed to acquire such abundance at a time when the islands suffered from dry weather and scarcity was unexplained, but the image of the enslaved feasting during periods of privation may have struck a particular chord among already panicked white people, furthering their fears of a world turned upside down by resistance of enslaved peoples. Regardless, such images featured prominently in planters' accounts of conspiracies among the enslaved, whether real or imagined.[37]

It is difficult to determine the extent to which severe shortages alone or in some combination with other factors prompted rebellions, or even if reports of conspiracy to rebel had any basis in reality.[38] The timing of several rebellions (or rumored rebellions) and commentary from colonists at the time, however, suggests a connection between drought, shortages of provisions, and rebellion, a link that distinguished drought from other forms of disaster. While white colonists often feared that the breakdown of order following hurricanes or earthquakes increased the possibility of enslaved people revolting, there is little evidence that the enslaved took advantage of the chaotic conditions to do anything more than salvage (panicked planters and officials would say loot) food and essential supplies. Most enslaved people were concerned with their own survival. Moreover, the relative suddenness with which hurricanes and earthquakes struck left little time to prepare any coordinated resistance. By contrast, lingering periods of drought not only generated steadily increasing suffering but also provided ample time for enslaved Africans to plan their actions. Far more than other kinds of disasters, drought appears to have generated active resistance among the enslaved and acute fears among white colonists. It is perhaps no coincidence that dry weather and shortages marked the years 1786 and 1788 in Saint-Domingue, and that conditions grew even worse in 1790, the year before the great slave uprising in 1791.[39]

Enslaved people in the Lowcountry at times suffered from provision shortages linked to drought, but famine did not stalk Lowcountry plantations as routinely as it did those in the islands. One key difference was that the Lowcountry staple crop—rice—was a foodstuff, and one that over the course of the eighteenth century became less vulnerable to drought. Enslaved Africans had access to damaged or discarded rice that was deemed unfit for sale abroad, which provided some food even in periods when corn and other provisions were in short supply. In addition, enslaved people in the Lowcountry spent a good deal of time hunting and fishing on their own, a situation resulting from the particulars of the Lowcountry environment and the task system of labor used in rice production. As the historian Philip Morgan notes, enslaved Africans and African Americans "hunted extensively" and were "keen fishermen." Both activities provided important sources of protein, and neither were linked to shifting weather conditions. Finally, Lowcountry planters had access to provisions from other parts of the mainland, locations closer and more readily accessible than was the case for the islands. Carolina planters often purchased corn and other provisions from backcountry farmers and had ready access to provisions in nearby colonies. This is not to suggest that enslaved people in the Lowcountry were immune from the consequences of extended periods of dry weather. As drought plagued South Carolina in the summer and fall of 1756, Henry Laurens and other planters received word from the "interior parts of the province . . . that their Negro provisions . . . are almost totally destroy'd by a drought attended with Violent hot Weather that has Scorch'd up every thing." Planters and enslaved Africans struggled to secure adequate provisions. Nevertheless, Lowcountry colonists and enslaved Africans generally had greater access to provisions than their island counterparts, and while shortages of food occurred at times, famine conditions—and the resistance associated with it— appeared less frequently.[40]

Colonists and colonial officials responded to the threat of drought in a number of ways. At times they sought divine intervention. Protestant colonists interpreted droughts and other major disasters as providential events, sent to punish sinful colonists or serve as warning of even greater punishments to come if they did not reform. The council in Jamaica, for example, referred to a "long and excessive drought" in 1726 as the "immediate hand of God upon us." As droughts lingered, political leaders and religious officials often called for a day of fasting during which colonists ceased work (as did enslaved peoples), refrained from food and drink, and attended church services marked by lengthy sermons interpreting the disaster and outlining the reforms needed to appease a just and angry God. Concerned about smallpox and an ongoing drought that threatened "a great scarcity of Provisions," Lieutenant Governor William Bull of South Carolina called for a day of fasting and prayer in July 1738. Such rituals were called most frequently in the Leeward Islands, where officials ordered fasts in 1711, 1725, 1726, 1731, 1736, and 1741. Indeed, although the evidence is fragmentary, it appears that drought may have occasioned the calling of fasts and thanksgivings more frequently than any other form of disaster. And at times such measures appeared successful. One report from Antigua noted that "a day of fast was appointed the 19th of May to beseech the Almighty to turne his wrath from us. God was graciously pleased to send us a fine Season [shower] the 17th and some the 19th, which put some watter in our ponds and greatly refreshd the canes, which gives hopes of a Crop the next year."[41]

How the majority of the population in these colonies—enslaved people of African descent—interpreted drought is less clear. Colonists made only passing reference to rituals and beliefs of the enslaved (in part because religious ceremonies often took place away from the white community), and when they did, their comments were often negative. That said, enslaved Africans, like Europeans, turned to the heavens to seek relief from drought. Because of high mortality rates and constant importation of enslaved people from West Africa, diverse African rituals and beliefs remained powerful in most of the islands. One of the more detailed accounts of enslaved people's rituals during a period of drought came from the Danish Leeward Islands. The Moravian missionary C. G. A. Oldendorp reported that during a period of extreme dryness in the 1730s, enslaved people from different ethnic groups invoked a variety of rituals. The Wawu (possibly Ewe speakers from the Bight of Benin) tied leaves around their heads and bodies and marched in a "sorrowful procession" to the "schambu hut" in which dwelled the "tiger" god, pleading with him to send rain. The Loango (from Kongo) sacrificed a cow in a ritual that concluded with penitents running home to escape the rain they expected to follow. "Karamnti" (likely Coromantee) women formed a procession that offered various fruits to a priest (called Udum), asking for rain. Many of these offerings took place in the houses of sacred figures or in "sacred groves" on the island. Such rituals highlighted both the powerful presence of varied African cultures in the Leeward Islands and across the region, and the extent to which providential interpretations characterized response of enslaved peoples to drought.[42]

In addition to prayer, colonists took more direct steps to alleviate shortages created by drought conditions. Local officials in Antigua hired a sloop in the summer of 1717 to bring water to the island from nearby Barbuda. They also purchased and distributed a hundred barrels of flour to poor whites whose crops had failed because of dry weather. Colonists sometimes looked to foreign colonies for assistance. Supplies came from Martinique and Guadeloupe during the drought years of the 1720s and 1730s. Governor William Burt, for example, opened Leeward Island ports to neutral nations during the disastrous late 1770s, which he believed "prevented insurrections among the slaves." Likewise, officials in Jamaica opened their ports to ships for the new United States to alleviate terrible suffering during the disastrous 1780s.[43]

The Revolutionary-era drought crisis also prompted planters in some places to dedicate more acreage to provision crops on their plantations, especially crops such as yams that were resistant to dry conditions. Planters in Barbados reduced the amount of land planted with canes, which opened up more land for provisions, especially Guinea corn (sorghum). Even when sugar output increased by the end of the 1780s, planters remained committed to growing more food on their plantations. Likewise, Clement Tudway, the absentee owner of the Parham plantation in Antigua, and his attorneys dedicated thirty acres of land to yams and reduced the production of corn and potatoes, which fared poorly during the dry conditions of the 1770s, a modest but still noteworthy shift. Drought was not the only factor pushing such shifts, but it did play a significant role in the process.[44]

In the longer term, colonists took steps to preserve existing water supplies, increase rainfall, and ensure a more regular supply of water to their fields. One of the earliest efforts occurred in 1724 when the Antigua assembly passed a law that prohibited cutting timber within thirty feet of public ponds to limit the evaporation of water. A gradually expanding awareness of a link between forests and rainfall in subsequent decades pushed other local and imperial officials to preserve sections of forests in some of the islands. In 1764 British officials laid plans for the preservation of a certain number of acres on the newly acquired ceded islands of Grenada, Tobago, Dominica, and Saint Vincent. These areas were to remain forested "in order to preserve the season [i.e., rainfall] so essential to the fertility of the islands." Barbados enacted a similar measure the following year "to prevent the drought which in these climates is the usual consequence of a total removal of the woods." The success of such plans on individual islands varied, but the ordinances represented a real attempt to ease the threat of drought.[45]

Finally, colonists sought ways to offset the lack of rainfall. Island planters often built ponds, some large enough to contain twenty to thirty thousand gallons of water, to ensure a steady supply of water for their distillery operations. Lowcountry planters, as noted above, turned to swamps and later tidal rivers to flood their rice fields. This option was less available in the Lesser Antilles, as many islands lacked significant rivers. In Jamaica, by contrast, planters had access to rivers, which some began to tap to irrigate their cane fields. In doing so they followed the example of French planters in Saint-Domingue, who first implemented large-scale irrigation projects during the middle of the eighteenth century. Their success—by the 1760s, Saint-Domingue produced more sugar than all the British islands combined—inspired British planters to experiment as well. The Jamaican planter Bryan Edwards noted that while Saint-Domingue had excellent soils, "above all" the island's output resulted from "the prodigious benefit which resulted to the French planters from the system of watering their sugar-lands in dry weather."[46]

Several Jamaican plantations began to irrigate their fields in the early 1770s. One was Hope Plantation, outside Kingston, owned by an absentee planter, Roger Hope Elletson. The overseer of the Hope Plantation suggested the possibility of using water from the Hope River in the 1760s, but Elletson was skeptical at first, concerned that increased water would erode the soil. He changed his mind by 1774 as drought continued to plague the island. Enslaved Africans constructed a series of aqueducts to redirect the water from the river to the fields, and by 1778 the overseer reported that Hope was the only plantation in the Liguanea Plain that did not suffer from the ongoing drought.[47]

℘

Such steps, of course, did not end the threat and effects of drought entirely, but they did represent recognition among colonists of the challenges posed by drought in the region and that adjustments could offset some of the worst effects of prolonged periods with little or no rain. Drought remained, and remains, an issue in many parts of the Caribbean. As this chapter has suggested, it also played a central and distinct role in the history of the region. Drought shaped the lives and fortunes of all colonists, and often had major economic consequences for rich and poor. The impact was especially severe for the region's enslaved population, as drought produced famine conditions, terrible suffering, and countless deaths. Unfolding slowly over time and without the tremendous physical destruction that accompanied other events, drought nonetheless exacted a heavy human and economic toll. The physical environment of the Caribbean presented a number of challenges for Europeans and enslaved Africans in the early modern period. Drought was not the most dramatic of those hazards, but it was certainly among the most devastating, and one that warrants greater attention from historians of the early modern British Caribbean.

NOTES

The author is grateful to Andrew Johnson, Blake Earle, and the other conference organizers for the invitation to participate, and to April Hatfield and other participants for thoughtful comments on the initial paper. Special thanks to Phil Morgan who shared his transcriptions of the McDowall letters, to Kate Johnston for references to the Hamilton Papers, and to Jordan Smith for sharing parts of his dissertation with me. Parts of this essay are drawn from a larger work in progress on natural disasters in the early modern Caribbean cowritten with Stuart Schwartz.

1. Robert Robertson, *A Detection of the State and Situation of the Present Sugar Planters of Barbadoes and the Leward Islands* (London: J. Wilford, 1732), 49.

2. David Watts, "Long-term Environmental Influences on Development in Islands of the Lesser Antilles," *Scottish Geographical Magazine* 109 (August 1993): 133–41. The historical geographer Bonham C. Richardson argues that next to hurricanes, drought was the "most grievous climatic hazard" in the minds of island residents in the nineteenth century. See Richardson, *Economy and Environment in the Caribbean: Barbados and the Windwards in the Late 1800s* (Gainesville: University Press of Florida, 1998), 83; Ashok K. Mishra and Vijay P. Singh, "A Review of Drought Concepts," *Journal of Hydrology* 391 (2010): 202–16. An argument for the Greater Caribbean as a region is Matthew Mulcahy, *Hubs of Empire: The Southeastern Lowcountry and British Caribbean* (Baltimore: Johns Hopkins University Press, 2014).

3. Sam White, *A Cold Welcome: The Little Ice Age and Europe's Encounter with North America* (Cambridge, Mass.: Harvard University Press, 2017); David W. Stahle, Malcolm K. Cleaveland, Dennis B. Blanton, Matthew D. Therrell, and David A. Gay, "The Lost Colony and Jamestown Droughts," *Science* 280 (April 1998): 564–67. See also C. J. Mock, "Paleodroughts and Society," *Encyclopedia of Quaternary Science* 3 (2006): 1958–64.

4. S. Max Edelson, *Plantation Enterprise in Colonial South Carolina* (Cambridge, Mass.: Harvard University Press, 2006); Bradford J. Wood, *This Remote Part of the World: Regional Formation in Lower Cape Fear, North Carolina, 1725–1775* (Columbia: University of South Carolina Press, 2004); Justin Roberts, *Slavery and the Enlightenment in the British Atlantic, 1750–1807* (New York: Cambridge University Press, 2013); Richard B. Sheridan, *Sugar and Slavery: An Economic History of the British West Indies, 1623–1775* (Baltimore: Johns Hopkins University Press, 1974); David Barry Gaspar, *Bondmen and Rebels: A Study of Master-Slave Relations in Antigua* (Durham, N.C.: Duke University Press, 1993).

5. Alexander Jorge Berland, "Extreme Weather and Social Vulnerability in Colonial Antigua, 1770–1890" (PhD diss., University of Nottingham, 2015); Alexander Jorge Berland and Georgina Endfield, "Drought and Disaster in a Revolutionary Age: Colonial Antigua during the American Independence War," *Environment and History* 24, no. 2 (March 2018): 209–35. See also Douglas Gamble, "The Neglected Climatic Hazards of the Caribbean: Overview and Prospects for a Warmer Climate," *Geography Compass* 8 (April 2014): 221–34. Sherry Johnson highlights issues of drought and hurricanes in eighteenth-century Cuba. See *Climate and Catastrophe in Cuba and the Atlantic World in the Age of Revolution* (Chapel Hill: University of North Carolina Press, 2012).

6. Mishra and Singh, "Review of Drought Concepts." See also Donald A. Wilhite and Michael H. Glantz, "Understanding the Drought Phenomenon: The Role of Definitions," *Water International* 10 (1985): 111–20.

7. Alexander Berland, Sarah Metcalfe, and Georgina H. Endfield, "Documentary-Derived Chronologies of Rainfall Variability in Antigua, Lesser Antilles, 1770–1890," *Climate of the Past* 9, no. 2 (2013): 1331–43; Douglas W. Gamble and Scott Curtis, "Caribbean Precipitation: Review, Model, and Prospect," *Progress in Physical Geography* 32 (June 2008): 265–76; David Watts, *The West Indies: Patterns of Development, Culture, and Environmental Change since 1492* (New York: Cambridge University Press, 1990), 17–25. A contemporary measurement of rainfall in the Lowcountry highlighting the summer and autumn rainy season is John Lining, "A Letter from John Lining, M.D. of Charles-Town, South-Carolina, to the Rev. Thomas Birch, D.D. Secr. R.S. concerning the Quantity of Rain Fallen There from January 1738, to December 1752," *Philosophical Transactions of the Royal Society* 48 (1752–53): 284–85. For modern data for Charleston in the period 1948–2005, see http://www.dnr.sc.gov/cgi-bin/sco/hsums/cliMAINnew.pl?sc1549, accessed April 29, 2019.

8. César Caviedes, *El Niño in History: Storming through the Ages* (Gainesville: University Press of Florida, 2001), 89–145. Recent research suggests the impact of El Niño–Southern Oscillation ENSO events varies significantly across the region. El Niño events can result in relatively heavy rainfall in parts of the Greater Antilles in May, June, and July, for example, but reduced late summer rainfall in the southern parts of the Lesser Antilles. See Berland et al., "Documentary-Derived Chronologies"; Michael Chenoweth, *The 18th Century Climate of Jamaica: Derived from the Journals of Thomas Thistlewood* (Philadelphia: American Philosophical Society, 2003), 2–4; Wenhong Li, Laifang Li, Rong Fu, Yi Deng, and Hui Wang, "Changes to the North Atlantic Subtropical High and Its Role in the Intensification of Summer Rainfall Variability in the Southeastern United States," *Journal of Climate* 24 (March 2011): 1499–1506.

9. For Antigua, see Berland et al., "Documentary-Derived Chronologies," 1332; Watts, *West Indies*, 17–25. On rainfall patterns in general, see Thomas Boswell, "The Caribbean: A Geographic Preface," in *Understanding the Contemporary Caribbean*, ed. Richard S. Hillman and Thomas J. D'Agostino (Boulder, Colo.: Lynne Rienner, 2009), 24–25. For Nevis, see Sheridan, *Sugar and Slavery*, 161; Tyrell to Stapleton, May 4, 1732, in Edwin Gay, "Letters from a Sugar Plantation in Nevis, 1723–1732," *Journal of Economic and Business History* 1 (November 1928): 170.

10. Simon Taylor to Chaloner Arcedeckne, April 14, 1769, and April 16, 1770, in *Travel, Trade, and Power in the Atlantic, 1765–1884*, ed. Betty Wood and Martin Lynn (New York: Cambridge University Press, 2002), 77, 89; Douglas H. Hall, *In Miserable Slavery: Thomas Thistlewood in Jamaica, 1750–1786* (Kingston, Jamaica: University of West Indies Press, 1989), 15. For Antigua, see Berland et al., "Documentary-Derived Chronologies," 1337. For Carolina, see Henry Laurens to Devonsheir, Reeve & Lloyd, October 16, 1755, in Philip M. Hamer, George C. Rogers Jr., and Maude E. Lyles, eds., *The Papers of Henry Laurens*, 16 vols. (Columbia: University of South Carolina Press, 1968–2003), 1:364 (hereafter *PHL*).

11. David Watts, "Cycles of Famine, in Islands of Plenty: The Case of the Colonial West Indies in the Pre-emancipation Period," in *Famine as a Geographical Phenomenon*, ed. Bruce Currey and Graeme Hugo (Dordrecht, Netherlands: D. Reidel, 1984), 62.

12. William Byam to William Lord Willoughby, 1670?, *Calendar of State Papers, Colonial Series* (London, 1860–), 205–6 (hereafter cited as *CSPC*); Governor Sir Nathaniel

Johnson to Lords of Trade and Plantations, June 2, 1688, *CSPC*, 553; "An Account of Governor Codrington's Proceedings as to the Settlement of St. Christopher," September 12, 1691, *CSPC*, 538; Mr. Nivine to Council of Trade and Plantations, May 27, 1718, *CSPC*, 256; Robertson, *Detection*, 49; Governor Hart to the Council of Trade and Plantations, May 20, 1726, *CSPC*, 74; Gregory Cushman, review of Johnson, *Climate and Catastrophe in Cuba and the Atlantic World* in *Hispanic American Historical Review* 93 (January 2013): 103–4.

13. Order of the Council of Jamaica, August 22, 1679, *CSPC*, 408; Address of the Present and the Council of Jamaica to the King, July 11, 1726, *CSPC*, 118–19; Edward Long, *The History of Jamaica* (London: T. Lownudes, 1774), 3:615; Veront M. Satchell, *Hope Transformed: A Historical Sketch of the Hope Landscape, St. Andrew, Jamaica, 1669–1960* (Kingston, Jamaica: University of the West Indies Press, 2012), 120–21; Chenoweth, *18th Century Climate of Jamaica*, 47–49.

14. "Extracts of Letters from Carolina," November 1671, *CSPC*, 279; Edelson, *Plantation Enterprise*, 104; Laurens to John Nutt, August 27, 1756, *PHL*, 2:303; Laurens to Henry Bright, September 9, 1762, *PHL*, 3:118.

15. *South Carolina Gazette*, January 19, 1738; Edelson, *Plantation Enterprise*, 108; Laurens to Sam Munckley, September 11, 1762, *PHL*, 3:120. Despite the "pernicious drought" in 1762, the harvest was better than early expectations. See Laurens to William Fisher, October 23, 1762, *PHL*, 3:142; Laurens to James Dennistoune, John Pagan, & Co., July 6, 1764, *PHL*, 4:327. For a discussion of challenges of inland swamps in Lowcountry Georgia, see Paul M. Pressly, *On the Rim of the Caribbean: Colonial Georgia and the British Atlantic World* (Athens: University of Georgia Press, 2013), 139. Joyce E. Chaplin notes that tidal irrigation became more common after the American Revolution. See Chaplin, *An Anxious Pursuit: Agricultural Innovation and Modernity in the Lower South, 1730–1815* (Chapel Hill: Published for the Institute of Early American History and Culture, Williamsburg, Virginia, by the University of North Carolina Press, 1993), 227–76.

16. Laurens to James Cowles, October 16, 1755, *PHL*, 1:361–62; Laurens to Devonsheir, Reeve, & Lloyd, August 26, 1756, *PHL*, 2:299–300. Carolina exported roughly 303,000 pounds of indigo in 1755, which dropped to 222,000 pounds in 1756, before rebounding with a bumper crop of 876,000 pounds in 1757. See *Historical Statistics of the United States, Millennial Edition Online* (Cambridge: Cambridge University Press, 2016), 5:749–50; John Lewis Gervais to Laurens, November 26, 1777, *PHL*, 12:86; *South Carolina Gazette*, February 13, 1762.

17. On reduced juice, see Lt. Governor Stede to Lords of Trade and Plantations, May 27, 1687, *CSPC*, 377; Tullideph to Wm. Dunbar, April 10, 1738, GD 205/53/8, National Archives of Scotland (NAS); Robert Calhoun to William McDowall, April 15, 1732, GD 237/12/35, NAS; Simon Taylor to Chaloner Arcedeckne, February 25, 1770, in Wood and Lynn, *Travel Trade, and Power*, 86; Alexander West Hamilton to Hugh Hamilton, September 21, 1797, and August 18, 1796, Hamilton Family Papers, Ayrshire Archives, Scotland, AA/DC/17/8 (hereafter HFP).

18. Gaspar, *Bondmen and Rebels*, 224. Gaspar cites export figures from Noel Deerr, *History of Sugar* (1949). Richard Sheridan's figures for sugar imported into England from Antigua differ somewhat but illustrate the same trend. See Sheridan, *Sugar and Slavery*, 490–91. See also Satchell, *Hope Transformed*, 120–21.

19. Frederick H. Smith, *Caribbean Rum: A Social and Economic History* (Gainesville: University Press of Florida, 2008), 45; Jordan Smith, "The Invention of Rum" (PhD diss., Georgetown University, 2018), 114–15.

20. On Saint Croix, see *South Carolina Gazette*, June 28, 1768; Robert Poole, *The Beneficent Bee, or a Traveller's Companion* (London: E. Duncomb, 1753), 270. On the general issue of fire, see Bonham C. Richardson, *Igniting the Caribbean's Past: Fire in British West Indian History* (Chapel Hill: University of North Carolina Press, 2004), 91–92; Hall, *In Miserable Slavery*, 62–63.

21. Lt. Governor Stede to Lords of Trade and Plantations, October 19, 1687, *CSPC*, 454–55. See also Nicholas Blake to Joseph Williamson, March 23, 1670, *CSPC*, 59–60. On the blast, see Griffin Hughes, *The Natural History of Barbados* (London, 1750), 245–46. For a larger discussion, see Matthew Mulcahy and Stuart Schwartz, "Nature's Battalions: Insects as Agricultural Pests in the Early Modern Caribbean," *William and Mary Quarterly* 75 (July 2018): 432–64.

22. Edelson, *Plantation Enterprise*, 101.

23. Governor Kendell to Lords of Trade and Plantations, August 22, 1690, *CSPC*, 311; Governor Hart to the Council of Trade and Plantations, May 20, 1756, *CSPC*, 311. On high prices, see also Alexander West Hamilton to Hugh Hamilton, July 22, 1796, HFP; J. L. Carstens, *A General Description of All the Danish, American or West Indian Islands*, edited and translated by Arnold R. Highfield (Saint Croix: Virgin Islands Humanities Council, 1997), 122–23; Watts, "Cycles of Famine," 62.

24. Laurens to Meyler & Hall, January 20, 1757, *PHL*, 2:423; Laurens to Devonsheir, Reeve, and Lloyd, August 26, 1756, *PHL*, 2:299–300. On slave sales, see Laurens to Augustus & John Boyd & Co., November 15, 1756, *PHL*, 2:351n3; Laurens to Gidney Clarke, October 13, 1756, *PHL*, 2:337; *Pennsylvania Gazette*, August 25, 1773.

25. Robertson, *State and Situation*, 45; Lt. Governor Stede to Lords of Trade and Plantations, *CSPC*, 377. See also *American Weekly Mercury*, August 22, 1734. For Carolina, see George Milligen-Johnston, "Additions" to *A Short Description of the Province of South Carolina* (London: John Hinton, 1770), in *Colonial South Carolina: Two Contemporary Descriptions*, ed. Chapman Milling (Columbia: University of South Carolina Press, 1951), 107; Lionel Chalmers, *An Account of the Weather and Diseases of South-Carolina* (London: E. and C. Dilly, 1776), 18–19; *South Carolina Gazette*, September 29, 1759; *Pennsylvania Gazette*, August 25, 1773; Long, *History of Jamaica*, 1:453; Berland, "Extreme Weather and Social Vulnerability," 139.

26. On drought and working conditions, see Roberts, *Slavery and the Enlightenment*, 95, 105–6; William Ramsay, *An Essay on the Treatment and Conversion of African Slaves in the British Colonies* (1784), 73–74, quoted in Sheridan, *Sugar and Slavery*, 160; Governor Sir Nathaniel Johnson to the Lords of Trade and Plantations, April 20, 1689, *CSPC*, 24. On slaves carrying water on their heads, see Alexander West Hamilton to Hugh Hamilton, July 22, 1796, HFP; Samuel Martin, quoted in Smith, *Invention of Rum*, 114–15.

27. On plantains, see Alexander West Hamilton, July 22, 1796, HFP. On the high cost of water, see Vere Lang Oliver, *The History of Antigua* (London, 1894), 1:xcvi; Rachel Tudway, quoted in J. R. Ward, *British West Indian Slavery, 1750–1835: The Process of Amelioration* (Oxford: Clarendon, 1988), 37; Rebecca Woolnough, quoted in Christine Walker, "To Be My Own Mistress: Women in Jamaica, Atlantic Slavery, and the Creation of Britain's American Empire, 1660–1770" (PhD diss., University of Michigan, 2014), 285.

28. Gay, "Letters from a Sugar Plantation," 155–57, 167–68.

29. David Stalker to William Stapleton, December 15, 1736 (quotation), 4/10, Stapleton Mss., John Rylands Library, University of Manchester; Tullideph to Wm. Dunbar, April

10, 1738, Tullideph Letterbook, GD 205/53/8, NAS. See also Keith Mason, "The World an Absentee Planter and His Slaves Made: Sir William Stapleton and His Nevis Sugar Estate, 1722–1740," *Bulletin of the John Rylands University Library of Manchester* 75 (1993): 103–31; Robertson, *Detection*, 44; Smith, *Natural History of Nevis*, 225.

30. For Barbados, see J. Harry Bennett Jr., *Bondsmen and Bishops: Slavery and Apprenticeship on the Codrington Plantations of Barbados, 1710–1838* (Berkeley: University of California Press, 1958), 38; Frank Klingberg, *Coddington Chronicle: An Experiment in Anglican Altruism on a Barbados Plantation, 1710–1834* (Berkeley: University of California Press, 1949), 71; Tullideph to George Thomas, May 22, 1746, in Richard Sheridan, ed., "Letters from a Sugar Plantation in Antigua, 1739–1758," *Agricultural History* 31 (July 1957): 14; Robert Colhoun to William McDowall, May 30, 1757, and Wm. Milliken to Capt. McDowall, June 2, 1757, GD 237/12/47, NAS.

31. Richard Sheridan, "The Crisis of Slave Subsistence in the British West Indies during and after the American Revolution," *William and Mary Quarterly* 33 (October 1976): 615–41; Berland and Endfield, "Drought and Disaster," 219–22; Ward, *British West Indian Slavery*, 66. See also Andrew Jackson O'Shaughnessy, *An Empire Divided: The American Revolution and the British Caribbean* (Philadelphia: University of Pennsylvania Press, 2000), 162.

32. Edward East to Roger Hope Elletson, March 19, 1777, Stowe-Brydges Papers, box 25, folder 43, Huntington Library, San Marino, Calif.; Simon Taylor to John Taylor, April 8, 1781, 1/A/14, Taylor Papers, Institute of Commonwealth Studies, London; Simon Taylor to Chaloner Arcedeckne, April 8, 1781, http://blog.soton.ac.uk/slaveryandrevolution/1781/04 /08/simon-taylor-to-chaloner-arcedeckne-8-april-1781-2/, accessed April 29, 2019.

33. William Taylor to Thomas Graham, August 8, 1786, Airth Mss 10924, f. 55– 56, National Library of Scotland; Simon Taylor to Chaloner Arcedeckne, December 14, 1786, http://blog.soton.ac.uk/slaveryandrevolution/1786/12/14/simon-taylor-to-chaloner -arcedeckne-14-december-1786/, accessed April 19, 2019; Report of the Jamaica Assembly, cited in Bryan Edwards, *The History, Civil and Commercial, of the British Colonies in the West Indies* (Dublin: Luke White, 1793), 2:394–97.

34. Wm. Milliken to Capt. McDowall, June 2, 1757, GD 237/12/47, NAS. A similar argument regarding the French colonies is advanced by Joseph Horan, "The Colonial Famine Plot: Slavery, Free Trade, and Empire in the French Atlantic, 1763–1791," *International Review of Social History* 55 (2010): 103–21.

35. Hall, *In Miserable Slavery,* 67–68; Robert Colhoun to William McDowall, May 30, 1757, GD 237/12/47, NAS.

36. Keith Mason, "The Absentee Planter and the Key Slave: Privilege, Patriarchalism, and Exploitation in the Early Eighteenth-Century Caribbean," *William and Mary Quarterly* 70 (January 2013): 79–102, quotation on 93; Gaspar, *Bondmen and Rebels,* 215–54; Richard Sheridan, "The Jamaican Slave Insurrection Scare of 1776 and the American Revolution," *Journal of Negro History* 3 (1975): 290–308; Berland, "Extreme Weather and Social Vulnerability," 132; *The West-India Merchant* (London: J. Almon, 1778), 118–19.

37. James Dator, "Search for a New Land: Imperial Power and Afro-Creole Resistance in the British Leeward Islands, 1624–1745" (PhD diss., University of Michigan, 2011), 232, 237, 339–43; Jason Sharples, "The Flames of Insurrection: Fearing Slave Conspiracy in Early America, 1670–1780" (PhD diss., Princeton University, 2010), 270–71. Feasts during the "hard winter" of 1740–41 also figured in the New York slave conspiracy. See Jill Lepore,

New York Burning: Liberty, Slavery, and Conspiracy in Eighteenth-Century Manhattan (New York: Vintage, 2006), 5–14.

38. On the need to read accounts of conspiracies with caution, see Jason T. Sharples, "Discovering Slave Conspiracies: New Fears of Rebellion and Old Paradigms of Plotting in Seventeenth-Century Barbados," *American Historical Review* 120 (June 2015): 811–43.

39. On hurricanes and threats of social disorder, see Mulcahy, *Hurricanes and Society in the British Greater Caribbean, 1624–1783* (Baltimore: Johns Hopkins University Press, 2006), 94–117. On drought and resistance, see Berland, "Extreme Weather and Social Vulnerability," who notes that "drought may have been more likely to produce overt, confrontational reactions to oppression, as severe hunger, thirst and high temperatures—all hallmarks of drought in colonial Antigua—are known to increase irritability and restlessness" (230). Likewise, Waldemar Westergaard, *The Danish West Indies under Company Rule, 1671–1754* (New York: Macmillan, 1917), argues that food shortages were the "most persistent motive that led to general unrest" (164). On Haiti, see Laurent Dubois, *Avengers of the New World: The Story of the Haitian Revolution* (Cambridge, Mass.: Harvard University Press, 2004), 93–94; *Pennsylvania Gazette*, July 5, 1786.

40. Philip D. Morgan, *Slave Counterpoint: Black Life in the Eighteenth-Century Chesapeake and Lowcountry* (Chapel Hill: Omohundro Institute of Early American History and Culture and North Carolina Press, 1998), 134–45, quotation on 138; Laurens to Richard Oswald, July 26, 1756, *PHL*, 2:270; see also Laurens to Devonsheir, Reeve, and Lloyd, August 26, 1756, *PHL*, 2:299–300; Laurens to Augustus & John Boyd & Co., November 15, 1756, *PHL*, 2:351n3; Laurens to Meyler & Hall, January 20, 1757, *PHL*, 2:423. South Carolina did experience drought and shortages of corn and other provisions in 1737–38, the years leading up to the Stono Rebellion, but it is not clear that such conditions lingered into 1739 or that they played a major role in precipitating that event. Robert Pringle reported that large crops of rice were harvested at the end of 1738 and that a large crop was expected in 1739. See Robert Pringle to Bartholomew Cheever, July 21, 1738, in *The Letterbook of Robert Pringle*, ed. Walter Edger (Columbia: University of South Carolina Press, 1972), 1:21–22; *South Carolina Gazette*, June 29, 1738. On large crops, see Pringle to Theodorus Hodshun, June 25, 1739, *Letterbook of Robert Pringle*, 1:103–4.

41. See Matthew Mulcahy, "Environmental Threats and Imperial Celebrations: Days of Fasting and Thanksgiving in the British Caribbean, 1670–1780," paper presented at "National Worship in International Perspective," Durham University, April 2010. "Address of the President and Council of Jamaica to the Kind," *CSPC*, 118–19; *South Carolina Gazette*, June 29, 1738. Although slaves did not attend church services, it appears that many owners did not require slaves to work on fast days. See Hall, *In Miserable Slavery*, 57. On Antigua fast, see Edward Byam to Abraham Redwood, May 22, 1731, in *The Commerce of Rhode Island, 1726–1800* (Boston: The Society, 1914), 1:20.

42. C. G. A. Oldendorp, *History of the Mission of the Evangelical Brethren of the Caribbean Islands of St. Thomas, St. Croix, and St. John*, ed. Johann Jakob Bossard, trans. Arnold R. Highfield and Vladimir Barac (Ann Arbor, Mich.: Karoma, 1987), 191–92.

43. Oliver, *History of Antigua*, 1:xc; Berland and Endfield, "Drought and Disaster," suggests that little specific evidence exists for formal liberalization of trade during periods of drought prior to the Revolutionary era, but it was common after that time. See also "Extreme Weather and Social Vulnerability," 140. Officials in other colonies in the region did the same thing. For the Spanish case, see Sherry Johnson, "El Niño, Environmental Crisis,

and the Emergence of Alternative Markets in the Hispanic Caribbean, 1760–70s," *William and Mary Quarterly* 62 (July 2005): 365–410.

44. Ward, *British West Indian Slavery*, 61–80.

45. Oliver, *History of Antigua*, 1:xcv; Richard Grove, *Green Imperialism: Colonial Expansion, Tropical Island Edens and the Origins of Environmentalism, 1600–1860* (New York: Cambridge University Press, 2003), 271.

46. Smith, "Invention of Rum," 116–17; Watts, *West Indies*, 299; Edwards quoted in Richard Sheridan, *Development of the Plantations to 1750* (Barbados, 1970), 52.

47. Satchell, *Hope Transformed*, 169–74.

Native Women Work the Ground

Enslavement and Civility in the Early American Southeast

HAYLEY NEGRIN

In the seventeenth century, English colonists considered civilizing Natives to be an important justification for the colonization of North America. The English aimed to create a hearty Protestant empire in the Americas that would enhance England's reputation on the world stage and provide what they thought to be a more civilized dominion over Native peoples than the popish, cruel Spanish. With this mission in mind, land use and labor roles were critical areas that the English felt they could improve on in Native societies. Gendered understandings of inappropriate labor roles among Algonquians became a flashpoint among writers and travelers who were disturbed by the agricultural labor of Native women and what they saw as the laziness of Native men for their lack of field work. The English planned to import English agricultural techniques and labor roles to their own communities as well as Native societies. However, the exigencies of colonization often forced colonists to adopt Native crops and techniques instead of crops favored by imperial authorities and the sponsors of English colonization. Additionally, as racial slavery became the labor system of choice in the growing tobacco and rice economies of the English Southeast, the agricultural labor of Native women, once the focus of settlers' disquiet, was actually put to use by colonial planters in the name of export crop production. This chapter traces the evolution of these ideas, arguing that the rise of the Native slave trade contributed to a transformation in English colonialism and conceptions of proper labor roles for Native women in the environments of southeastern North America over the course of the seventeenth century.

Historians have documented not only the physical labor but also the legal, cultural, and intellectual labor that went into fashioning early American land to be fit for English colonization. As scholars such as William Cronon and Carolyn Merchant, among others, have shown, part of laying claim to Native land was rejecting or modifying existing Native epistemologies in favor of colonial ideas about ownership, property, and the nature of the landscape itself.[1] Less explored in this literature is how early American ideas about female Native agricultural labor evolved in the developing plantation societies of the early Southeast. As colonists came up against Native agricultural methods that had been successful for centuries alongside ideas from the sponsors of English imperialism from across the Atlantic, they struggled to define what appropriate and profitable land use would look like. Imperialists hoped that English crops such as wheat would take hold. They also assumed that the gendered division of labor in England between male field workers and female housewives would flourish in the colonies and that Natives—whose societies were conceived by the English through the lens of European-style property relations and the spread of Protestant empire abroad—would conform to this vision. Over the course of the seventeenth century, however, in spite of the distaste the English had once displayed for Native women doing field work in their own societies and resistance from across the Atlantic, Chesapeake and Carolina colonists incorporated female Natives from a variety of polities across the region into plantations as enslaved field laborers. They adopted many Native crops and rejected plans from imperial authorities to civilize Native women by bringing them around to proper European labor roles.

While fewer in number than enslaved African women, enslaved Native women appear consistently in laws, inventories, probate records, records of the Society for the Propagation of the Gospel, and diplomatic discourse across Virginia and South Carolina in the early colonial period. Scholars have devoted considerable time to understanding gendered and racialized conceptions of labor roles for African and English women in the early colonial Southeast, but less is known about how colonists configured enslaved Native women into their plans and what this incorporation meant for colonial conceptions of English imperialism.[2] While southern planters would maintain a variety of relationships with Native polities in the region—including peoples who would be their suppliers in the slave trade—they made a statement about the limitations of the English colonial project to transform Native people when they decided Native women were fit for racial slavery. Investigating the role of Native female labor in defining the English colonial project reveals how English colonialism evolved to fit the needs of a patriarchal plantation society.

In Anglo-Protestant culture farming was the domain of men. Work that took place outside the home was thought of as a masculine endeavor, as opposed to household labor, which was the domain of women. As historian Mary Prior argues, in early modern England "whatever a man did was work and what a woman did was her duty."[3] Early modern English people followed Christian cosmological teachings that ascribed profound spiritual importance to the productive working of land and the particular assignment of gender roles that, in their view, went along with it. Biblical patriarchs such as Abraham, Isaac, and Noah as described in Genesis were rewarded by a male God when they tilled the earth, while women such as Rebecca and Rachel were in charge of producing a male heir to inherit the patriarch's mantle. As Genesis says, "Isaac sowed seed in that land, and in the same year reaped a hundredfold. The LORD blessed him."[4] In early discovery narratives some English writers presented a conflicted narrative about Native farming techniques. On the one hand, they were disturbed by the fact that Native women were the primary agricultural producers in their societies because this went against early modern English mores about the sexual division of labor. On the other hand, however, early modern English observers and writers were invested in showing how productive the land could be in order to promote colonization.[5] This often meant a grudging acknowledgment of the contributions of Native women. As Thomas Hariot explained in 1588 in *A Brief and True Report of the New Found Land of Virginia*, Algonquian women were involved in "husbandry" using "short peckers or parers" to till the ground. Their crops were highly productive. As he assured readers: "An English acre containing forty pearches in length, and foure in breadth, doeth *there* [Virginia] yeeld in croppe or of corne, beanes, and peaze, at the least two hundred London bushelles . . . Whenas in England fourtie bushelles of our wheate yeelded out of such an acre is thought to be much."[6]

In general colonists could expect an easy time producing corn, beans, and squash. As Hariot promised, "The increase is so much that small labour and paines is needful." But while Hariot pointed to the abundance of American crops and was aware of the contribution Native women made to production, as he described how the English would fare when colonists began to plant crops in Virginia he was quick to think in terms of English gender roles instead of Native ones. As he explained, *"one man* may prepare and husband so much grounde (hauing once borne corne before) with lesse then foure and twentie houres labour, as shall yeelde him victuall in a large proportion for a twelue moneth."[7] Although the land was productive under the direction of Algonquian women, as Hariot saw it, when the English came men would take over farming. In the eyes of many early European observers, Native men were lazy because they managed to avoid farming, which in the eyes of the English was the highest form of labor, biblical in its significance. Native women, on the other hand, suffered deeply. As George Archer, an early Jamestown colonist complained, Algonquian women "do all the labour and the men hunt and goe at their pleasure."[8] In explorer William Strachey's eyes, "The men bestowe their tymes in fishing, hunting, wars, and such man-like exercises without the doores, scorning to be seen in any effeminate labour, which is the Cause that the women be very paynefull, and the men often idle."[9] John Smith agreed, saying disdainfully that besides hunting and warring, "The women and children do the rest of the worke."[10]

Gendered critiques of labor roles in Algonquian society were often paired with one of the most precious justifications Englishmen had for colonization: that land in America was ill used by Natives and would be better off in the hands of Englishmen. In his detailed discussion of farming techniques, Hariot found it difficult not to acknowledge Native women's successful work. But most writers were dubious about how well Natives were doing with women at the helm of agricultural production. According to Smith, Native women's agricultural labor was inappropriate and did not produce enough food for Algonquian societies. "When all their fruits be gathered, little els they plant, and this is done by their women and children; neither doth this long suffice them, for neare three parts of the yeare, they onely obserue times and seasons, and liue of what the Country naturally affordeth from hand to mouth."[11] Algonquian women were treated terribly by men because they had to do an extensive amount of labor that took place outside the household. According to one Englishman, William Wood, New England Algonquian women had "gurmandizing husbands" who would eat seed corn before they could even plant it. When their people moved to accommodate seasonal hunting, Algonquian women "like snailes" had to "carrie their houses on their backs." Native women dug shellfish, "where by her lazie husbands guts shee crams."[12] When early writers pointed out the supposed poor treatment of Native men toward their wives, the ensuing outrage supported English goals for colonial projects. Algonquian men were harming the women in their communities by forcing them to do "male work," and Englishmen would teach them to do better once they arrived in greater numbers.[13] This concern over what Englishmen perceived to be an unequal and damning division of labor in Native societies was often accompanied by sympathetic descriptions of Native women. As Smith said, "The women are always covered about their middles with a skin, and very shamefast to be seene bare." In spite of the horrible labors they had to endure, Algonquian women were modest and possessed propriety. Smith also pointed to their bodily integrity, saying they were "fat and well favoured."[14] Children were also described as well behaved and hardworking as they were spotted planting and weeding beside their mothers. Children had the potential to learn English ways, perhaps more so than men who, in the English view, were problematic because they ignored their patriarchal responsibilities and led their dependents in unnatural, uncivilized directions.

As early travel writers and explorers lamented the sad place of Native women in Native societies, legal theorists made the transformation of Algonquians and other Natives into civilized beings a stated goal of English colonization. As authors of the Virginia charter promised, Englishmen "may in time bring the Infidels and Savages, living in those parts, to human Civility, and to a settled and quiet Government."[15] Similar language found its way into most early colonial charters. The Carolina charter stated that the Lords Proprietor were establishing the colony because they were "excited with a laudable and pious zeal for the propagation of the Christian faith."[16] In the well-known liberal religious freedom clause in the Fundamental Constitutions of Carolina, John Locke also included a conversion clause that included Jews and other heathens. "Jews, heathens, and other dissenters from the purity of Christian religion may not be scared and kept at a distance from it, but . . . may, by good usage and persuasion . . . suitable to the rules and design of the gospel, be won ever to embrace and unfeignedly receive the truth."[17] Promises to civilize provided a convenient justification for English colonialism that carried real legal and cultural weight for many early modern English people. Indeed, the first clause of Carolina's charter laid out a justification for colonization by stating that this new colony to the south of Virginia was "not yet cultivated or planted, and only inhabited by some barbarous people, who have no knowledge of Almighty God."[18] It also fit with ambitions begun in the Tudor court to create a vast Protestant empire, a task that the Stuart monarchs and then Oliver Cromwell would pick up again through his western design scheme in the 1650s.[19] While gender roles were not explicitly mentioned in legal discourse, early modern audiences would have associated the turn to Christianity and civility with Native women giving up their agricultural labor for housewifery.[20] Just as Native men would need to give up hunter-gather techniques or "the chase," as theorists like John Locke termed it, Native women would soon see the virtue in leaving "mens work" behind.[21]

The move to bring civility to "barbarous" people on lands that were "not yet cultivated" was a legal imperative but also a cultural one. As conceived of by Europeans, the transformation to civility—moving from a barbarous hunter-gatherer to the farming patriarch—was a process the English themselves had endured when the Romans conquered ancient Britain. As William Strachey explained in justifying the English presence in Virginia, though some destruction had occurred, the Romans had brought order and civility to the English, which was a gift. The Romans "reduced the conquered partes of our barbarous island into provinces." They also built "castells and townes, and in every corner teaching us even to knowe the powerfull discourse of divine reason (which makes us only men and distinguisheth us from beasts, amongst whome we lived as naked and beastly as they)." For Strachey these ideas about civilization and intensive farming were also linked to appropriate gender roles. Without the Romans, Strachey thought that the English "might yet have lyved as overgrowne Satyrs, rude, and untutored, wandering in the woodes, dwelling in Caves, and hunting for our dynners, (as the wyld beasts in the forests for their prey) prostituting our daughters to straungers, [and] sacrificing our children to idols."[22] In this view, a hunter's attachment to the land divorced from cultivation was animalistic and barbaric. This barbarism was in turn associated with disordered gender roles where fathers rejected their duty to maintain the sexual purity of their daughters and their role as protector of children. However, after being conquered themselves, ancient Britons set aside these practices. They rejected seasonal foraging, adopted intensive farming techniques to make the best use out of the land, and organized their families in the image of biblical patriarchs. In short, ancient Britons were better off just as the Natives of America would be.

Anglicans who believed in spreading Protestantism abroad thought carefully about how their goals could be achieved through the transformation of Natives' domestic lives and the establishment of formal conversion programs. When George Thorpe, a missionary and member of Parliament, came to Virginia and met with Powhatan leaders, he wrote to the Virginia Company to send "apparel and househoudestufe" to speed along the conversion process.[23] King James I directly involved himself in efforts to bring civility to Natives in ways that would affect their day-to-day domestic life, ordering a collection be taken up in 1618 for the "planting of a college for the training up of the children of those infidels in true religion and moral virtue and Civility and for other godly uses."[24] When Pocahontas traveled to London, her marriage to John Rolfe and baptism as Rebecca Rolfe was hailed as a great success for the English colonial project. It was not only her turn from heathen religious practice to Christianity that was significant for audiences but also the fact that she appeared to embrace the domestic life of an Englishwoman. Pocahontas—or Matoaka, as she referred to herself—adopted not only an English name but also an English style of dress. After her London visit, along with a title highlighting her baptism, Smith's writings on Virginia circulated a well-known portrait of her wearing clothes that might adorn any female member of the Stuart court. She also gave birth to a son who was baptized Thomas Rolfe, which completed the image of English womanhood.[25] This was quite a distance from the vision that Englishmen first had of Algonquian women who covered themselves decently enough but only with a "skin" as they worked the fields.

In the early years of colonization legislators promised to pay English families to take in Native children and teach them English ways. The Virginia Company, a joint stock company led by a group of wealthy aristocrats and noblemen mostly located in England, was the original entity that led the colonization of Virginia. In 1620 an anonymous donation of £500 was received by the company "for the maintenance of a convenient number of young Natives taken at the age of seven years or younger." The donor, likely a wealthy devotee of the Anglican church, had a plan for the development of the children. First, they were to be instructed in reading the Bible and the tenets of Christianity until they turned twelve, when they were to be instructed "in some lawful trade with all humanity and gentleness." Finally, when they turned twenty-one these Natives were to "enjoy like liberties and privileges with our native English." In order to be sure that the money was being put to proper use, the donor requested that the names of the children be taken down as well as "their foster fathers and overseers."[26] But English attacks on the Powhatan and the Natives' retaliation in 1622 resulted in the deaths of a quarter of the colonists of Virginia, which made the building of King James's school impossible. English attempts to foster Native children on a meaningful scale were also unsuccessful. In that same year, before the attack on the colony, a settler reported to the Virginia Company that Natives would not give their children up for "feare of hard usage by the English."[27] The Brafferton Indian School at the College of William and Mary did finally come to fruition at the end of the seventeenth century. Designed specifically to cater to young boys, the plan reflected English gender ideals by prioritizing male education. But the college also focused on the domestic life of the boys. Directions for the funding of the school, which developed out of a bequest from the estate of scientist Robert Boyle, included that the board of governors of the school keep the children in "books and education" but also "in Meat drink Washing Lodgeing Cloaths [and] Medicines."[28] The idea was even circulated for the Native boys to "have a careful Indian man of their own country to wait upon them and serve them" to mimic English domestic life, which privileged the use of servants in well-off households.[29]

English desires to implant civility in the Americas also manifested itself through land-use practices. Hopeful of maintaining civilized behavior among colonists and transferring the best of Englishness overseas to their new possessions, most funders of colonization projects and some early colonists envisioned a profitable, orderly crop organized in neat English-style rows to be the ideal. In 1672, for instance, only two years after the first 150 settlers anchored their ships at Ashley River, executive council member Joseph Dalton wrote optimistically back to one proprietor of Carolina that the colony was "excellent for English grain, and will afford us the convenient husbandry of wheat."[30] The Lords Proprietor of Carolina argued that mulberry trees would be ideal in order to make a refined, profitable product such as silk. In 1680 planter and Native trader/slaver Maurice Mathews noted that "the clime is moderat and *wee believe* pleasing to Silk wormes."[31] However, the harsh realities of colonization meant that the English ended up depending on local Natives for food in the early years and struggling to get refined crops such as silk off the ground. In 1670 colonist Stephen Bull wrote to one of the Lords Proprietors saying that he had reached out to the local Cusabo people for food. "The Last yeare in our extreme wants of Provisions I was imployed by the Collony to Get some Corn from the Indians to supply our wants."[32] Colonists would also take agricultural guidance from locals, more likely than not looking to Native women for help as they cultivated maize and other North American crops.[33]

In the years before rice emerged as a profitable export crop, huge swaths of land remained completely uncultivated in the Carolinas, contrary to the European biblical ideal. Carolina colonists raised and sold cattle in land that the proprietors hoped they would sow. As one early pamphlet author explained, "The marshes and meadows are very large from 1500 to 3000 acres, and upwards, and are excellent food for cattle."[34] Mathews admitted, "Our plantation have not as yet admitted us to make triall of several Inglish grains." He claimed that "they had some good wheat" but still "nothing of this nature yet worth the relation." Finally, he said grimly, "Our ground generallie are not clear of stumps of trees." While "English graines" remained elusive, Indian corn adapted from local Natives was a success. Mathews may have written somewhat disparagingly about English wheat cultivation, but he wrote proudly about hogs, saying, "wee have great store" and also "plenty of corn." In fact, domestic livestock cultivation worked well as a complement to maize. According to Mathews, the "country . . . is so plentifull of corn and hath so short and moderate a winter that it will afford aboundance of poultry."[35] In 1674 Lord Ashley, one of the Lords Proprietor, expressed his concern about the grazing economy that was developing in Carolina, arguing that the plan was to have "planters there and not Graziers."[36] In the minds of men such as the proprietors, raising cattle wasted significant acres of land that was left uncultivated while wild animals roamed. The adoption of maize, or what colonists called "Indian corn," was perhaps necessary to avoid starvation in the early years, but it was also antithetical to orderly English styles of agriculture and a lucrative mercantilist vision. Both conceptions of land use were perhaps too close to Strachey's vision of uncivilized satyrs who roamed and hunted in a savage land. This, however, did not stop colonists from pursuing grazing. In Carolina, even as rice was adopted, Native food crops remained critical. In 1710 Carolina colonist Thomas Nairne described a ninety-acre plantation as an ideal, with forty-five acres devoted to rice and the other forty-five to be sowed with "Indian corn, peas, pumpkins, potatoes, melons and other eatables, for the use of the family."[37] English colonists embraced Native methods and continued to go against English models of agriculture even after they managed to stabilize their food supply.[38]

Colonization strategies developed on the ground, and colonists heeded the advice of funders and authorities only when it was convenient for them. In Virginia the first colonists were at odds with members of the Virginia Company leadership, who considered tobacco to be a temporary choice for cultivation because of its reputation as a barbarous plant owing to its association with Na-tives. Even before the establishment of Jamestown, in his 1604 pamphlet "A Counterblast to Tobacco," King James I asked his subjects "what honour or pol-icie can move us to imitate the barbarous and beastly maners of the wilde, god-lesse, and slavish Indians, especially in so vile and stinking a custome?"[39] As Virginia's burgeoning tobacco economy would show, tobacco advocates pre-vailed even though the king drew an association between uncivilized behavior, Natives, and the crop. In 1621 colonists wrote feverishly to England about tobac-co's importance, arguing that there essentially would not *be* a Virginia without it.[40] Just like Carolinians, in the early years Virginians also depended on local Natives for food. Virginians had also adopted local Native crops such as maize, beans, and melons to supplement their staple crop output so they could con-tinue to feed themselves long after food shortages had passed. Hariot's advice about the possibilities of American agriculture was taken to heart. Indentured servants, the enslaved, and free men and women would all end up taking some time out of tobacco production to work with Native crops. As Lorena Walsh has shown, Virginia planters rarely had the luxury of having enough laborers to split up their forces between tobacco production and food crops.[41] As James Rice has argued in his environmental history of early Virginia, "Approaching an English farm in early summer, a traveler from England would have been struck by the similarities between colonists' and Algonquians' fields."[42]

Maintaining English cultural values was still a concern, perhaps even more so as colonists adopted Native agricultural methods and lived in such close proximity to Indigenous peoples. Naturally, Virginians became concerned about the implications of consigning women to field labor just as Hariot, Smith, and other early writers were concerned about women's work in Native society. As Kathleen M. Brown has shown, gender roles were under stress in the Chesapeake as colonists struggled to develop a social order that was in line with early modern English mores as well as labor needs.[43] Faced with the neces-sity of consigning newly arrived Englishwomen with backbreaking work in to-bacco fields because of labor shortages, colonists enforced tithing on European women in a limited capacity and focused on taxing enslaved African women just as they would European male laborers. These laws helped ensure that as Virginians came to adopt slavery on a wide scale by the beginning of the eigh-teenth century, enslaved African-descended "wenches" would actually come to bear the brunt of the field work and the stigma that went along with it, while English women were more protected. Masculinizing enslaved black women and shepherding white women into wife and daughter roles ensured that civil-ity and English gender roles could be maintained in a palatable-enough form for concerned patriarchs.

However, as colonists adopted American crops, they also adopted American labor practices. After the Native slave trade enveloped the Southeast in the second half of the seventeenth century, Native women who were once in charge of agricultural production in societies throughout the Southeast became producers in English plantation societies in Carolina and Virginia. After the entrance of Europeans on the continent, Native communities competed with one another for captives, space, and European trade goods such as guns, which became critical in the increasingly violent postcontact world—the world of the "shatter zone," as anthropologist Robbie Ethridge has described it.[44] Natives from a variety of groups had labored in Virginia prior to mid-century, but they did so in greater numbers after the settlement of Carolina and the rise of commercial Native slave trading throughout the South. Scholars working on southeastern Native history have documented the distinctly gendered nature of the trade; colonists provided a robust market for Native male warriors/captive raiders who delivered the women and children of their rivals into their hands.[45] But enslaving Native women and children was also directly taken up by colonial men in both Virginia and South Carolina to meet their financial interests. For example, in 1662, when Virginia governor William Berkeley was struggling to fill Virginia tobacco fields with enough hands, he gave specific instructions to attack troublesome Rappahannock towns and capture Native women and children to sell into slavery.[46] Several decades later as Carolina was shifting toward rice production, in 1704 former Carolina governor James Moore proudly wrote to the Lords Proprietor that he had managed to take 325 Apalachee men and 4,000 Apalachee women and children as slaves in a raid on Spanish Florida "without one penny charge to the publick."[47] Historian Alan Gallay estimates that between thirty and fifty thousand Natives were enslaved by the British from 1670 to 1715.[48] One scholar argues that one-fourth of Carolina's early enslaved labor force was made up of Natives. This population skewed toward women and children. A 1708 Carolina census recorded a higher number of Native women and children as opposed to men.[49] In Henrico County, Virginia, which became a central hub of the Native slave trade in the Southeast, there were more people described as being enslaved Natives than any other laborer between 1677 and 1692.[50] As Native labor became available, planters expressed no problem with having Native women take on agricultural labor even though it had come off as disturbing to the English at the outset of colonization. Instead, in 1711 one pamphlet writer in Carolina even argued that Native women were the ideal agricultural laborers for plantations. Skipping over white indentured servants and female African slaves as the main female labor force, he argued that in Carolina "Fifteen good Negro Men" and "Fifteen Indian women to work in the field" would be needed in order to establish a successful plantation.[51] Planters rejected the idea of sparing Native women from arduous, masculine field work in order to civilize them. They established their own vision of colonial land use and labor roles for Native women instead.

Long before the Native slave trade reached its apex in the Southeast with the colonization of Carolina, increasing wars in the Piedmont, and raiding into Spanish Florida, Virginians had already established Native women as taxable laborers. In a colony that revolved economically and politically around tobacco production, taxation was tied to the export crop and to those who produced it. Indentured servants and enslaved people were the most profitable items in colonial estates outside of the crop itself, and the public purse was fueled by taxing masters on each individual laborer. Establishing tithability based on whether or not an individual "worked in the ground" began quite early. As a 1629 Virginia law stated, colonists "thought fitt that all those that worke in the ground of what qualitie or condition soever, shall pay tithes to the ministers." European colonists developed policies over the course of the seventeenth century that ensured that both Native men and women who were indentured or enslaved would need to be tithed. Often, Natives and Africans were approached in overlapping ways. In 1658 the first act specifically positioning "Indian servants male or female however procured" as "tythables" was passed.[52] Another act positioning Natives as "tythables" was passed in 1672. It ensured that "each county shall take an account of all negro, molatto, and Indian children, within their severall precincts, and the masters and owners of such children are to make appeare upon oath or evidence the ages of them." After a commercial trade in Native slaves was legalized in Virginia in 1682, yet another act was passed that specifically targeted Native women. "Whereas it hath bin doubted whether Indian women servants sold to the English above the age of sixteene yeares be tythable, Bee it enacted and declared, and it is hereby enacted and declared by the governour, councill and burgesses of this generall assembly and the authority thereof, that all Indian women are and shall be tythables, and ought to pay levies in like manner as negroe women brought into this country doe."[53] The act was particular about both the age of the Native women being targeted and the fact that Native women should be seen in the same category as African women.

"Indian" became a racialized legal and social category that Virginians and Carolinians included in slave codes. Carolina's 1690 slave code, which enacted harsh disciplinary measures, defined enslaved people as "any negroe or Indian slave."[54] Virginia's well-known 1705 slave code, which scholars credit as offering a comprehensive definition of blackness and whiteness, was broadly worded to include not only African and African American people but Natives as well.[55] Throughout most of the seventeenth century, Virginians attempted to restrain Native slavery, especially against local tributary Natives. When enslavement was sanctioned by authorities it was practiced in the context of what were perceived to be just wars or punitive measures such as Berkeley's order in 1662. This changed in 1682, however, when trade routes expanded into the Piedmont and Virginians began to take advantage of strife in southeastern Native communities to the south, siphoning off what they could from the Piedmont-Carolina trade. The 1682 law legalized enslavement as well as a broadly defined commercial "trafiqueing" of Native people that lay outside any just war arguments.[56] Virginians did manage to escape taxes by hiding field laborers—of all kinds—but it seems that after Native slavery was legalized, the taxation of Native females was enforced at least in Henrico County, where Native slavery was prevalent. Because tithing policies reflected whether or not individuals were engaging in field labor, they are an important indicator of how gendered and racialized categories were developing in Virginia. White Englishwomen were slated to be the potential "good wives" engaging in housewifery. As one writer explained, housewifery was for most respectable women while "wenches that are nasty, beastly and not fit to be so imployed are put into the ground."[57] They would not have a primary association with field work and could therefore avoid the degrading term "wench" as long as they did not engage in other forms of improper womanly behavior. However, these policies not only resigned African women to take on the traditionally male role of field work and the stigma that went along with it. Enslaved Native women and African women were often viewed in overlapping ways as laboring women who were thus degraded by field work and their taxability. In 1685 the Henrico County court penalized Anne Morris for not adding her "Indian servant wench" to tithability lists. In 1686 Amy Kent brought a twelve-year-old enslaved Native girl named Doll to court to have her age judged so the court could establish when she would have to pay tithes on her. The court recorder referred to Doll as an "Indian wench."[58]

Concerns about Native women laboring in the fields in their own societies at the beginning of colonization apparently did not extend to colonial uses of Native female agricultural labor. Instead of devoting energies to civilizing Native women by removing them from field work, planter-legislators protected the rights of planters to use Native and African women in planting, processing, and packing tobacco as well as for work on provisioning crops. They became part of a plantation system built on racial patriarchy and the work that had once provided them with status in their own societies and helped define them as women now stigmatized them as masculine. Colonists subverted critical ideas about land use and female authority in Native societies. Like European stories about the beginning of the world, Native cosmologies defined crop cultivation along gendered lines. Native women—who were by and large in charge of agricultural production in the southeastern Native societies that became wrapped up in the slave trade—were politically and culturally tied to the land both through their lead roles in agricultural production and in the ceremonial life that surrounded it. For many groups the passing of another year was marked by the Green Corn Ceremony where entire clans came together to fast, dance, and purify themselves all under the celebratory setting of the ripening of corn. Most groups worshipped a corn mother who was a female god responsible for agriculture. For example, according to Creek and Cherokee cosmologies, the first corn grew from a combination of the body Selu, the first female goddess, and the earth. In this understanding of the world Native women had a critical physical relationship to the land and to agricultural production. Without the sacred joining of the body of the first woman, Selu, with the land, there would be no corn, just as without a woman's labor in day-to-day life in the fields there would be no corn.[59] In Virginia and Carolina enslaved Native women such as Doll worked on some similar crops that they had labored over as free women, but they now did so under the legal authority of English colonial masters and mistresses who claimed the fruits of their labor for themselves.

By adopting Native crops and the labor of Native women, southern planters established a different vision for colonial land use and labor roles than imperial theorists had originally proposed. But while colonists may have brushed aside original plans, English imperial authorities were still concerned about the impact that enslaving Natives could have on the gendered vision they had of the English civilizing mission. When the Lords Proprietor realized the extent of the slaving going on in Carolina, they expressed concern—and their arguments against the practice were distinctly gendered in nature. In the 1680s Carolinians encouraged the Savannah Natives to join them in attacking another polity known as the Waniah with the promise of booty in slaves and trade goods. When the proprietors learned of the plot—led by men such as council member and future colonial governor James Moore—they were horrified. To the Lords Proprietor, "by buying Indians of the Savannahs you induce them . . . to make war upon their neighbors, to ravish the wife from the husband, kill the father to get the child."[60] As the proprietors expressed it, their fury stemmed from the attack on Native dependents and the destruction of the nuclear patriarchal family—as the English conceived of it. Targeting women and children made colonists just as bad as, if not worse than, Native men who also did not know how to treat these dependents. It showed a lack of appropriate behavior on the part of colonial men who were supposed to lead Natives along the path to civilization instead of dragging them down into illegal acts that put Native women and children in danger.

Even as authorities and intellectuals across the Atlantic wrote copiously about civilizing Natives, as time wore on early colonial successes such as the baptism of Pocahontas were few and far between. Colonists had strayed from the original plan to bring Native women and children under the patriarchal English mantle by rescuing them from the drudgery of field work and exposing them to English ways. The Society for the Propagation of the Gospel (SPG), an organization that came to be because leaders in the Church of England felt that churches and ministers in the colonies were badly tended, responded to calls to Christianize and spread English values to Natives. But when Dr. Francis Le Jau, the SPG preacher sent to Charlestowne in 1706, attempted to make contact with Natives, he met with little success. According to Le Jau, this was in large part due to Native slave traders who did not believe in the value of his work. In a letter to the bishop of London in 1712, Le Jau explained why he was making little progress.

> The Indian traders have always discouraged me by raising a world of Difficultyes when I proposed any thing to them relating to the conversion of the Indians. It appears they do not care to have clergymen so near them who doubtless would never approve those perpetual wars they promote amongst the Indians for the onley reason of making slaves to pay for their trading goods; and what slaves! Poor women and children, for the men taken prisoners are burnt most barbarously. I am informed it was down so this last year and the women and children were brought among us to be sold.[61]

Just like the Lords Proprietor, Le Jau was particularly concerned about how slaving affected southeastern Native women and children. The very type of savagery that writers such as Strachey abhorred based on disordered gender roles and irresponsible patriarchs was enacted by slaving. Organizers and funders supporting imperial projects from across the Atlantic envisioned the extension of patronage over helpless heathen women and children that promoted civilizing processes. Because of the focus on women and children in particular, slaving went against a moralizing patriarchal sensibility that men coming from an imperial viewpoint often articulated.

Imperial officials and dedicated Church of England believers continued to support Native schools, but by the end of the century, after Native slavery became institutionalized in Virginia, colonial planters were less enthusiastic. In the early eighteenth century, when Virginia lieutenant governor Alexander Spotswood turned to the legislature for funding for his Native school at Fort Christana, he was refused. Spotswood was raised in a family invested in the English presence abroad. He was born in the English colony of Tangier in Morocco, and his elder half-brother was the first governor of Gibraltar. Spotswood's extensive correspondence with SPG officials indicates his belief that civilizing heathens was part of good imperial policy. It could help maintain diplomatic relationships with unruly tribes, and it reflected Church of England ideals. But Spotswood wrote with frustration to the Board of Trade in 1711 that his attempts to attract Natives to his school at Fort Christana through diplomacy were being thwarted by the governors of the college who "have chosen rather to be at a great expense for buying Indians of remote nations taken in war."[62] Enslavement had become so important to how planters conceived of Virginia's relationships to Natives that it could not be separated from civilizing projects. At a meeting of the board of governors of the Brafferton School in 1716, it was decided that English children would be taken on by the schoolmaster. A petition was erected "at the charge of the college to separate the English children from the Indians."[63] Unlike earlier in the century, when plans were put forward to have Native children live within English homes under father figures, by 1716 the prospect of Native students living side by side with English students was problematic. In this vision of the domestic life of Natives, they were evidently too different to live alongside colonists even though they were theoretically on the road to civilization. In 1728 William Byrd II, son of well-known Native slave trader William Byrd I, lamented that civilization and education schemes were not working on the Native boys at the Brafferton School because Natives always reverted back to their natural "barbarism." "They have been taught to read and write, and have been carefully Instructed in the Principles of the Christian Religion, till they came to be men. Yet after they return'd home, instead of civilizing and converting the rest, they have immediately relapt into Infidelity and Barbarism themselves. . . . They are apt to be more vicious and disorderly than the rest of their countrymen."[64] Virginians had always been tempted to make the most of the Native children they were "fostering," but the House of Burgesses in the 1650s specifically tried to address this, warning against a trade in Native children and stating that Native children should not be used as slaves.[65] Over the course of the century, since ideas for schools had first been proposed, colonists had developed a cadre of laws institutionalizing Native slavery, and these protections vanished along with support for imperial projects to convert Natives.

In the early colonial Southeast, divisions between imperialists across the Atlantic and colonists in Virginia and Carolina led to competing ideas of what civilized land use and labor roles should look like in the region. Adopting Native land-use practices and enslaving Native women raised questions about the direction of English imperialism and what "civilized" agricultural production would look like. As colonists developed plantations centered around export crop production in Virginia and Carolina, they rejected Native visions of land use centered on the leadership of women *on top of* plans from authorities abroad. Instead, they developed their own interpretations of civilized agricultural production grounded in the adoption of "Indian corn" and women's labor under expansive patriarchal control. They brushed aside civilization ideas, rejecting a model in which Native men would be civilized along with Native women who would then fall under the patriarchal supervision of Native men. Instead, they developed a legal chain of reasoning that linked Native women directly to themselves and to plantation land as enslaved property, or as one Virginia law dictated in 1705, as real estate.[66]

NOTES

1. Carolyn Merchant, *Ecological Revolutions: Nature, Gender, and Science in New England* (Chapel Hill: University of North Carolina Press, 1989); William Cronon, *Changes in the Land: Indians, Colonists and the Ecology of New England* (New York: Hill & Wang, 1983); Timothy Silver, *A New Face on the Countryside: Indians, Colonists, and Slaves in South Atlantic Forests, 1500–1800* (Cambridge: Cambridge University Press, 1990); Michael Oberg, *Dominion and Civility: English Imperialism, Native America, and the First American Frontiers, 1585–1685* (Ithaca, N.Y.: Cornell University Press, 2003).

2. Scholars have undertaken the critical work of locating the positions of English and African women in the developing gender hierarchies of southern plantations. See Kathleen Brown, *Good Wives, Nasty Wenches, and Anxious Patriarchs* (Chapel Hill: University of North Carolina Press, 1996); Jennifer Morgan, *Laboring Women: Reproduction and Gender in New World Slavery* (Philadelphia: University of Pennsylvania Press, 2004); Lois Green Carr and Lorena Walsh, "The Planter's Wife: The Experience of White Women in Seventeenth-Century Maryland," *William and Mary Quarterly*, 3rd ser., 34 (1977): 542–71; Mary Beth Norton, "The Evolution of White Women's Experience in Early America," *American Historical Review* 89, no. 3 (1984): 593–619; Carole Shammas, "Black Women's Work and the Evolution of Plantation Society in Virginia," *Labor History* 36 (1985): 5–28. On the agricultural roles of enslaved Native American women in early South Carolina, see D. Andrew Johnson, "Enslaved Native Americans and the Making of South Carolina, 1659–1739" (PhD diss., Rice University, 2018), chap. 6.

3. Mary Prior, "Women and the Urban Economy: Oxford, 1500–1800," in *Women in English Society, 1500–1800*, ed. Mary Prior (London: Routledge, 1985), 95.

4. Genesis 26:12 (New Revised Standard Version).

5. As Joyce Chaplin has shown, in the early settlement period the English believed that the environment shaped an individual's body. If the English hoped to live in Virginia and attract other English people to the space, it was important to show that the environment was yielding healthy, strong bodies. This helps explain why English travel writers painted a favorable portrayal of Algonquian physicality in Virginia. Though writers remarked that like African women, Native women did not feel the pain of childbirth, early writers consistently remarked on their beauty and strength. Joyce E. Chaplin, "Natural Philosophy and an Early Racial Idiom in North America: Comparing English and Indian Bodies," *William and Mary Quarterly*, 3rd ser., 54, no. 1 (1997): 229–52.

6. Thomas Hariot, *A Brief and True Report of the New Found Land of Virginia* (London, 1588), 20.

7. Ibid., 20, 21.

8. Gabriel Archer, *A Relatyon of the Discovery of our River*, in *Jamestown Voyages under the First Charter, 1606–1609*, ed. Philip Barbour (Cambridge: Cambridge University Press, 1969), 1:96.

9. William Strachey, *The Historie of Travell into Virginia Britania* (1612; London: Printed for the Hakluyt Society, 1953), 81.

10. John Smith, *The Complete Works of Captain John Smith, 1580–1631*, vol. 1, ed. Philip Barbour (Chapel Hill: University of North Carolina Press, 2011), 162.

11. Ibid., 158–59.

12. William Wood, *New England's Prospect* (London, 1634), 33, 94–95.

13. As Karen Kupperman has argued, "The coming of the English would help Indian men to see their errors, and, as they became civilized, they would learn to esteem the contributions of their wives. Only large-scale settlement, with a full representation of English society, would allow such learning to take place." Karen Ordahl Kupperman, *Indians and English: Facing Off in Early America* (Ithaca, N.Y.: Cornell University Press, 2000), 150. Scholars have explored the role of gendered language in discovery narratives. Early male writers often feminized land in the "New World," thereby presenting it as ripe for conquering by male settlers. See Louise Montrose, "The Work of Gender in the Discourse of Discovery," *Representations* 31 (Winter 1991): 1–41; Anne McClintock, *Imperial Leather: Race, Gender, and Sexuality in the Colonial Contest* (New York: Routledge, 1995).

14. John Smith, *The Complete Works of Captain John Smith, 1580–1631*, vol. 2, ed. Philip Barbour (Chapel Hill: University of North Carolina Press, 2011), 115, 116, 90.

15. William Hening, ed., *The Statutes at Large, Being a Collection of All the Laws of Virginia from the First Session of the Legislature in the Year 1619*, 3 vols. (Richmond, Va.: Franklin Press, 1809), 1:57–66. The first charter of Virginia is dated April 10, 1606.

16. William L. Saunders, ed., *The Colonial Records of North Carolina, 1662 to 1712*, vol. 1 (Raleigh, N.C.: P. M. Hale, 1886), 20–33. The first charter of Carolina is dated March 24, 1663.

17. Thomas Cooper, *The Statutes at Large of South Carolina*, vol. 1 (Columbia: A. S. Johnston, 1836), 54.

18. Saunders, *Colonial Records of North Carolina*, 1:20–33.

19. Karen Ordahl Kupperman, "Errand to the Indies: Puritan Colonization from Providence Island through the Western Design," *William and Mary Quarterly* 45 (January 1988): 70–99; David Armitage, "The Cromwellian Protectorate and the Languages of Empire," *Historical Journal* 35, no. 3 (1992): 531–55; Kenneth Andrews, "The English in the Caribbean, 1560–1620," in *The Westward Enterprise: English Activities in Ireland, the Atlantic, and America, 1480–1650*, ed. Kenneth Andrews, Nicholas P. Canny, Paul Edward Hedley Hair, and David B. Quinn (Liverpool: Liverpool University Press, 1978).

20. For insight into how labor roles were constructed along gendered lines in early modern England, see Susan Dwyer Amussen, *An Ordered Society: Gender and Class in Early Modern England* (Oxford: Basil Blackwell, 1988); Lawrence Stone, *The Family, Sex and Marriage in England, 1500–1800* (New York: Harper, 1977). The importance of housewifery to English notions of appropriate feminine labor roles in the colonies was perhaps most clearly articulated by John Hammond in *Leah and Rachel; or, The Two Fruitfull Sisters Virginia, and Maryland* (London, 1656).

21. For discussion of Locke's policies and Native people from a political theory perspective, see Nagamitsu Miura, *John Locke and the Native Americans: Early English Liberalism and Its Colonial Reality* (Cambridge: Cambridge Scholars Publishing, 2013), 65.

22. Strachey, *Historie of Travelle into Virginia*, 18–19.

23. George Thorp to Sir Edwin Sandys, May 15 and 16, 1621, in *Records of the Virginia Company of London*, ed. Susan Myra Kingsbury, 4 vols. (Washington, D.C., 1906–35), 3:446–98.

24. Instructions to George Yeardley from the Virginia Company in London, November 18, 1618, in Kingsbury, *Records of the Virginia Company*, 3:102.

25. For discussion of how Pocahontas presented the ideal of English womanhood on her visit to England, see Karen Kupperman, *The Jamestown Project* (Cambridge, Mass.: Belknap Press of Harvard University Press, 2007), 245, 269–80; Helen Rountree, *Pocahontas, Powhatan, Opechancanough: Three Indian Lives Changed by Jamestown* (Charlottesville: University of Virginia Press, 2006), 160–80.

26. Anonymous letter dated February 2, 1620, in Kingsbury, *Records of the Virginia Company*, 1:309.

27. Kingsbury, *Records of the Virginia Company*, 1:588.

28. "Supplementary Documents Giving Additional Information Concerning the Four Forms of the Oldest Building of William and Mary College," *William and Mary Quarterly*, 2nd ser., 10 (1930): 68–69.

29. Instructions to Mr. Robert Hicks and Mr. John Evans from Lieutenant Governor Francis Nicholson, May 1700, in *Historical Collections Relating to the American Colonial Church: Virginia*, ed. William Perry, vol. 1 (Hartford, Conn.: Church Press Company, 1870), 123–24.

30. Joseph Dalton to Lord Ashley, January 20, 1672, in *The Shaftesbury Papers*, ed. Langdon Cheves (1897; Charleston, S.C.: Home House Press, 2010), 376.

31. Maurice Mathews, "A Contemporary View of Carolina in 1680," *South Carolina Historical Magazine* 55, no. 3 (July 1954), 153–59, quote on p. 156, emphasis added.

32. Stephen Bull to Lord Ashley, March 1670, in Cheves, *Shaftesbury Papers*, 273–75.

33. In a 1670 communication, colonists explained that local natives were "assisting them to cleare and plant their land." Barbados Proclamation, November 4, 1670, in Cheves, *Shaftesbury Papers*, 210–13.

34. Robert Horne, *A Brief Description of the Province of Carolina* . . . (London, 1666), reprinted in *Narratives of Early Carolina, 1650–1708*, ed. Alexander S. Salley Jr. (New York, 1911), 66–73.

35. Mathews, "Contemporary View of Carolina," 156, 157.

36. The Lords Proprietors to Governor and Council, May 18, 1674, *Shaftesbury Papers*, 437.

37. Thomas Nairne, *A Letter from South Carolina: giving an account of the soil, air, product, trade, government, laws, religion, people, military strength, & of that province; together with the manner and necessary charges of settling a plantation there, and the annual profit it will produce* (London: A. Baldwin, 1710), 54.

38. In his detailed study of early plantation agriculture in South Carolina, historian Max Edelson has shown how colonists embraced Native agricultural methods even after they were no longer starving and dependent on local Natives. S. Max Edelson, *Plantation Enterprise in Colonial South Carolina* (Cambridge, Mass.: Harvard University Press, 2011), 30–47. Also see Johnson, "Enslaved Native Americans."

39. King James I, *A Treatise on Scottis Poesie: A Counterblaste to Tobacco*, ed. Robert Rait (1616; Westminster, U.K.: A. Constable, 1900), 36; also see Melissa Morris, "Spanish and Indigenous Influences on Virginian Tobacco Cultivation," in this volume.

40. Governor and Council in Virginia to Virginia Company, January 21, 1621, in Kingsbury, *Records of the Virginia Company*, 3:424–25.

41. Lorena Walsh argues that with labor supplies being low in the colony, there were rarely enough hands to split a labor force between corn and tobacco cultivation. Laborers had to switch back and forth to manage both export crops and food crops. Lorena Walsh, *Motives of Honor, Pleasure, and Profit: Plantation Management in the Colonial Chesapeake, 1607–1763* (Chapel Hill: Omohundro Institute of Early American History and Culture and University of North Carolina Press, 2010), 72, 161.

42. James Rice, *Nature and History in the Potomac Country: From Hunter-Gatherers to the Age of Jefferson* (Baltimore: Johns Hopkins University Press, 2009), 114.

43. Brown, *Good Wives*, 119–20.

44. Robbie Ethridge and Sheri M. Shuck-Hall, eds., *Mapping the Mississippian Shatter Zone: The Colonial Indian Slave Trade and Regional Instability in the American South* (Lincoln: University of Nebraska Press, 2009). For a discussion of slaving in the 1680s, see Ethridge, *From Chicaza to Chickasaw: The European Invasion and the Transformation of the Mississippian World, 1540–1715* (Chapel Hill: University of North Carolina Press, 2013), 156.

45. William Ramsey, *The Yamasee War: A Study of Culture, Economy, and Conflict in the Colonial South* (Lincoln: University of Nebraska Press, 2010), 34, 40–46; Christina Snyder, *Slavery in Indian Country: The Changing Face of Captivity in Early America* (Cambridge, Mass.: Harvard University Press, 2010), 49, 55, 60–66; Alan Gallay, *The Indian Slave Trade: The Rise of the English Empire in the American South, 1670–1717* (New Haven, Conn.: Yale University Press, 2002), 297–318. See also Johnson, "Enslaved Native Americans."

46. H. R. McIlwaine, ed., *Minutes of the Council and General Court of Colonial Virginia, 1622–1632, 1670–1676*, 2nd ed. (Richmond: Virginia State Library, 1924), 488–89.

47. James Moore to the Lords Proprietors of Carolina, April 16, 1704, Library of Congress. These numbers are debated, but Moore's pride over the accumulation of Native dependents is an important example of how early southern planters considered their rights to Indian female slaves. For a discussion of Moore's exaggeration, see John Hann and Bonnie McEwan, *The Apalachee Indians and Mission San Luis* (Gainesville: University Press of Florida, 1998); Mark Boyd, *Here They Once Stood: The Tragic End of the Apalachee Missions* (Gainesville: University Press of Florida, 1999).

48. Gallay, *Indian Slave Trade*, 298–99.

49. South Carolina Population as Reported by the Governor and Council, September 17, 1708, in *Records in the British Public Record Office Relating to South Carolina, 1663–1710*, 5 vols., ed. Alexander S. Salley Jr. (Columbia: Printed for the Historical Commission of South Carolina by Foote & Davies Company, 1928–47), 5:203–9; Ramsey, *Yamasee War*, 34, 40–46. D. Andrew Johnson argues that in the early eighteenth century, one-third of the enslaved women in South Carolina were Native American. See "Enslaved Native Americans," chap. 4.

50. Analysis drawn from calculating the number of indentured servants, enslaved Africans, and enslaved Natives in all inventories and wills in Henrico County Court Records, Wills and Deeds, 1677–92.

51. John Norris, *Profitable Advice for Rich and Poor*, in *Selling a New World: Two Colonial South Carolina Promotional Pamphlets*, ed. Jack P. Greene (Columbia: University of South Carolina Press, 1989), 88.

52. Hening, *Statutes at Large*, 1:144, 454.

53. Ibid., 2:296, 491–92. Owen Stanwood has argued that Natives were not field laborers because planters saw them as better suited for other tasks. Stanwood, "Captives and Slaves: Indian Labor, Cultural Conversion, and the Plantation Revolution in Virginia," *Virginia Magazine of History and Biography* 114 (2006): 450. This interpretation is at odds with the multiple laws Virginians passed making Natives tithable. Stanwood also minimizes labor shortages in the period and the value of laborers in general in an agricultural export society where there was a large amount of land and not enough people to work it.

54. Thomas Cooper, *The Statutes at Large of South Carolina*, vol. 7 (Columbia: A. S. Johnston, 1837), 343.

55. Hening, *Statutes at Large*, 3:447–62.

56. Hayley Negrin, "Possessing Native Women and Children: Slavery, Gender and English Colonialism in the Early American South, 1670–1717" (PhD diss., New York University, 2018); Negrin, "Interconnected Regimes: The Indian Slave Trade in Carolina and Plantation Slavery in Virginia after the Westo War of 1679" (paper presented at the Region and Nation in American Histories of Race and Slavery, Omohundro Institute of Early American History Conference, Mount Vernon, Virginia, October 6–9, 2016).

57. Hammond, *Leah and Rachel*. For Kathleen Brown's analysis of wench terminology drawn from this text, see chap. 3 of *Good Wives*.

58. Henrico County Court Orders 1678–93, 83, 99.

59. Historians have documented the status that southeastern and northeastern woodlands women drew from their roles as the primary agricultural producers in their communities. They were responsible for most material wealth in Native societies, including crops, houses, and tools. The Green Corn Ceremony, which centers around the celebration of the female corn goddess, was and still is a highly important ceremony for many groups across the Southeast. Helen Rountree, *The Powhatan Indians of Virginia: Their Traditional Culture* (Norman: University of Oklahoma Press, 1989), 88–99; Theda Purdue, *Cherokee Women: Gender and Culture Change, 1700–1835* (Lincoln: University of Nebraska Press, 1998), 13, 14–27, 103–5; Michelene Pesantubbee, *Choctaw Women in a Chaotic World: The Clash of Cultures in the Colonial Southeast* (Albuquerque: University of New Mexico Press, 2005), 124–28; James Merrell, *The Indians' New World Catawbas and Their Neighbors from European Contact through the Era of Removal* (Chapel Hill: University of North Carolina Press, 1989), 37, 130–31, 230; Charles Hudson, *The Southeastern Indians* (Memphis: University of Tennessee Press, 1978), 296–98; James Mooney, *Myths of the Cherokee* (New York: Dover, 1900), 242–50; Jean Chaudhuri, *A Sacred Path: The Way of the Muscogee Creeks* (Los Angeles: UCLA American Indian Studies Center, 2001), 45, 59, 103.

60. Lords Proprietors, September 30, 1683, in Salley, *Records*, 1:255.

61. Dr. Francis Le Jau to Henry Compton Bishop of London, May 27, 1712, in *The Carolina Chronicle of Dr. Francis Le Jau, 1706–1717*, ed. Frank J. Klingberg (Berkeley: University of California Press, 1956), 116.

62. R. A. Brock, ed., *The Official Letters of Alexander Spotswood*, vol. 1 (Richmond: Collections of the Virginia Historical Society, 1973), 129–30, quotation on 122.

63. "A general meeting of the visitors and governors of the college of William and Mary held the 13 of June, 1716." Manuscript. Lee Family Papers Sect. 78 Mss1 L51 F132–34, Virginia Historical Society, Richmond.

64. Kevin Berland, ed., *The Dividing Line Histories of William Byrd II of Westover* (Williamsburg, Va.: Published for the Omohundro Institute of Early American History and Culture, 2013), 119–22.

65. Hening, *Statutes at Large*, 1:396.

66. Ibid., 3:447–62.

Ocean Graveyards and Ulterior Atlantic Worlds

The Experience of Colonial North Carolina

BRADFORD J. WOOD

More than five thousand vessels are believed to rest in the ocean grave-yard near North Carolina's Outer Banks.[1] They are there because North Carolina's history has been shaped by a coastline of more than three hundred miles of shallow openings, sandy inlets, and other conditions that proved forbidding to mariners. The area around the Cape Fear River near South Carolina is a partial exception to this pattern and allows more of an opening to the Atlantic, but even there shallow water and shoals inhibited shipping and slowed the growth of trade. Today the North Carolina coast warns seagoing vessels with a conspicuous array of lighthouses.[2] During the first few centuries of colonization, few places in the Americas faced more difficulty in accessing the ocean. Some colonists found more remote or distant places in the Americas, but it is unlikely that any other comparable group of people knew what it was like to be so close to the Atlantic Ocean itself and yet so far from its other shores.

Still, somehow, in the middle of the eighteenth century more than a hundred thousand colonists lived in the North Carolina colony, beyond the Outer Banks. By the 1760s a diverse and growing mass of colonists had penetrated far into the interior of the continent, outstripping almost all of the transatlantic ties that remained precious, if fragile, along the coast. Roughly half of the colony's population resided in the interior region, referred to by Atlantic-looking contemporaries as "the backcountry." The most complete but probably still understated population estimates for the colony indicate that in 1767, more than 160,000 people resided in the colonized areas, with more than 50,000 on the Piedmont and another 40,000 even further to the west. By that time the colony's population was growing by more than 5 percent per year.[3]

These two impressive numbers—5,000 sunken vessels and more than 160,000 people—reveal a tension in scholarship that has highlighted the Atlantic Ocean as a means of connection. Decades of scholarship have emphasized the central role of the Atlantic in connecting early modern peoples, but it has distracted from the very real difficulties of ocean travel and from the sometimes more important connections across land. Colonial North Carolina offers a clear example of an Atlantic world locale that remained separate in important ways because it could not be readily connected to the ocean. North Carolina's most distinctive traits are directly related to its treacherous coastline. The Outer Banks and other environmental features shaped North Carolina in significant ways that made it unlike most colonies in the Americas. First, and most obviously, regular transatlantic connections became much more difficult to maintain. North Carolina became more separate and isolated than other British colonies in the Americas, with tremendous consequences for colonists. Second, the different coastal environment encouraged those on shore to adapt their relationship to the sea. Along the Outer Banks people known as "Bankers" eked out a marginal existence that met with contempt from authorities, while farther west in the Carolina Piedmont, a vast farming world was created with little reference to transatlantic trade or migration. Third, the disruption of shipping circumscribed opportunities to participate in the broader Atlantic world. Most notably, efforts to integrate the colony's farms into the Atlantic plantation system met with relatively limited results. In all of these ways, North Carolina's coast offers scholars a different vantage point on the relationship between early modern peoples and the Atlantic.

Following historian W. Jeffrey Bolster's insight, we need to put the actual ocean in our discussions of the Atlantic world. But along with focusing on the life of the ocean and its creatures—biomass, in Bolster's terminology—we also need to pay more attention to oceans as geographic spaces between—and separating—continents.[4] An Atlantic perspective depends on one's understanding of the environmental variations along the shores of the ocean, and scholars who write about connections across the Atlantic littoral need to consider the roles of currents, shoals, sandbars, sounds, and fall lines. North Carolina's Atlantic world was defined by its difficult coastline, and, at least in the early modern period, both ocean and shore remained changeable and beyond the control of humans.

Scholarship on the southern mainland colonies of North America, however, has never focused much on North Carolina, and for decades historians have sought evidence of Atlantic world crossings in the most oceanic and coastal places.[5] In short, historians who are relentlessly focused on processes of transatlantic connection have had little use for a place that is strikingly disconnected. Increasingly, historians have begun to realize that there were other worlds in addition the Atlantic world. Some of those worlds were deep in the hearts of continents, but others developed within sight of the ocean itself, separated from it by sandbars, shoals, and other physical obstacles.

Colonial North Carolina, and places like it, can most fully be understood with what might be called an "ulterior Atlantic" perspective. They were "ulterior" to the Atlantic in the sense that geography put them "beyond" the

Atlantic Ocean.[6] The ulterior Atlantic remained separated from much of the Atlantic world, primarily because of the geography of the Atlantic littoral, which interfered with colonial movement and communication over distance. In this sense, ulterior Atlantic worlds emerged because of specific relationships between colonists and the coastal environments that controlled access to Atlantic infrastructure. The emergence of ulterior Atlantic spaces was a complicated process involving varying historical contexts, so it is not possible to write comprehensively about them in one essay, but North Carolina can be treated as paradigmatic of the process.

Studying early North Carolina specifically, and the ulterior Atlantic more generally, allows scholars to understand places beyond the ocean graveyard. Studying colonial outposts disconnected from the Atlantic Ocean means studying peoples who were part of ulterior Atlantic places. Scholars have tended to ignore most ulterior Atlantic worlds in order to write about port towns, islands, and riverine tidewaters. It is easy to miss how many people were involved in ulterior Atlantic places. North Carolina, for example, actually had a larger population than South Carolina until the middle of the eighteenth century. It had a larger European population than any other European mainland colony south of Virginia and east of the Mississippi until the end of the eighteenth century.[7] Beyond North Carolina, ulterior Atlantic worlds included much of the colonial population of the Americas. North Carolina's relationship to the Atlantic was distinctive, but it was not merely an anomaly. Its ports received as much shipping as most of the thirteen colonies that would declare independence in 1776, and many colonists throughout British America experienced similar difficulties accessing the Atlantic.[8]

Ulterior Atlantic histories can be more fully explicated by invoking the concept of infrastructure. The term initially gained favor from scholars studying science and technology, but it has recently attracted considerable attention in anthropology and a variety of other disciplines.[9] In common usage, infrastructures typically refer to systems such as roads, plumbing, or electric grids, but scholars have made use of a much broader definition of infrastructures that has been applied to issues that are as much social, intellectual, or aesthetic as they are material.[10] In this sense, the bundle of cultural assumptions, networks, and institutions that made up the first British Empire can be considered a form of infrastructure. But infrastructures are closely related and sometimes almost indistinguishable from nature, and the Atlantic provided important assistance to the British Empire by making it more connected.[11] Scholars have intuitively sensed the usefulness of this conceptualization when they have frequently described the ocean as functioning like a highway instead of a barrier. But if the Atlantic world was built with forms of infrastructure, the ocean was less reliable and less fully available than our interstate highway system. Consequently, when access to the Atlantic was disrupted, much that made British colonies part of larger British and Atlantic worlds either attenuated or ceased to function altogether.[12] Without the Atlantic, the infrastructure of the British Empire became mostly unavailable, too. The absence, or at least the scarcity, of infrastructure therefore defined much of ulterior Atlantic worlds.

In this context, ulterior Atlantic experiences such as those in North Carolina emerged as an important part of early modern colonization. As colonists expanded into areas not as accessible by water, movement and basic communication and exchange between peoples adapted to overland routes. In many cases, ulterior Atlantic places were "colonies of colonies." The slave trade bore more resemblance to the intercolonial migrations described by Gregory E. O'Malley than the transatlantic trades described by scholars such as David Eltis, John Thornton, and Stephanie Smallwood.[13] Extended families were broken apart and transformed. Empires became weaker, but colonists filled the gap by seizing opportunities to make more decisions for themselves. Disconnection from Atlantic systems made transatlantic connections even more potent for those that had them and limited the possibilities for those less connected. Transatlantic connections conferred a form of power. Material conditions also proved especially dependent on ocean access because trade and other economic concerns played a vital role in keeping the Atlantic world together. Ulterior Atlantic spaces had to be reorganized over time. They also became places with a high degree of cultural variation, because mainstream metropolitan influences proved less important. At the same time, local worlds and communities played an even larger role for those unable to maintain compelling but difficult ties across water and long distances. Consequently, broader processes characteristic of the ulterior Atlantic played out in many locales, but they did so with considerable variation because of different environmental and historical contexts.

When Europeans first interacted with North Carolina's Outer Coastal Plain in the sixteenth and seventeenth centuries, two specific features of its environment separated it from other places and powerfully shaped their experience. When North Carolina met the Atlantic the distinction between land and water was often blurry, prompting some scholars to describe it as a "Land of Water."[14] On the one hand, the land along the coast had too much water. Swamps, rivers, and other bodies of water hindered European travelers and colonists throughout the Tidewater.[15] On the other hand, there was an imprecise division between the shore and the sea itself, as islands, shoals, and other coastal features intruded into shallow ocean waters. The overabundance of water made North Carolina harder to reach and travel through by land, but the coastal geography proved to be a much more severe obstacle to ocean shipping.

The first permanent colonists who came south into North Carolina's Albemarle region had to find a way past the forbidding Great Dismal Swamp, which straddled the present-day border between Virginia and North Carolina. Both the sheer physical difficulties of crossing a swamp of more than two thousand square miles and the intimidating appearance and lore of the Great Dismal probably deterred many from heading south toward Albemarle Sound. The Great Dismal and the many smaller swamps in the Outer Coastal Plain hindered human contact at times, but they never completely stopped it—even for some who dwelled in the swamps.[16] Many other bodies of water, such as Albemarle and Pamlico Sounds and the Outer Coastal Plain's many rivers, blocked easy land transportation but resulted in more regular travel in boats.

The North Carolina shoreline along the Atlantic Ocean offered a sharp visual contrast to the stark and dreary appearance of the Great Dismal, but to early modern Europeans it presented more significant challenges and, at least at the time, even greater terrors. Nothing else that Europeans encountered on the western shores of the Atlantic prepared them for the difficulties of navigating the Outer Banks of North Carolina. The Outer Banks themselves are a long series of small islands, stretching hundreds of miles southward from near the boundary of Virginia. North Carolina as a whole has a distinctive "coastal system" that includes about 325 miles of barrier islands, 24 inlets, 3,500 square miles of inland seas and estuaries, and 10,000 miles of estuarine shorelines.[17] Numerous sandbars, some above water as islands and some just below, put mariners navigating near the coast in danger even in the best of conditions. Those who tried to enter the narrow openings to the Outer Banks faced the toughest tests, but even ships passing along the coast had to navigate carefully, partly because of the Gulf Stream.[18] Strong currents and hurricanes created risks of a different order, as a meeting of ocean currents made weather patterns more volatile. Both hurricanes and nor'easters have devastated eastern North Carolina from time to time, and more shipwrecks have occurred during storm seasons.[19] Scholars have described the coastal system as "dominated by and a product of energetic storms that build, maintain, and drive its evolution."[20]

Those who tried to enter the Outer Banks, instead of just passing by them, had to make their way through small inlets that one authority has described as "about as restless and unpredictable as bodies of water can ever be."[21] At least two dozen inlets in the Outer Banks have been named and mapped at some time, and many more have opened and closed before acquiring such notoriety, with only Ocracoke Inlet remaining open throughout recorded history. At least four inlets closed between the Roanoke voyages and the arrival of permanent colonists in the mid-seventeenth century. During the 1730s, one Currituck Inlet closed and another opened. These shifting inlets are merely the best documented of a variety of changes at work along the shifting and steadily eroding North Carolina coast.[22] Conditions were somewhat better to the south of the Outer Banks, and the Cape Fear River offered the colony's best port, but even there nothing came easily or without risk to sailors. Shoals jutted out into the ocean at Cape Fear as well as at Cape Lookout and Cape Hatteras along the Outer Banks. Barrier islands and shallow estuaries typified the whole coastline. Prudent mariners often avoided the North Carolina coast as much as they could.

The failed Roanoke colonies of the late sixteenth century struggled with the difficulties of access to the North Carolina coast, and by the time (what became) permanent colonies were in place in the middle of the seventeenth century, many realized that the Outer Banks were a dangerous place for people at sea.[23] Sir Robert Dudley's 1647 map included important new details for the use of those navigating the North Carolina coast, including prevailing winds, ocean currents, and soundings of the depths of water in the sounds and near the banks.[24] Within two decades colonists, customs officials, and agents for the Carolina proprietors began sharing bad news about shipping prospects near the first settlements on Albemarle Sound.[25] The inlets along the Outer Banks and the harbors in northern North Carolina could only accommodate small vessels. Sustained transatlantic shipping was not an option, and what little was exported often went along the coast in slight, opportunistic vessels from New England or Virginia. As early as 1663 authorities lost confidence in shipping through Albemarle Sound and hoped to discover better conditions in Pamlico Sound, but it took almost half a century before substantial colonization extended that far south. When it did, Pamlico Sound's harbors involved many of the same problems.[26] After North Carolina became a royal colony, in the early 1730s Governor George Burrington gave repeated assessments of obstacles to the colony's trade, distilling what must have been generations of frustration, anxiety, and desperate hope for sailors, merchants, and officials. By then, the trade of most of the province was "miserable," the old Currituck Inlet had closed, and the port of Roanoke was "so dangerous that few people care to use it." As the governor of North Carolina, Burrington sometimes tried to sound positive notes, praising the relatively good conditions at Cape Fear and Pamlico and expressing optimism about opening a new port at Ocracoke, but he could not deny the problems and probably did not change many minds.[27] A more objective commentator, the Moravian bishop August Gottlieb Spangenburg, wrote in 1752 that there was little potential for commerce in North Carolina because "there are difficulties in the way of shipping."[28]

Over time, the dangers of North Carolina's coast changed patterns of interaction and became a part of the colony's reputation even for those elsewhere in the Atlantic world. More than one colonist shared the frustration expressed in a letter from North Carolina that apologized for the disappearance of "at least" four transatlantic letters sent from different ports, including one on the James River.[29] Transatlantic ties were too important to be abandoned, but sometimes more than four letters became necessary. Some optimistically continued to try to overcome the challenging environment but often learned the hard way, such as the captain of a 120-ton vessel that somehow made it to Edenton to load tobacco but remained stuck in shallows there for more than a year when the water returned to normal depths.[30] Many more vessels must have followed the lead of the *Friends' Adventure*, which gave up on trying to get past a sandbar and decided to sail up the coast from North Carolina to a different colony.[31] Cautionary tales of the Outer Banks spread fast in Atlantic coastal communities. Between 1737 and 1775 more than thirty news updates in the *Pennsylvania Gazette* reported ships damaged or in danger going to and from North Carolina.[32] Many of these accounts focused on the area's volatile weather as well as the difficult geography of the coast, as exemplified by the young Massachusetts merchant Robert Treat Paine, who described one Albemarle port as "calm one Hour Hurricane the next."[33]

In other colonies the coastline became the site of bustling port towns, typically the most prosperous and cosmopolitan centers, but in North Carolina the barren and dangerous stretches of land along the Outer Banks became remote and marginal places of exile or refuge. The islands along the coast could not sustain productive agriculture, fisheries arrived belatedly, and relatively few colonists braved the difficult living conditions along the ocean. The people known as Bankers usually went unnoticed by the mainstream of colonial society, but they took on greater importance when ships became trapped on the banks. They attracted the attention of British official Edward Randolph during the 1690s. When a British navy ship, the HMS *Hady*, became stuck on the sandy shore between Currituck and Roanoke Inlets, Randolph wrote about nearby settlers robbing, vandalizing, and immobilizing the vessel.[34]

Randolph might have conflated the story of the *Hady* with a very similar incident involving the HMS *Swift Advice*. In 1696 the *Swift Advice* was forced away from Virginia in an icy winter storm. When the crew abandoned the vessel at sea, it wrecked in the sands of North Carolina, only to be plundered and damaged by residents.[35] More and more people came to see what they could take from the ship. According to Deputy Governor Thomas Harvey, some who came to the ship were "great Rogues" but "opportunity made others but little better," until twenty people were taken into custody and eventually prosecuted for participating in this "Riot," while others disappeared into Currituck County. Items taken from the *Swift Advice* had been hidden in homes and even buried in the ground, and papers left on board were burned. A committee dispatched to the banks determined that the ship was beyond repair.[36] A large number of people participated in the sacking of the *Swift Advice*, and the attitude of authorities indicates that the coastal areas that made up much of Currituck County were seen as remote and strange. According to one minister trying to describe the colony's Anglican parishes, as late as 1709, nearly fifty years after it was first colonized, Currituck had no church and had never received any religious books from missionaries. Significantly, in contrast to the other parishes, the minister had never been to Currituck and admitted to knowing little about it.[37] The following year the first minister sent there described himself as struggling "with Lawless and Barbarous People."[38] The most Atlantic places in North Carolina were the least connected and most peripheral.

More than fifty years after the wreck of the *Swift Advice*, colonists near Ocracoke thwarted authorities again by trying to take advantage of another disaster at sea. A total of five ships in a Spanish flotilla came ashore in North Carolina in August 1750 after they were all caught in a ferocious storm. One sank in the water near Cape Hatteras and another ended up in pieces and partly buried in sand at Topsail Inlet. Spanish ships had raided the Outer Banks in the past, and in 1748 they sailed into the Cape Fear River and attacked the town of Brunswick, so these Spaniards were not likely to be greeted with sympathy, especially when more than one of the ships carried valuable cargo, including pieces of eight, hides, and cochineal. The survivors and cargo continued on through various improvised routes and means of transportation, but one ship, the *Nuestra Señora de Guadalupe*, became a source of controversy after it limped into Ocracoke.[39] When the Spaniards came ashore, relations between Britain and Spain were fragile, the nations having just signed a peace treaty ending almost a decade of war in 1748, but some of the remaining crew mutinied and paid little attention to diplomatic protocols. In this chaotic situation, residents of the Outer Banks, probably filled with either anger or greed or both, descended on the wreckage. Governor Gabriel Johnston sent Spanish-speaking council member James Innes to Ocracoke, but Innes heard that some Bankers, people described as "a set of People who live on certain sandy Islands lying between the Sound and the Ocean, and who are very Wild and ungovernable," were coming to pillage the wreckage in large numbers. The governor considered the Bankers to be virtually beyond the rule of law because "it is seldom possible to Execute any Civil or Criminal Writs among them." The North Carolina government did manage to get involved, but only after the Spanish imprudently trusted some of their cargo to local sailing vessels and were robbed.[40]

If the colony's challenging coastline provided a haven for ungovernable Bankers across generations, it also offered more temporary respite for other kinds of exiles and lawbreakers. Smuggling pervaded the maritime worlds of colonial British America, but even in this context North Carolina acquired a notable reputation for illicit trade.[41] North Carolina also rivaled other colonies for notoriety as a "pirates' nest." In fact, the colony does not seem to have attracted as many pirates as more affluent Atlantic ports such as Port Royal, Newport, or Charles Town. However, when the British Empire eventually drove most pirates out of more connected ports, many of them found they could hide in North Carolina. The capture of Stede Bonnet and the final defeat of Blackbeard, both near the colony's coast, in 1718 and 1719 provides some indication of the role North Carolina played for pirates by that time. In Blackbeard's case there are indications that he received support from both residents on the coast and officials in the North Carolina government.[42] But the presence of famous pirates along the North Carolina coast did not mean that North Carolina enticingly offered access to valuable transatlantic goods and connections. Instead, once-formidable pirates were being pushed into the most remote of maritime places, as their way of life declined and their enemies pursued them with success in more hospitable Atlantic venues. Pirates joined sandbars, shallow waters, strong storms, and anti-authoritarian Bankers to make maritime North Carolina a distinctive and separate place. David Cecelski has shown that by the antebellum period the coastal waters of North Carolina sometimes also provided a place of refuge for enslaved African Americans. To Cecelski, remote maritime places enabled the existence of diverse and varied cultures.[43]

Harsh conditions along the Outer Banks made for a sparse population along the coast, but just inland denser populations sought to recreate conditions that appeared to have been successful in other British American colonies. Their ability to do so was powerfully constrained by their difficulty accessing the Atlantic. North Carolina's growth as a colony took place during decades when the Atlantic plantation system began to spread and expanded across the Greater Caribbean and eventually to areas of the mainland. The adjacent colonies of Virginia and South Carolina were each remade into places dominated by exportable, agricultural plantation produce, but North Carolina continued to be a colony of small farms and relatively small plantations. Many explanations have been given for North Carolina's different path, and later scholars would reflect on what it meant for North Carolina to be "in" but not "of the South." While various factors were involved in the colony's economic development, the lack of normal transatlantic shipping placed clear limits on the development of North Carolina's plantation system.

By the late seventeenth century, colonists in the Albemarle region hoped to imitate the success of nearby tobacco planters in Virginia. Albemarle settlers must have taken it for granted that tobacco would provide the basis for any export wealth they could generate in the region, and they began planting it shortly after they arrived. Thomas Miller wrote that in 1677 the Albemarle was producing 800,000 pounds of tobacco a year.[44] A tobacco crop of this magnitude would have required the labor of between 500 and 1,000 laborers in a region with only 5,000 or so colonists.[45] North Carolina appeared to be a burgeoning tobacco colony, and colonists cleared land for plantations and remade the landscape to more closely resemble the Virginia Tidewater. As it turned out, however, Albemarle planters had reached their limit and would not even maintain the same level of production. At the end of the colonial period, North Carolina still only exported a little more tobacco than these early harvests from all of its ports, while Virginians and Marylanders had dramatically expanded their export production.[46] Geography put planters in the Albemarle at a severe comparative disadvantage because of the challenges of transporting bulky hogsheads of tobacco to a location where they could be shipped across the Atlantic. Tobacco either had to be on a vessel that could get past the Outer Banks or moved overland past the Great Dismal Swamp. When additional expenses and regulations were imposed by British authorities or by Virginia, tobacco became even less promising. The Albemarle became an area of the Greater Chesapeake that historian Lorena Walsh's framework for understanding the regional variances in Chesapeake tobacco production would categorize as marginal.[47] Tobacco became unimportant to all but a handful of the wealthiest planters who continued to grow it in these areas, and per capita export wealth fell to less than half that for other parts of the Chesapeake.[48] In the Albemarle, the absence of connections intensified the limits of tobacco cultivation still further.

After 1725 some wealthy South Carolinians and others tried another way to make North Carolina into a plantation colony. They hoped to migrate to land near the mouth of the Cape Fear River and build rice plantations. Some of those planters became very wealthy through diverse economic activities, but not much rice was sold from the Cape Fear in the eighteenth century. North Carolina never achieved the kind of profitable rice cultivation associated with the South Carolina Lowcountry. The limits of rice cultivation in the colony weren't merely a matter of soil, climate, or some other aspect of agriculture, because the Cape Fear became well known for its rice in the nineteenth century. The Cape Fear was too far from the rice entrepôt of Charles Town, and it was not practical to try to build a transatlantic rice-trading network from the Cape Fear. Cape Fear planters could send rice directly across the Atlantic themselves, but the costs and obstacles were too great and the opportunities for profit too small. The allure of rice plantation wealth from farther south was strong enough that colonists imported and experimented with the latest rice technologies, putting considerable effort into meeting the distinctive requirements of rice cultivation, but Cape Fear rice planting was insignificant for a century and small in scale even after that.[49]

Some North Carolinians did develop a profitable export system despite these limits to tobacco and rice cultivation, however. Many of them put most of their resources into developing the most extensive and profitable forest industries system in North America. They burned wood into tar and pitch, extracted turpentine, cut lumber, and made barrels, in a system unlike anything else in the many forests of colonial America.[50] Colonists opted to destroy vast forests of longleaf pine, because it was their best opportunity for short-term success in the Atlantic economy. Ten workers producing naval stores might have used up a thousand acres of forest in three years.[51] The largest of these operations may have been an exception to the general pattern of deforestation in colonial America in which colonization and the clearing of land for farms destroyed more trees than lumbering or other forest industries.[52] Therefore, they may have changed and exploited their environment even more fully than rice and tobacco planters, who typically cleared smaller areas of land. This forest-based economy rarely matched the prosperity associated with large Virginia and South Carolina plantations, but it made some men in the Cape Fear region, at least, quite wealthy. Despite these possibilities, most naval stores and other forest exports were only fully successful in a small area along the Cape Fear River.[53] Bulky naval stores and lumber proved hard to move and were only profitable near navigable waterways, because they still had to be sold to transatlantic or intercolonial markets. In eastern North Carolina, only the Cape Fear River met these transportation requirements, and the Cape Fear became wealthier and proportionally more politically powerful than the rest of the colony. Those who had access to the Atlantic reaped impressive benefits, while the absence of Atlantic connections frustrated and thwarted most North Carolinians.

The Pollock family, perhaps the earliest family of successful plantation owners in North Carolina, struggled to export commodities for most of the first half of the eighteenth century. By 1712 Thomas Pollock, the patriarch of the North Carolina Pollocks, found it so difficult to get freight that he had his own vessel built in the Albemarle, but he still complained of his inability to find sufficient freight for years afterward.[54] Even as too few vessels were willing to thread their way into Albemarle Sound, other environmental challenges frustrated Pollock, as when one year's hard rains made it impossible to move bulky naval stores three miles in a cart across difficult terrain so it could reach a landing.[55] Many of the same difficulties continued to plague Thomas

Pollock's son Cullen in the 1740s. The problems with navigating Albemarle Sound made freight scarce and therefore prohibitively expensive. By the time shipping was available, commodities sometimes spoiled, keeping their value down in the available markets and their price low throughout the region itself.[56] The Pollocks continued to consider whether to build their own ships for their own exports, but doing so was expensive and risky.[57] Ship captains who were unfamiliar with the complicated watery landscape of North Carolina or not flexible enough to deal with its peculiar requirements caused additional frustration.[58] Even after decades of trying to streamline the process, the Pollocks still also found that sometimes "getting the tar to a landing will be as difficult as burning the kiln."[59] Yet the Pollocks represented the best-case scenario. As perhaps the wealthiest and best-positioned landowners in the colony outside of the Cape Fear, they could afford to alternate between forest industries and tobacco planting, tap into commercial networks in a number of Atlantic world ports, and build their own small fleet of trading vessels for good measure. Despite having what seem to be the makings of cosmopolitan Atlantic merchants and planters, the Pollocks remained in the ulterior Atlantic and never had the same opportunities as the elite families of Virginia's tobacco counties or of the South Carolina Lowcountry.

Frustrated Albemarle tobacco farmers, limited Cape Fear rice planters, and adaptable North Carolina naval stores producers all understood that colonial participation in the Atlantic economy depended heavily on export commodities. Much of the research on the economies of British America has also focused on the wealth produced by the exportation of agricultural commodities. More recently, the emphasis on agricultural commodities has been challenged, but transatlantic connections remain at the center of interpretations of early American economic history, and in plantation colonies, these commodities were undeniably important. The widely used set of British customs records for the years 1768 to 1772 makes it relatively easy to compare North Carolina's seaborne export wealth.[60] Based on these records, North Carolina's ports clearly shipped much fewer profitable commodities than many ports in British America. Estimates of per capita wealth from seaborne exports indicate that many North Carolinians made less than colonists in the adjacent plantation colonies and even compared unfavorably with the poorest mainland colonies in New England. The Cape Fear region proved to be a partial exception because of its substantial shipping advantages.[61]

Scholars looking beyond the Atlantic might evaluate the economy of early North Carolina based on different criteria, however. Export commodities may have been less important than the development of local and internal economies. Internal economic developments are neglected by colonial historians partly because they are notoriously difficult to measure or study. This level of economic output arises from building more local infrastructures for exchange and communication and for supplying provisions and consumer goods for growing populations.[62] In early North Carolina, the Moravians in Wachovia kept careful enough records to provide some sense of the level of local economic activity, and the evidence is impressive. A relatively small group of Moravians moved into an uncolonized region; cleared land; farmed; built houses, mills, and other structures; made roads; and established extensive and wide-ranging trade networks, all within a few years.[63] Colonists such as the Moravians remade the North Carolina Piedmont through little interaction with transatlantic markets or assistance. By the middle of the eighteenth century, North Carolina's population was growing at an undeniably rapid pace even by the standards of colonial British America. Economic activity tied to population growth may well have enabled North Carolina to develop a thriving domestic economy in the absence of much transatlantic trade. Colonists in the ulterior Atlantic understood that colonial economic growth did not depend solely on overseas trade. Where transatlantic trade opportunities ran out, colonists shifted their attention and resources to internal markets and intercolonial trade possibilities that did not depend on crossing the ocean.

The same contrast between the necessarily connected Atlantic plantation system and the more fragmented and localized economic worlds of the ulterior Atlantic can also be expressed in more environmentally oriented terms. The movement of colonists past the Outer Banks and into the area now known as North Carolina took place as part of a profound environmental transformation, as Europeans and all they brought with them made their mark on the Western Hemisphere. At least initially, and for a long time afterward, that transformation mattered to differing degrees from place to place and could take several different directions. Scholars differ about the magnitude and timing of aspects of the Columbian exchange in the southeastern area of North America, but much of the change associated with microbes and other new organisms predated the arrival of permanent colonies. When colonies were started, Europeans quickly focused on the extraction of resources. In some places in North Carolina or wherever the Atlantic plantation system could take root, the drive to produce valuable commodities encouraged planters to remake landscapes and ecologies in the ways described by a number of scholars. Rice plantations, which required elaborate technologies to control water, provide the most familiar examples of the ways that plantation landscapes had to be altered, but an intense focus on any crop was bound to require some important ecological changes.[64] Most landowners in North Carolina ultimately could not exert the sort of economic power required to build viable plantations and had to accommodate themselves to certain challenges. Significantly, they did not all give up on transatlantic trade, and they certainly did not opt to leave the environment as they found it. The slow growth of populations, communities, and local infrastructures attracted less metropolitan attention and created less wealth for elites than plantation commodities, but they probably involved at least as much environmental change.

Further from critical transportation infrastructure, in this case the ocean, for most North Carolina landowners, local markets became more important. North Carolinians lived in a world of more farms than plantations. They produced crops that they could use themselves or market locally instead of commodities for transatlantic export. In the short term this was a more subsistence-oriented and perhaps therefore a more sustainable world than the more extractive-oriented and monocultural plantation sites.[65] But there were also long-term tensions between sustainability and rapid development. Studies of early American agriculture indicate that for a long time—at least into the eighteenth century in the Chesapeake and much of New England—little damage was done to soil ecologies and other farming conditions.[66] Still, as time went on the sustainability of expanding colonial farming practices proved limited, and increasing population densities and growing markets proved to be the most important agents of environmental change.[67] As newcomers poured into the western settlements, no one bothered to worry about how many resources they would use, how much land they would take, or what they would do to ecosystems.

Along these lines, after the initial arrival of European germs and other organisms, the environmental changes that transformed North Carolina owed less to the Atlantic plantation system and more to processes related to population growth. If North Carolina failed to participate regularly in the Atlantic world, it experienced stunning population growth, driven by immigration to the west of the early Tidewater area of colonization, which contemporaries repeatedly noted.[68] In 1766 Governor William Tryon wrote to the Board of Trade, "I am of opinion this province is settling faster than any on the continent," and he went on to describe more than a thousand wagons from the north passing through the town of Salisbury and mostly bringing new colonists.[69] A newspaper item originating in Williamsburg, Virginia, where observers were close enough to notice the massive movement into North Carolina, noted, "There is scarce any history, either antient or modern, which affords an account of such a rapid and sudden increase in inhabitants in a back or frontier county, as that of North Carolina." It cited the example of Orange County where, in twenty years, "not twenty taxable persons" had become part of four thousand on the tax lists.[70] One contemporary heard Benjamin Franklin estimate that forty thousand people left Pennsylvania for North Carolina in the space of a few years alone.[71] All of these estimates were necessarily imprecise, but they all identify a clear trend toward surprising and rapid growth. All of them also describe a pattern of populations rising almost entirely from immigration, though much of North Carolina may have been relatively healthy by this time. All agreed that the population was coming overland, especially from colonies to the north, usually along the Great Wagon Road. Consequently, North Carolina's impressive expansion owed little directly to Atlantic crossings and depended heavily on the development of the continent. Along the same lines, while these immigrants had many motivations, the most consistent and powerful reason for the movement into North Carolina was a desire to obtain land.[72] The intense land hunger that attracted thousands to the North Carolina Piedmont starting in the mid-eighteenth century was distinctive to North America even in the long and varied global history of European colonialism, and eventually it would transform North American environments, no matter if resources continued to seem plentiful in both the Tidewater and the Piedmont for generations.[73]

If different narratives about the environmental history of North Carolina converge to show how European attitudes toward nature transformed North Carolina, they are, nonetheless, different narratives. During these generations colonists not only continued the long story of movement across the Atlantic, they also began new stories about their own interactions with specific environments. They began stories about what we now call "the Outer Banks" or "the Piedmont." They began stories about the Ocean Graveyard, and about the distinctive and different worlds they were making, for better or for worse, beyond the Atlantic.

NOTES

1. Richard W. Lawrence, "An Overview of North Carolina Shipwrecks with an Emphasis on Eighteenth-Century Vessel Losses at Beaufort Inlet," 11, Research Report and Bulletin Series, QAR-R-08–01, North Carolina Underwater Archaeology Branch, State of North Carolina, Raleigh, N.C.

2. Many writers have commented on North Carolina's difficult coastline. See, for example, David Stick, *The Outer Banks of North Carolina* (Chapel Hill: University of North Carolina Press, 1958), 1–10; C. C. Crittenden, *The Commerce of North Carolina, 1763–1789* (New Haven, Conn.: Yale University Press, 1936), 1–20; H. R. Merrens, *Colonial North Carolina in the Eighteenth Century: A Historical Geography* (Chapel Hill: University of North Carolina Press, 1964), 90–91.

3. Marvin Michael Kay and Lorin Lee Cary, *Slavery in North Carolina, 1748–1775* (Chapel Hill: University of North Carolina Press, 1995), 226–28.

4. See W. Jeffrey Bolster, *The Mortal Sea: Fishing the Atlantic in the Age of Sail* (Cambridge, Mass.: Harvard University Press, 2012); Bolster, "Putting the Ocean in Atlantic

History: Maritime Communities and Marine Ecology in the Northwest Atlantic, 1500–1800," *American Historical Review* 113, no. 1 (February 2008): 19–47.

5. The historiography of colonial North Carolina is perhaps as limited as that for any British mainland colony. For some exceptions dealing with the colonial populations, see Bradford J. Wood, *This Remote Part of the World: Regional Formation in Lower Cape Fear, North Carolina, 1725–1775* (Columbia: University of South Carolina Press, 2004); Merrens, *Colonial North Carolina*; Kay and Cary, *Slavery in North Carolina*; Kirsten Fischer, *Suspect Relations: Sex, Race, and Resistance in Colonial North Carolina* (Ithaca, N.Y.: Cornell University Press, 2002); A. Roger Ekirch, *"Poor Carolina": Politics and Society in Colonial North Carolina, 1729–1776* (Chapel Hill: University of North Carolina Press, 1981); Marjoleine Kars, *Breaking Loose Together: The Regulator Rebellion in Pre-Revolutionary North Carolina* (Chapel Hill: University of North Carolina Press, 2002).

6. In this usage "ulterior" is intended in the sense of "beyond," because it is literally and metaphorically far from the Atlantic, but to a lesser degree it also suggests the sense of "hidden" because it has involved neglect by both contemporaries and modern scholars.

7. For various population estimates that all support the comments here, see John J. McCusker, "Population, by race and by colony or locality: 1610–1780," Table Series Eg1–59, in *Historical Statistics of the United States, Earliest Times to the Present: Millennial Edition*, ed. Susan B. Carter, Scott Sigmund Gartner, Michael R. Haines, Alan L. Olmstead, Richard Sutch, and Gavin Wright (New York: Cambridge University Press, 2006); Peter H. Wood, "The Changing Population of the Colonial South: An Overview by Race and Region, 1685–1790," in *Powhatan's Mantle: Indians in the Colonial Southeast*, ed. Gregory H. Waselkov, Peter H. Wood, and M. Thomas Hatley (Lincoln: University of Nebraska Press, 2006), 60–61, 66–70; Jack P. Greene, *Pursuits of Happiness: The Social Development of Early Modern British Colonies and the Formation of American Culture* (Chapel Hill: University of North Carolina Press, 1988), 178–79.

8. The six were Massachusetts, New York, Pennsylvania, Virginia, Maryland, and South Carolina. New Hampshire, Rhode Island, and Connecticut received comparable shipping tonnages. New Jersey and Georgia received substantially less. See Table Series Eg461–483, in Carter et al., *Historical Statistics*.

9. For some general discussions on this work on infrastructures, see Casper Bruun Jensen and Atsuro Morita, "Infrastructures as Ontological Experiments," *Ethnos* 82, no. 4 (2017): 1–12; Cymene Howe, Jessica Lockrem, Hannah Appel, Edward Hackett, Dominic Boyer, Randal Hall, Matthew Schneider-Mayerson, et al., "Paradoxical Infrastructures: Ruins, Retrofit, and Risk," *Science, Technology, and Human Values* 41, no. 3 (2015): 547–565; Brian Larkin, "The Politics and Poetics of Infrastructure," *Annual Review of Anthropology* 42, no. 1 (2013): 327–43; Ashley Carse, "Nature as Infrastructure: Making and Managing the Panama Canal Watershed," *Social Studies of Science* 42, no. 4 (2012): 539–63.

10. On broader definitions of infrastructure, see Howe et al., "Paradoxical Infrastructures," 2–3, 12; Carse, "Nature as Infrastructure," 540–42; Larkin, "Politics and Poetics of Infrastructure," 328.

11. See Carse, "Nature as Infrastructure."

12. On this point, see Matthew Mulcahy, "'Miserably Scorched': Drought in the Plantation Colonies of the British Greater Caribbean," in this volume.

13. For "a colony of a colony," see Peter H. Wood, *Black Majority: Negroes in Colonial South Carolina from 1670 through the Stono Rebellion* (New York: W. W. Norton, 1974);

Gregory E. O'Malley, *Final Passages: The Intercolonial Slave Trade of British America, 1619–1807* (Chapel Hill: Omohundro Institute of Early American History and Culture and University of North Carolina Press, 2014); Stephanie Smallwood, *Saltwater Slavery: A Middle Passage from Africa to American Diaspora* (Cambridge, Mass.: Harvard University Press, 2008); David Eltis, *The Rise of African Slavery in the Americas* (Cambridge: Cambridge University Press, 1999); Linda M. Heywood and John K. Thornton, *Central Africans, Atlantic Creoles, and the Foundation of the Americas, 1585–1660* (New York: Cambridge University Press, 2007); John K. Thornton, *Africa and Africans in the Making of the Atlantic World, 1400–1680* (New York: Cambridge University Press, 1992).

14. Stanley R. Riggs and Dorothea V. Ames, "An Uncompromising Environment: North Carolina's 'Land of Water' Coastal System," in *New Voyages to Carolina: Reinterpreting North Carolina History*, ed. Larry E. Tise and Jeffrey J. Crow (Chapel Hill: University of North Carolina Press, 2017), 14–40.

15. Merrens, *Colonial North Carolina*, 37–38. Also see Frances Kolb, "Profitable Transgressions: International Borders and British Atlantic Trade Networks in the Lower Mississippi Valley, 1763–1783," in this volume.

16. Some commentators have been skeptical of stories about people living in the Great Dismal, but archaeological evidence has now proven that many people did in fact reside there on a long-term basis under varying circumstances and at different times. Sylvia A. Diouf, *Slavery's Exiles: The Story of the American Maroons* (New York: New York University Press, 2014), 209–29; Daniel O. Sayers, *A Desolate Place for a Defiant People: The Archaeology of Maroons, Indigenous Americans, and Enslaved Laborers in the Great Dismal Swamp* (Gainesville: University Press of Florida, 2014), 1–26, 84–113. For contemporary discussions of the Great Dismal and its environs, see the relevant passages in Kevin Joel Berland, ed., *The Dividing Line Histories of William Byrd II of Westover* (Chapel Hill: University of North Carolina Press, 2013), and "A Journal of the Proceedings of the Commissioners for Settling the Bounds betwixt Virginia and Carolina," 1727/28, William L. Saunders, ed., *Colonial Records of North Carolina* (Raleigh: State of North Carolina, 1886–1890), 2:750–757. The Saunders edition will hereafter be given as *CR*.

17. Riggs and Ames, "Uncompromising Environment," 15.

18. Stick, *Outer Banks of North Carolina*, 1–10; David Cecelski, *The Waterman's Song: Slavery and Freedom in Maritime North Carolina* (Chapel Hill: University of North Carolina Press, 2001), 3–4; Lawrence, "Overview of North Carolina Shipwrecks."

19. Lawrence, "Overview of North Carolina Shipwrecks," 3–6; Jay Barnes, *North Carolina's Hurricane History* (Chapel Hill: University of North Carolina Press, 2013); Stick, *Outer Banks of North Carolina*, 107–16; Roy T. Sawyer, *America's Wetland: An Environmental and Cultural History of Tidewater Virginia and North Carolina* (Chapel Hill: University of North Carolina Press, 2010), 47–48, 53–55; Riggs and Ames, "Uncompromising Environment."

20. Riggs and Ames, "Uncompromising Environment," 15.

21. Stick, *Outer Banks of North Carolina*, 6.

22. Ibid., 7–10; Riggs and Ames, "Uncompromising Environment," 26–29.

23. For an introduction to the study of the famous "Lost Colony of Roanoke" and its broader context, see David Beers Quinn, *The Roanoke Voyages: Documents to Illustrate the English Voyages to North America under the Patent Granted to Walter Raleigh in 1584*, 2 vols. (New York: Dover, 1990–91); Karen Ordahl Kupperman, *Roanoke: The Abandoned Colony*

(Lanham, Md.: Rowman & Littlefield, 2007); Michael Leroy Oberg, *The Head in Edward Nugent's Hand: Roanoke's Forgotten Indians* (Philadelphia: University of Pennsylvania Press, 2007).

24. Sir Robert Dudley, "Carta particolare della Virginia Vecchia é Nuoua," in W. P. Cumming, *The Southeast in Early Maps*, 3rd ed. (Chapel Hill: University of North Carolina Press, 1998), 147, plate 27; Philip D. Burden, *The Mapping of North America: A List of Printed Maps*, 2 vols. (Rickmansworth, U.K.: Raleigh, 1996–2007), 1:357–58.

25. Letter from George Monck, Duke of Albemarle to William Berkeley, September 8, 1663, *CR*, 1:54; letter from Thomas Woodward to John Colleton, June 2, 1665, *CR*, 1:99; letter from the Commissioners of the Customs of England to the Lords of the Treasury of England, April 14, 1679, *CR*, 1:243.

26. Letter from George Monck, Duke of Albemarle to William Berkeley, September 8, 1663, *CR*, 1:54.

27. Petition from George Burrington concerning Quit Rents in North Carolina, March 1730, *CR*, 3:78; Description by George Burrington concerning his Actions as Governor, July 2, 1731, *CR*, 3:156; letter from George Monck, Duke of Albemarle to William Berkeley, September 8, 1663, *CR*, 1:54; letter of George Burrington to the Board of Trade, September 4, 1731, *CR*, 3:210; letter from George Burrington to the Commissioners of the Customs, *CR*, 4:169–73.

28. "Diary of Bishop Spangenburg—Location of the Moravian Settlement," September 13, 1752, *CR*, 5:1.

29. Letter from William Gale to his Father, August 5, 1703, *CR*, 22:732.

30. Eleazer Allen to James Abercromby, 1743, Abercromby Letterbook, 1743–50, North Carolina State Archives, Raleigh, N.C.

31. Minutes of Council of Virginia, April 19, 1700, British National Archives, CO 5/1410, 412–13.

32. These items were identified with an electronic search for "North Carolina" and therefore may not have included every reference. The items were part of a sample of 266 items, which excluded routine announcements about the arrival and departure of vessels. Therefore, more than every tenth item readers of the *Gazette* encountered about North Carolina associated it with shipping difficulties.

33. Paine to James Allen, Joseph Palmer, and Richard Cranch, March 1, 1750/51, *The Papers of Robert Treat Paine*, ed. Stephen T. Riley and Edward W. Hanson (Boston: Massachusetts Historical Society, 1992), 1:130–31.

34. Report by Edward Randolph concerning illegal trade in the proprietary colonies, 1701, *CR*, 1:546.

35. Report by Edward Randolph concerning illegal trade in North Carolina [extract], March 24, 1700, *CR*, 1:527. There are no other references to the *Hady*, and Randolph's descriptions of the two incidents are very similar. Compare with Report by Edward Randolph concerning illegal trade in the proprietary colonies, 1701, *CR*, 1:546.

36. Copy of a Letter from Deputy Governor Thomas Harvey to Governor Archdale, *North Carolina Historical and Genealogical Register* 3, no. 1 (January 1903): 35–38; Council Order [1698 March], in Mattie Erma Edward Parker et al., eds., *The Colonial Records of North Carolina, Second Series*, 11 vols (Raleigh: Carolina Charter Tercentenary Commission, 1963–2007), 7:375 (hereafter *CR2*); Report to the Deputy Governor and Council, June 8, 1698, *CR2*, 7:376; His Majesty's Ship Swift Advice, Wrecked and Plundered on the Coast of North Carolina, *North Carolina Historical and Genealogical Register*, 3:33–34.

37. Rev. William Gordon to Society for the Propagation of the Gospel, May 13, 1709, *CR2*, 10:86.

38. Rev. James Adams to _____ Hoar, March 27, 1710, *CR2*, 10:104.

39. Report by Thomas Child concerning the Spanish ship *Nuestra Señora de Guadalupe* landed in North Carolina, February 25, 1752, *CR*, 4:1300–1303; letter from Gabriel Johnston to James Abercromby, including report concerning Spanish ships wrecked in North Carolina [Extract], September 18, 1750, *CR*, 4:1304–5.

40. Report by Gabriel Johnston concerning the Spanish ship *Nuestra Señora de Guadalupe* landed in North Carolina, including petition from Juan Manuel de Bonilla, November 17, 1750, *CR*, 4:1305–8; letter from Gabriel Johnston to James Abercromby, including report concerning Spanish ships wrecked in North Carolina [Extract], September 18, 1750, *CR*, 4:1304–5.

41. For some examples among many, see Petition from Timothy Biggs concerning rebellion in Albemarle County, May 1678, *CR*, 1:325–26; Report by Edward Randolph concerning illegal trade in proprietary colonies [Extract], 1701, *Colon CR*, 1:546–47; letter from George Burrington to the Commissioners of Customs, July 20, 1736, *CR*, 4:169–73.

42. *CR*, 2:333–49; Baylus C. Brooks, "'Born in *Jamaica*, of Very Creditable Parents' or 'A *Bristol* Man Born'? Excavating the Real Edward Thache, 'Blackbeard the Pirate,'" *North Carolina Historical Review* 92, no. 3 (July 2015): 235–77. For some classic but not necessarily reliable accounts of pirates in North Carolina, see Manuel Schonhorn, ed., *A General History of the Pyrates* (Columbia: University of South Carolina Press, 1972), 75–84, 92–93, 96–97, 137, 669–70. Photocopies of a variety of relevant manuscript materials can be found in the Edward Teach (Blackbeard the Pirate) Papers in the North Carolina State Archives, Raleigh. On pirates in the British Empire more generally, see Mark G. Hanna, *Pirate Nests and the Rise of the British Empire, 1570–1740* (Chapel Hill: University of North Carolina Press, 2015); Robert C. Ritchie, *Captain Kidd and the War against Pirates* (Cambridge, Mass.: Harvard University Press, 1989).

43. Cecelski, *Waterman's Song*, 12–14, 20–21. Readers interested in life in maritime North Carolina after 1800 should begin with Cecelski.

44. Memorandum from Thomas Miller and Henry Hudson to the Commissioners of Customs concerning the tobacco customs collected in Albemarle County from 1675 to 1677, *CR*, 1: 265–67. Miller specified 2,000 hogsheads a year with 400 pounds per hogshead. For comments on his estimate, see John McCusker, Table Series Eg1054–56, English colonial tobacco imported into England: 1615–1701, documentation, in Carter et al., *Historical Statistics*; Lindley S. Butler, "Culpeper's Rebellion: Testing the Proprietors," in *The North Carolina Experience: An Interpretative and Documentary History*, ed. Lindley S. Butler and Alan D. Watson (Chapel Hill: University of North Carolina Press, 1984), 56–57. This rough estimate suggests that the Albemarle's tobacco crop amounted to about one-twentieth that of Virginia or one-eighth that of Maryland. Virginia produced 18,157,000 pounds in 1688, and Maryland seems to have been producing about 36 percent as much as Virginia through this period. Even given the region's small population, it was not as concentrated on—or successful with—tobacco cultivation as the older Chesapeake Bay colonies, but this was still a substantial crop that required the investment of effort and valuable land and labor.

45. For various estimates of tobacco productivity per laborer in Virginia and Maryland at this time, see Lorena S. Walsh, *Motives of Honor, Pleasure, and Profit: Plantation Management in the Colonial Chesapeake, 1607–1763* (Chapel Hill: University of North Carolina Press, 2010), 639–57. Given these estimates and conditions in the Albemarle, I

have assumed labor productivity of between 800 and 1,500 pounds of tobacco per worker per year. These numbers therefore indicate that the Albemarle employed less than half as large a share of its population growing tobacco as Virginia or Maryland. John J. McCusker, "Population, by race and by colony or locality: 1610–1780." Table Eg1–59, and Table Eg1054–1056 English colonial tobacco imported into England: 1615–1701, in Carter et al., *Historical Statistics*.

46. John McCusker, Table Eg1057–1134, Tobacco exported and imported, by colony and by origin of destination: 1768–1772, in Carter et al., *Historical Statistics*. Of course, this comparison does not take into account a variety of differences, including any amount of tobacco that North Carolinians exported through Virginia ports. See also the supporting evidence in Merrens, *Colonial North Carolina*, 120–24.

47. See Walsh, *Motives of Honor*, 5–6, 293–393, 539–623.

48. While the peripheral areas only included about a fifth of the Chesapeake population, they included the counties in the Lower James River area that had been home to most of the original Albemarle settlers and that were adjacent to the North Carolina border. Settlers on the periphery of tobacco areas adapted by diversifying their economies. See Lorena S. Walsh, "Summing the Parts: Implications for Estimating Chesapeake Output and Income Subregionally," *William and Mary Quarterly*, 3rd ser., 56, no. 1 (January 1999): 53–94; Walsh, *Motives of Honor*, 19, 212–13; April Lee Hatfield, *Atlantic Virginia: Intercolonial Relations in the Seventeenth Century* (Philadelphia: University of Pennsylvania Press, 2004), 5, 88, 92–93.

49. Wood, *This Remote Part*, 181–84.

50. Ibid., 174–216; Michael Williams, *Americans and Their Forests: A Historical Geography* (Cambridge: Cambridge University Press, 1989); Lawrence S. Early, *Looking for Longleaf: The Rise and Fall of an American Forest* (Chapel Hill: University of North Carolina Press, 2006).

51. Timothy Silver, *A New Face on the Countryside: Indians, Colonists, and Slaves in the South Atlantic Forests, 1500–1800* (New York: Cambridge University Press, 1990), 128.

52. John Brooke notes this pattern in "Ecology," in *A Companion to Colonial America*, ed. Daniel Vickers (Malden, Mass.: Blackwell, 2003), 52. More generally, see Williams, *Americans and Their Forests*.

53. Wood, *This Remote Part*, 177–81.

54. Thomas Pollock to Gentlemen, September 9, 1712; Thomas Pollock to Mr. Walsted and Company, June 6, 1716, both in Pollock Family Papers, North Carolina State Archives, Raleigh (hereafter PFP). On Thomas Pollock's career as a plantation owner, see Bradford J. Wood, "Thomas Pollock and the Making of an Albemarle Plantation World," in *Creating and Contesting Carolina: Proprietary Era Histories*, ed. Michelle LeMaster and Bradford J. Wood (Columbia: University of South Carolina Press, 2013), 211–33.

55. Thomas Pollock to Messrs., March 16, 1719/20, PFP.

56. Cullen Pollock to Sir, August 2, 1740, PFP.

57. Cullen Pollock to Messrs. Thos. Hutchinson and Goldthwait, March 30, 1744; Cullen Pollock to Mr. Malachy Salter, Jr., November 14, 1748, PFP.

58. Cullen Pollock to Messrs. Thos. Hutchinson and Goldthwait, February 10, 1743/4, PFP.

59. Cullen Pollock to Joseph Anderson, May 11, 1747, PFP.

60. For the classic discussion of the staples theory of colonial economic development, see John J. McCusker and Russell R. Menard, *The Economy of British America, 1607–1789*

(Chapel Hill: University of North Carolina Press, 1985), 17–34. For a perspective that challenges the staples theory, see Marc Egnal, *New World Economies: The Growth of the Thirteen Colonies and Early Canada* (New York: Oxford University Press, 1998).

61. See the analysis of these records and North Carolina's position in them in Wood, *This Remote Part*, 178–81; Merrens, *Colonial North Carolina*, 201–2. On these records more generally, see James F. Shepherd, "Commodity Exports from the British North American Colonies to Overseas Areas, 1768–1772," *Explorations in Economic History* 8, no. 3 (Fall 1970): 5–76. Of course, as historians have long noted, these estimates exclude substantial quantities of exports from North Carolina that traveled overland first and left from ports in adjacent Virginia or South Carolina. Surviving source materials provide little sense of the scale of North Carolina's export trade through ports in nearby colonies, but however large this trade might have been, some of its profitability would have been lost because of the expenses of overland transportation and its maintenance would have underscored the colony's frustrations with limited access to the Atlantic. For discussion of this problem, see Crittenden, *Commerce of North Carolina*, 75–76; Ekirch, *"Poor Carolina,"* 14–18. While any conclusions about the scale of this trade must seem speculative, it strikes me that both Crittenden and Ekirch provide estimates that seem likely to be high.

62. For two classic discussions of colonial internal economies, see Richard B. Sheridan, "The Domestic Economy," in *Colonial British America: Essays in the New History of the Early Modern Era*, ed. Jack P. Green and J. R. Pole (Baltimore: Johns Hopkins University Press, 1984), 43–85; McCusker and Menard, *Economy of British America*, 10–11, 32–34. James E. McWilliams has provided the most complete case study of internal economic development in a British American colony in *Building the Bay Colony: Local Economy and Culture in Early Massachusetts* (Charlottesville: University of Virginia Press, 2007). McWilliams found that a lack of export staples encouraged Massachusetts settlers to concentrate more on internal economic developments. This proved to be a relatively successful economic strategy in Massachusetts, and it is reasonable to assume that it would have been at least as successful in North Carolina, which had more fertile farmland and probably a more promising export economy.

63. Adelaide L. Fries, ed., *Records of the Moravians in North Carolina* (Raleigh: Edwards & Broughton, 1922–). For some examples, see 1:85–86, 104, 127, 132, 156, 206, 211.

64. See, for example, Mart Stewart, *What Nature Suffers to Groe: Life, Labor, and Landscape on the Georgia Coast, 1680–1920* (Athens: University of Georgia Press, 1996); S. Max Edelson, *Plantation Enterprise in Colonial South Carolina* (Cambridge, Mass.: Harvard University Press, 2006).

65. Silver's discussion of the environmental consequences of agriculture in North Carolina describes relatively limited damage to ecosystems compared to that in other colonies, but this is partly because he focuses on the period before 1750 when populations were smaller, on the Tidewater areas of the colony, and especially on soil exhaustion from tobacco cultivation. Silver, *New Face on the Countryside*, 166–68.

66. Brooke, "Ecology," 59–60. For studies of long-term agricultural trends, see Walsh, *Motives of Honor*; Brian Donahue, *The Great Meadow: Farmers and Land in Colonial Concord* (New Haven, Conn.: Yale University Press, 2007).

67. Brooke, "Ecology," 59–63.

68. See some of the examples cited in Merrens, *Colonial North Carolina*, 53–55, and Ekirch, *"Poor Carolina,"* 6–9.

69. William Tryon to the Board of Trade, August 2, 1766, *CR*, 7:248.

70. *Connecticut Courant*, November, 30, 1767, cited in Merrens, *Colonial North Carolina*, 54.

71. Election, Connecticut, May 4, 1767, in *Extracts from the Itineraries of Ezra Stiles, D.D. LL.D., 1755–1794, with a Selection from His Correspondence*, ed. Franklin B. Dexter (New Haven, Conn.: Yale University Press, 1916), 64; Merrens, *Colonial North Carolina*, 54.

72. Ekirch, *"Poor Carolina,"* 7; Merrens, *Colonial North Carolina*, 63–64.

73. For the differing of attitudes toward land and their consequences in sites of European colonialism, see Paul Grant-Costa and Elizabeth Mancke, "Anglo-Amerindian Commercial Relations," in *Britain's Oceanic Empire: Atlantic and Indian Ocean Worlds, c. 1580–1850*, ed. H. V. Bowen, Elizabeth Mancke, and John G. Reid (Cambridge: Cambridge University Press, 2012), 370–406.

Profitable Transgressions

International Borders and British Atlantic Trade Networks in the Lower Mississippi Valley, 1763–1783

FRANCES KOLB

In 1763, by dictate of treaty, the Mississippi River became a boundary between British and Spanish North America. In 1681 René-Robert de La Salle claimed all of the lands drained by the Mississippi River for France. By virtue of La Salle's actions, French territorial claims were built on the river systems of the Mississippi Basin. Thus, French territory overlapped with the existing Indigenous routes for transportation and trade, which were largely determined by the waterways of the Mississippi and its tributaries. The Treaty of Fontaine-bleau in 1762 and the Treaty of Paris in 1763 altered the situation by designating the Mississippi River a European imperial boundary. Britain received former French land claims east of the Mississippi, and Spain received the claims west of the river and the Isle of Orleans. The Mississippi River, then, and the series of waterways that separated the Isle of Orleans from West Florida became an international border.[1]

The Mississippi River, however, lent itself much more to bringing the regions and peoples of the river's drainage basin together than to dividing them. By imposing an international border on the Mississippi, European policy makers unintentionally created opportunities for the region's inhabitants to cross the imperial border for personal, economic, and political reasons. British merchants eager to tap into the market of the Lower Mississippi anticipated employing these waterways-turned-boundaries to expand their commercial activity. In short, conceptions of metropolitan policy makers quickly came into conflict with practices of the Lower Mississippi Valley's diverse inhabitants.

The Lower Mississippi River is often viewed by historians as a peripheral zone where empires competed with one another for territory. The social and cultural histories of the region have remained on the whole divorced from larger North American and Atlantic stories. By interrogating the importance of shifting commercial connections in the region of the Mississippi River system during the aftermath of the Seven Years' War along a new imperial boundary, this article suggests a different and more contingent story replete with significant North American and Atlantic connections.[2] When the Mississippi River, together with its tributaries, waterways, and swamplands, is considered, borderland inhabitants emerge as competitors with official imperial structures for control of the region. Borderlanders sought the preservation of their established fluid and flexible social and economic networks as a means to negotiate the uncertainty and instability inherent in a region subject to shifting imperial territorial claims. Although two empires were divided by the Mississippi River in 1763, the peoples on both sides of the river continued to engage their local networks of trade, alliance, and kinship. The Mississippi River system had long been and would continue to be especially important for borderland trade practices. The Mississippi and its tributaries were a defining force, determining the natural paths for transportation and communication. Connecting vast hinterlands of the Mississippi to New Orleans and defining many channels of trade, the waterways were the region's best infrastructure and friend to life in the borderland. The intricate system of waterways worked much more in favor of the borderlanders whose lives and livelihoods were built around it than in favor of those attempting to enforce the new imperial border whose very project was at odds with the greater forces of nature itself.[3]

William Cronon's classic work, *Nature's Metropolis*, focuses on the impact of markets on forests, fields, and waterways. It advances our understanding of how commerce altered the natural world, and how a city altered its hinterland by its commercial and industrial development.[4] Humans and the natural environment have exerted their influence on one another in myriad ways throughout history, and this is true of the Lower Mississippi as well.[5] In this chapter I explore the ways commercial use of a particular ecology of wetlands and waterways, triggered by people in the region adapting to shifting geopolitical contexts after the Seven Years' War, influenced the social and economic history of the region and influenced how the region was connected to the ongoing competition for territory in North America.

To do so, I trace the new ways that British merchants quickly tied the Lower Mississippi Valley to the Atlantic world after the French abandoned their territorial claims in 1763. When British merchants extended their operations into the Lower Mississippi Valley during the years of partition between 1763 and 1783, they linked to the existing trade practices of the frontier exchange economy and anticipated using the Mississippi and her tributaries to extend the reaches of their projects. The river system, then, became integral to extensive British mercantile trade networks, just as it had been to the existing borderland networks.[6] These British merchants brought regional trade into new and different Atlantic connections that ultimately had intense effects both locally and far into the continent. Tracing these trade networks through the American Revolution, in particular, will show how the emerging regional trade of British merchants actually contributed to Spain's support of the rebel British colonies to the east. During the years of partition, then, by exploiting the Mississippi and its tributaries, borderlanders and British merchants had great advantages in their competition with empire. The porous landscape of the Lower Mississippi drainage facilitated profitable boundary crossing. As they transcended borders, British trade networks connected with existing borderland networks, integrated those networks, and forever changed trade and society in the region.

British officials and merchants recognized the importance of the waterways of the Lower Mississippi to the profitability of their ventures. The river and its environs played a great part in facilitating that profitability and the interaction of British traders with local networks. British officials and merchants anticipated supplying manufactured goods to the region and capturing a flow of furs, skins, and raw goods. They accepted that West Florida would benefit the British Empire economically as a base for illicit trade with Spanish colonies.[7] In contrast, Spain issued all manner of policies that emphasized the imperial boundary and understood enforcement of that boundary as connected with building up Louisiana as a defensive border. Indeed, Louisiana's significance for the Spanish Empire lay in its role as a defensive border colony. By ignoring the value of the environment of the Mississippi basin, Spanish policy created impediments to the realization of its imperial goals. Finally, the inhabitants of the region saw little reason to pay heed to restrictions of empire and instead sought to maintain something that appeared more stable to them—their local networks of alliance and exchange, which were influenced by the geography of the region. Louisiana's inhabitants recognized British channels of trade as outlets for their traditional exports, most of which did not find legal markets in the Spanish world.[8] Britain occupied West Florida soon after the Seven Years' War, establishing its claims in 1763, which facilitated the stream of British merchants and opportunists to the Lower Mississippi. In contrast, the first Spanish governor, Antonio de Ulloa, did not arrive in Louisiana until March 1766. British merchants had the upper hand in tapping into the trade networks that stretched into Louisiana in part because the British took possession in the region sooner and Ulloa never took formal possession of Louisiana, leaving its colonial status and Ulloa's authority in an ambiguous state until the arrival of General Alejandro O'Reilly in August 1769.

O'Reilly's expulsion of merchants from New Orleans in 1769 provides one example of the conflict between imperial policy with borderland and British networks. In 1768 Louisiana colonists had united in a revolt that ousted Ulloa. Although numerous grievances contributed to colonists' rejection of Ulloa, who seemed to embody the new centralization of empire in the post–Seven Years' War world, one of the significant motivations for colonists taking part in the revolt was Spanish commercial policy. Louisiana colonists across the socioeconomic spectrum feared that enforcement of such restrictive policy would rip them from their traditional Caribbean and Atlantic networks and leave them without markets for their goods.[9]

O'Reilly arrived in Louisiana with the explicit purpose of bringing the colony into the Spanish Empire by securing the loyalty of its colonists and enforcing commercial policies, which included the suppression of the contraband trade that reigned in Louisiana. Illegal trade had long been the dominant commercial activity in New Orleans. British merchants had participated in this trade throughout the French period.[10] Following the 1763 partition of French Louisiana and the arrival in the Lower Mississippi of an ever-growing number of British merchants, the Caribbean and Atlantic networks of Louisiana colonists underwent a significant shift. By the time O'Reilly reached New Orleans in August 1768, he lamented that he "found the English entirely in possession of the commerce of this colony." After only a few weeks in New Orleans, O'Reilly issued an order expelling merchants known for participating in contraband trade. The list of perpetrators included British and Jewish merchants along with several men who had resisted the efforts of O'Reilly's predecessor, Ulloa, to implement Spanish commercial policy.[11] These expulsions proved only a minor setback, as offending merchants had only to remove to strategic locations in British West Florida to interact with trade networks throughout the Mississippi Valley.

A key for British trade networks of the Lower Mississippi was the trading post established near Fort Bute on the Mississippi at its confluence with the Iberville River, a place then called Manchac.[12] Capturing substantial Mississippi River trade meant that Britain needed to bypass the port city of New Orleans and develop an alternative route to the Gulf of Mexico that could handle the volume of commerce diverted from the Mississippi.[13] The Indigenous name for the Iberville River was Bayou Manchac, meaning "rear entrance," a reflection of the waterway's use by local navigators.[14] And indeed, British merchants intended to use it in a similar manner, as a rear entrance to the vast trade of the Mississippi Valley. British officials, cartographers, and merchants alike had already recognized the advantages of an imperial presence at Manchac, where one traveler described the bayou as amounting to little more than a "ditch."[15] They planned to expand the water route in a way that would increase its profitability in serving as a channel by which the empire could siphon off the wealth of the Mississippi trade. Plans for the post in 1765 envisioned that engineers would clear and open the Iberville to divert the fur and deerskin trade away from New Orleans by channeling it through Lakes Maurepas, Pontchartrain, and Borgne, a more ancient delta of the Mississippi. The journey from Pensacola to Manchac by this route would take only eight to ten days, whereas the journey from Pensacola via the Mississippi took roughly seven to eight weeks.[16] Although these plans faltered, Manchac nonetheless became a hub of British commercial activity. When projects to alter the Iberville failed, British West Florida compensated by constructing a road to the Mississippi that bypassed the low waters of the Iberville.[17] British surveyor and cartographer Thomas Hutchins rightly anticipated the significance of Manchac's location: "This place, if attended to, might be of consequence to the commerce of West-Florida; for it may with reason be supposed, that the inhabitants and traders who reside at Point Coupee, at Natchitoches, Attacappa, the Natchez, on the East side of the Mississippi and above and below the Natchez, at the Illinois, and St Vincents on the ouabashe, would rather trade at this place than at New Orleans, if they could have as good returns for their peltry and the produce of their country."[18] British trade benefited much in the way Hutchins predicted. After their expulsion from New Orleans, merchants relocated to Manchac, transforming it into a bustling trading post from which they engaged the trade routes that converged there. Like Hutchins, these merchants recognized that business would be conducted largely through exchange, as one put it, "in Deer Skins Indego Cotton Tobaco [and] rice."[19] For people already inhabiting and currently migrating into the Lower Mississippi Valley, this alternative linkage of the Mississippi with the Gulf of Mexico through British channels quickly became a pivotal point for exchange and commerce and defied Spain's imperial policies.

Isaac Monsanto provided an example of a man embedded in local trade networks who quickly teamed up with British merchants and so allowed them to link to these extensive regional circuits of trade and to penetrate Spanish territory. The Monsantos, along with the Britto and Fastio families, were Jewish merchants who had also been expelled by O'Reilly's mandate.[20] Isaac Monsanto and his siblings had begun building their commercial network in the Caribbean in 1755 on Curaçao. One brother, Joseph, moved to Santo Domingo while Isaac and other family members went to New Orleans in 1758. By 1765 most of Isaac Monsanto's siblings—brothers Manuel, Jacob, and Benjamin, and sisters Gracia, Angelica, and Eleanora—were also living in New Orleans. Isaac Monsanto, who was the leader among his siblings, became a merchant with regional, Caribbean, and Atlantic trade connections and was a target of Governor O'Reilly's actions against contraband trade. Monsanto received furs and flour from Illinois; he was involved in the illegal trade through Natchitoches; with two Havana merchants, he sent shipments to Veracruz and Campeche; he had business dealings with the Gradis firm of Bordeaux, the place of origin of his friend Isaac Fastio, and with Paris, LaRochelle, Cadiz, and London; and he was in contact early on with British military officials in West Florida and supplied them in their attempt to go to Illinois in the winter of 1764–65. Like other borderlanders, the Monsantos recognized opportunity in operating across the porous borders of empire. The Monsantos joined the exiled British merchants who only needed to remove to British Manchac or to Pensacola in order to continue their outlawed trade. After O'Reilly left Louisiana in 1770, some of these merchants began to trickle back into New Orleans. The Monsantos continued to operate in the Lower Mississippi for the rest of their lives and all ultimately returned to Louisiana.[21]

The strategic situation of British merchants at Manchac provided an Atlantic channel for a wide variety of regional exports. John Fitzpatrick's commercial activity illustrates how British merchants at Manchac used the location and connections with men such as the Monsanto brothers to expand the reaches of their trade deep into the Mississippi Valley, including across the riverine imperial boundary and into Spanish Louisiana. Additionally, many merchants engaged in the trade with Native Americans in Lower Louisiana received supplies and credit through men such as Fitzpatrick. Like Monsanto and many others, Fitzpatrick was forced to remove from New Orleans and chose to operate out of Manchac. There he supplied Native traders with goods from Pensacola and Mobile and funneled their skins to the British ports on the Gulf of Mexico. Fitzpatrick also supplied traders near Natchez.[22] Besides supplying Native traders, Fitzpatrick attempted to supply Charles Descoudreaux, first commandant at Spanish Manchac and later at Pointe Coupée. Descoudreaux informed Fitzpatrick that he was unable to supply licensed traders with goods purchased at New Orleans.[23] Although peddlers, such as men by the names of Morel and John Hamilton, operated with the permission of the Spanish regime in the Indigenous trade in Louisiana's western districts of Opelousas and the Attakapas, they brought their pelts and skins to Fitzpatrick, who helped resupply them.[24] Traders such as Jacob Monsanto and Hamilton were known to have reached Natchitoches, and Hamilton was suspected of penetrating the border with Texas.[25] Fitzpatrick also received tobacco from French-speaking planters at Pointe Coupée and from Jacob Monsanto, who obtained it at Natchitoches. Fitzpatrick then sent goods to Peter Swanson, John Ritson, and Philip Livingston at Pensacola along with wine he obtained clandestinely through prominent New Orleans merchants Louis Ranson and Jean Lafitte.[26]

British merchants sought plots of land on both sides of the Mississippi River to increase their presence at locations whose geographies made them strategic for commerce and exchange. The imperial boundary actually increased business opportunities for British merchants. Many merchants took advantage of the chance to own land on both sides of the Mississippi River, which also multiplied their interaction with local networks. The well-known Oliver Pollock, for example, employed dual identities to facilitate land ownership across empires:

he was both a British citizen and a man who had taken an oath of loyalty to the Spanish Crown.[27] The grants that Pollock procured for himself included tracts at Tangipahoa, British Manchac, New Orleans, and Spanish LaFourche, and in British West Florida across the Mississippi River from Pointe Coupée. Many other merchants connected to the Atlantic trade obtained similarly located lands in both the competing (but neighboring) empires, including John Waugh, Francis Murphy, and Patrick Morgan. Because of the regional waterways, these places where such merchants held land were already prime locations for trade and exchange and had been long before there was any British presence on the river. Located to the east of Lake Pontchartrain, Tangipahoa provided access to New Orleans. Use of this location for both Indigenous and contraband trade had persisted for some time.[28] Besides possessing fertile lands, the area above Pointe Coupée also provided fairly easy access to trade with colonists and Native Americans in proximity to Spanish Louisiana and access to traffic from the Red River.

The Mississippi River served as a space where British merchants conducted business. Manchac merchants extended their influence by employing "floating warehouses" from which they could trade with borderland inhabitants from both sides of the river. By 1770 numerous "floating warehouses" dotted the Mississippi from New Orleans to Pointe Coupée, much to the consternation of Spanish governors Ulloa, O'Reilly, Unzaga, and, later, Bernardo de Gálvez.[29] Some of these watercraft were used as part of slave-trading operations connected to the Caribbean. Vessels often belonged to merchants operating stores at Manchac. The *Rebecca* was one such vessel belonging to a British colonist by the name of Stephen Shakespeare. Anchored in the Mississippi in 1778, the *Rebecca* bore gunpowder, buckles, sixty sets of shirts and trousers, bundles of women's clothes, remnants of cotton, medicines, scales, and inkstands. Men such as Shakespeare exchanged these items for deerskins, indigo, and beaver pelts.[30]

Planters, farmers, traders, the enslaved, and Native Americans took advantage of the backdoor passageways to British Atlantic commerce. British trade networks provided an outlet for Louisiana produce outside the confines of the Spanish Empire. Indeed, a significant amount of produce and pelts bypassed New Orleans. The products of Louisiana exported to British markets included "lumber, indigo, cotton, furs, and some corn and rice."[31] Louisiana colonists traded their surplus grain to British West Florida merchants instead of sending it to New Orleans, a cause for concern for Spanish governor Luis de Unzaga. For example, the man on whom Henry Wadsworth Longfellow based the character Gabriel from his epic poem *Evangeline*, Pierre Arceneaux, "sold [grain] to the English of Manchac," as did his compatriots who were also settled on the

Mississippi.[32] Because the Spanish had set price controls for grain in New Orleans, the Acadians living along the Mississippi fared better by trading their surplus with British subjects, and transporting the grain to Manchac proved less costly than transporting it to New Orleans.[33] During the corn and rice shortage of 1770, Unzaga bemoaned the fact that "the farmers do not wish to descend to sell them."[34] Officials wrote that amid the scarcity of grain, the habitants sold their produce to the "*anglais*, with the excuse of being occupied with their harvest."[35] Although the commandant at Saint James de Cabahannocé, a Spanish post on the Mississippi, Nicolas Verret, protested that the residents of his post had not traded the precious grain, he did not convince Unzaga, who instructed Verret to inventory the grain on the farms in his district and to send excess grain to New Orleans.[36]

For *petites nations*, small Indigenous polities, access to British trade goods flowing into the Lower Mississippi Valley provided a special political opportunity, as did the location of the imperial border.[37] As France relinquished its claim to lands east of the Mississippi, *petites nations* formerly allied with the French such as the Taensas, Mobilians, Biloxis, and Alibamons relocated westward to the Mississippi River and to waterways such as Bayou Lafourche and even west of the Atchafalaya basin, lands already home to Houmas, Chetimachas, Attakapas, and Opelousas.[38] They did not settle permanently, however. The years of partition were years of frequent migration for many *petites nations*. The primary colonial negotiators in local competition among the empires for Native allies were local officials such as Charles Descoudreaux at Spanish Manchac, Balthasar DeVilliers at Spanish Pointe Coupée, and John Thomas, the deputy superintendent for Indian affairs on the Mississippi and justice of the peace at British Manchac. These same officials were frequently drawn into *petites nations'* customs and ceremonies, more often negotiating on Native terms. Relying on supplies of trade goods to negotiate ongoing alliances with Mississippi Valley Native Americans, these officials complained frequently of the ease with which *petites nations* acted in friendship with both empires.[39] The location of British merchants at their strategically placed stores encouraged migration, although access to trade goods and alliances with local officials were not the only motivations for migration by *petites nations*. Other motivations included desire to maintain ties with French traders and long-standing mutual hostility between the *petites nations* and the British and Chickasaws. Later pressures that influenced migration included the Creek-Choctaw War and the American Revolution. The location of British merchants also encouraged the political activities of the Indigenous peoples of the region and revealed that during the era of partition, diplomatic power rested in their hands.

The *petites nations* did not have to remain within the borders of Spanish Louisiana, nor of British West Florida, for that matter. Their frequent relocation during the 1770s made this matter abundantly clear to the officials vying for their loyalty.[40] The Alibamons left British West Florida, established themselves for a time at Spanish Opelousas, and then resettled with two other *petites nations* near Manchac.[41] In March 1772 they settled with the Taensas, Mobilians, and Pacanas on land above Pointe Coupée on the British side of the river, a decision encouraged by Thomas. He noted that "they gave me the United dance and are now clearing a spot of ground."[42] Meanwhile, Alibamons continued to visit Spanish Manchac, smoking the calumet with Descoudreaux.[43] Later, the Alibamons and Pacanas returned to Spanish Louisiana, some settling in Opelousas and others on the Red River at Rapides.[44]

During the years of partition, both Spain and Britain vied for the exclusive loyalty of the *petites nations*, but neither side with marked success. The Mobilians, the Alibamons, the Pacanas, the Taensas, and the Tunicas all received gifts and medals from officials representing the two competing empires.[45] Indeed, groups such as the Pacanas and Alibamons hoped to benefit from friendship with both empires and demonstrated adeptness in using the imperial rivalry and the desperation of officials to obtain loyal allies from among the region's Native peoples for their own benefit.[46] In February 1772 the Alibamon chief arrived at the Iberville and attempted to enter into alliances with both the British and the Spanish at their respective forts. When Charles Descoudreaux, then commandant at Spanish Manchac, refused to give the chief provisions of two loaves of bread and two bottles of wine, the chief sent a letter to Devilliers, arguing that Descoudreaux's actions indicated that Spain rejected an alliance with his people. Perhaps this interaction contributed to the chief's decision to settle, at least for a time, in British territory.[47] When Descoudreaux suggested that the Pacana chief was disloyal and fickle for migrating with the Alibamons to British Manchac, the chief responded by reminding Descoudreaux that Britain and Spain were at peace. Surely, then, he should not have to pick between empires. Why not ally with both?[48]

Indigenous leaders made their power known to imperial representatives, happily recounting to local officials of one empire the benefits they enjoyed from alliance with the other. Two groups long allied with the French, the Chetimachas and the Tunicas, told stories of the gifts that Thomas dispensed to them at British Manchac as they bargained with Spanish officials at Pointe Coupée and Spanish Manchac.[49] After the Pacanas and Alibamons had left Louisiana for British West Florida in 1772, Descoudreaux begged them to cross to Spanish Manchac and dine with him, hoping to win them over from the British influence. When they did indeed cross the river, the Pacanas and

Alibamons told Descoudreaux of their reasons for relocating to British Manchac. The primary factor was access to better and less expensive supplies than they were able to obtain through French-speaking traders at Opelousas.[50]

During the years of partition, commercial and political success belonged to the merchants and to the *petites nations* rather than to either the Spanish or British imperial designs. The ease with which these merchants, their trading partners, and the *petites nations* navigated the Lower Mississippi was a significant factor that influenced their successes. Neither the Spanish nor British could negotiate with Indigenous polities without trade goods. Spanish officials were plagued by the sense that they simply could not offer Natives access to the same quality of goods that they received at British Manchac.[51] Once he was appointed to Pointe Coupée, Descoudreaux attempted to deal with this problem by gaining access to supplies through Fitzpatrick. Perhaps other Spanish officials attempted to bypass approved suppliers in favor of British merchants.[52] The demand for trade goods through the active British networks operating on the banks of the Mississippi concentrated power in the hands of those with access to these channels of trade. The competition between the British and Spanish for Native alliances allowed the power to decide alliances to reside in the hands of each Native polity. Until the American Revolution extended its reach to the Lower Mississippi in 1778, access to goods on both sides of the Mississippi River gave the diplomatic advantage to the Natives and encouraged the *petites nations* to visit, trade, and hold ceremonies with representatives of the British and Spanish Empires.[53]

Besides opening new channels for trade goods and enslaved people, British merchants connected the region in new ways to the Atlantic world and to British North American port cities. O'Reilly's enforcement of Spanish commercial policy was not absolute. In fact, he sanctioned trade between British North American ports and New Orleans. Before leaving Havana to take possession of the colony of Louisiana in 1769, O'Reilly turned to a man from Northern Ireland, Oliver Pollock, to secure flour for the city of New Orleans. At the time, Pollock was operating throughout the West Indies on behalf of several Philadelphia firms.[54] After reaching New Orleans with the requested flour, Pollock stayed on and supplied flour through his connections in Philadelphia, particularly the firm of Willing and Morris, which was expanding during the 1770s and giving greater attention to Spanish ports.[55] Unlike most British merchants operating in Louisiana, Pollock gained licit entry to the Spanish colony. At Pollock's suggestion, Thomas Willing's brother, James, migrated to partner with Pollock in starting an indigo plantation on the Mississippi.[56] Willing and Morris regularly sent ships laden with flour and manufactured goods from Philadelphia to Spanish New Orleans, participating in the first consistent flow of such

cargo to the Lower Mississippi.[57] During the American Revolution, this particular channel of trade developed into an important wartime conduit of Spanish-
American diplomacy and trade.

Another significant accomplishment of expanding British trade networks
was the development of a more regular flow of trade along the Ohio and Mississippi Rivers. George Morgan, the junior partner of Philadelphia's Baynton,
Wharton, and Morgan, pioneered the route in 1767.[58] Taking advantage of
America's great rivers until 1775, the firm established a circuitous trade from
Philadelphia to the borderlands in the Ohio River basin, down the Ohio to
the Illinois Country, from there to the Lower Mississippi, and back again via
the Gulf of Mexico and the Atlantic.[59] Bartholomew Macnamara, Fitzpatrick, and Pollock all served as contacts for Baynton, Wharton, and Morgan
in the Lower Mississippi Valley.[60] Other firms also developed versions of this
trade. For example, Francis Murphy came to New Orleans as a representative
of Barnard and Michael Gratz, an American branch of a London-based trade
network that stretched form the East Indies to the interior of North America
where the Gratz brothers participated in land speculation and in supplying the
Native trade.[61]

The networks that connected the region to the British Atlantic world were
inextricably linked to the forced migration of hundreds of enslaved Africans
and Creoles to the Lower Mississippi River Valley. Some of the trading and
shipping networks that transported enslaved people to the Lower Mississippi
were closely associated with Willing and Morris and Baynton, Wharton, and
Morgan. Merchants along the Mississippi often served as middlemen in the
slave trade, including Fitzpatrick and planter William Dunbar.[62] Slaving ships
coming to the Mississippi usually originated in or at least made port in the Caribbean, with Jamaica serving as the most significant entrepôt for slavers des-
tined for the Lower Mississippi. Small-scale operations, such as those of West
Florida planter-merchants Dunbar and Patrick Morgan, outfitted vessels with
goods and enslaved people in Jamaica before sailing to the Mississippi, where
they would sell some of their cargo to finance the establishment of a plantation in West Florida.[63] Exemplifying this branch of contraband trade in human
cargo were the Scottish brothers Robert, George, and David Ross. The Ross
brothers held land grants in West Florida and traded enslaved people throughout the region, at posts such as Pensacola, Natchez, Pointe Coupée, and New
Orleans.[64] Ships bearing enslaved people also came from Saint-Domingue,
Martinique, Antigua, and Barbados.[65] At Barbados, Thomas and James Willing's brother, Charles, actively participated in the business of Willing and Morris and sent slaving ships to New Orleans. Pollock then sold these people at
New Orleans and Manchac.[66]

The activities of British merchants on the Lower Mississippi, the opportunities that their trade offered to the region's inhabitants, and the peoples and commodities that flowed into the Lower Mississippi contributed to long-term changes in the region. During this period of competition and transition, the commerce bypassing imperial oversight and control helped accelerate the growth of the nascent plantation economy while also encouraging frontier exchange. Slaving to the region would continue to escalate during the Spanish colonial period as the Lower Mississippi transitioned eventually to a plantation society based on enslaved labor. British commercial activity also influenced the increase in the number of enslaved people from the Caribbean and Africa arriving in Louisiana and the beginning of the re-Africanization of the enslaved population.[67]

Native diplomacy and trade experienced both short- and long-term effects in the wake of the expansion of British trade networks. In one of several ironies associated with British commercial activity during the years of partition, British merchants at Manchac actually facilitated the migration into Spanish Louisiana of Native groups leaving Florida when it suddenly became a British colony. In the long term, after the American Revolution, the *petites nations* migrated west of the Mississippi permanently, many settling along the Red River. At the same time, the British trade networks established east of the Mississippi, especially among the Choctaw, Chickasaw, Creek, and Cherokee, persisted with great vitality and would become caught up in the ensuing competition for the southern trans-Appalachian West.[68]

The second great irony of the success of the contraband trade was that by disobeying Spanish law, colonists of Spanish Louisiana and subjects of the British Crown furthered the interests of the Spanish Empire by strengthening colonial outposts, population, and economies of Louisiana. And so, on the eve of Spain's official entry into the American Revolutionary conflict in 1778 and 1779, Louisiana colonists were prepared to participate as loyal Spanish subjects, which was a dramatic shift from the act of rebellion Louisiana colonists had perpetrated in October 1768.[69]

The expansion of British trade networks also influenced the political future of Spanish Louisiana and intersected with the Spanish Empire's role in the American Revolution. British merchant networks that took root in the Lower Mississippi during the years of partition became central to the Spanish-American alliance during the American Revolution. British trade with Louisiana tied the Spanish colony to merchants in Philadelphia. As the thirteen colonies declared their independence, rebels sought assistance from Spain through channels already available to them. Channels of communication followed channels of trade. Ultimately, these networks also facilitated diplomatic relations that produced wartime alliances between Spain and the United States. The connections developed through Oliver Pollock and Willing and Morris were among the most significant. Pollock became the representative for the United States and for the state of Virginia at New Orleans and a central figure in the flow of arms and supplies to American forces through New Orleans. Between the declaration of American independence in July 1776 and the Spanish declaration of war in June 1779, Spain embraced an official policy of neutrality, while providing the Americans with access to supplies. One of the most important branches in the exchange of American flour for supplies and aid grew out of the connection between New Orleans and Philadelphia. The trade and diplomacy conducted through New Orleans was only one piece of a larger alliance between Spain and the United States that spanned the Atlantic and built on existing trade connections.[70]

Connection between the rebel colonies and the Lower Mississippi also influenced the wartime experience of the region's inhabitants. Ideas for an American campaign against British West Florida built on the experiences of American merchants who had traveled the interior waterways of the continent to New Orleans and along the Gulf Coast. In 1776 James Willing returned to Philadelphia, where he advocated for an invasion of West Florida that would secure navigation of the Mississippi for the Americans and easy access to New Orleans. In 1777 George Morgan brought before the Continental Congress a plan for such an expedition. Robert Morris used his position on the Committee of Commerce to influence the project but with Captain James Willing, instead of Morgan, leading a small force of men. The goals of the expedition included an exchange for supplies at New Orleans.[71] Willing and his party of about thirty left Pittsburgh in January 1778, and others joined their force along the way. They followed the path that Morgan had pioneered before them.[72] When Willing's party struck West Florida, it embroiled the Lower River in unanticipated conflict before Spain had finished preparing for war.[73]

Finally, the British trade networks, both licit and illicit, that merchants helped create were purposefully entangled with the local networks of the frontier exchange economy and opened a long-term sustained trade to the Lower Mississippi, especially to New Orleans. Eventually the influence of American merchants in New Orleans and the Lower Mississippi Valley would contribute to American possession by the dawn of the next century. In this instance, the power of the environment to contribute to the shaping of history remained on the side of North American trade networks, both those emanating from the Atlantic port cities and those connected by the water routes of the vast subregions of the Mississippi basin. Many of the same British and American merchants and members of their networks continued to operate in the Lower Mississippi for the remainder of the 1700s, including Patrick Morgan, James Mather, Arthur Strother, Francis Murphy, Daniel Clark Sr., Daniel Clark Jr., the Ross brothers, and the Jones brothers. These individuals perpetuated the trade relationships with the Anglophone Atlantic, especially with ports such as Philadelphia, Baltimore, and New York. The trade route developed by Morgan in the 1760s would also shift in its significance and be transformed in the 1780s and 1790s to include even more extensive networks linking the edges of American western expansion, the Mississippi River Valley, New Orleans, and other American port cities. The question of access to the river and New Orleans encouraged Americans in the trans-Appalachian West to cooperate and collaborate with Spanish New Orleans and her spies for the remainder of the Spanish colonial period. The power of the river system and of the Atlantic and continental connections developed during the years of partition could not be contained by any imperial policy—though Spain attempted to regulate trade in the decades to come.

Spanish policy, however, never succeeded in surmounting the power of the Mississippi River Valley to unite peoples and sustain trade relationships. Spain enjoyed its greatest success in its attempts to claim and shape the borderland when its policies and interests overlapped with those of the borderlanders, as they did in the American Revolution, and when they unwittingly cooperated with the river system. Policy seldom employed the natural environment as an asset; rather, it more often competed with the power of the region's rivers and waterways to shape the borderland and with the inhabitants' knowledge of the topography. Indeed, borderlanders would continue to use the waterways of the Lower Mississippi to thwart Spanish efforts to exert control. And the alliance between borderlanders and their region would haunt Spanish officials as they attempted to stamp out maroon communities in the 1780s, stem the flow of the "contagion" of the Age of Revolutions in the form of slave rebellion and conspiracy throughout the 1790s, and manage American use of the Mississippi River.

During the years of partition, the British trade networks expanded rapidly throughout the Lower Mississippi largely because they tapped into and then incorporated the existing borderland trade networks that took advantage of the environment of the region. The rapid transformation of an intricate chain of waterways into a strong commercial connection to the Atlantic world during the 1760s and 1770s had a significant influence on the Lower Mississippi Valley, in unexpected and long-lasting ways.

NOTES

1. Craig E. Colten, *Southern Waters: The Limits to Abundance* (Baton Rouge: Louisiana State University Press, 2014), 27–28; David Narrett, *Adventurism and Empire: The Struggle*

for Mastery in the Louisiana-Florida Borderlands, 1762–1803 (Chapel Hill: University of North Carolina Press, 2015), 11–20. For a discussion of the diplomacy and understanding of western lands in 1762 and 1763, see Paul W. Mapp, *The Elusive West and the Contest for Empire, 1713–1763* (Chapel Hill: University of North Carolina Press, 2011), 359–427.

2. François Furstenberg, "The Significance of the Trans-Appalachian Frontier in Atlantic History," *American Historical Review* 113 (June 2008): 652–55.

3. William Cronon, *Nature's Metropolis: Chicago and the Great West* (New York: W. W. Norton, 1991), 23; Stephen Aron, *American Confluence: The Missouri Frontier from Borderland to Border State* (Bloomington: Indiana University Press, 2006), xvii; Shannon Dawdy, *Building the Devil's Empire: French Colonial New Orleans* (Chicago: University of Chicago Press, 2008), 4, 78–79, 102–15; for a discussion of Indigenous and transatlantic understandings of the Mississippi basin, see Colten, *Southern Waters*, 11–38.

4. Cronon, *Nature's Metropolis*, xvi, 12, 61, 267.

5. Craig E. Colten, "Introduction," in *Transforming New Orleans and Its Environs: Centuries of Change*, ed. Craig E. Colten (Pittsburgh: University of Pittsburgh Press, 2001), 1–6.

6. For a full discussion of the frontier exchange economy, see Daniel H. Usner Jr., *Indians, Settlers, and Slaves in a Frontier Exchange Economy: The Lower Mississippi Valley before 1783* (Chapel Hill: University of North Carolina Press, 1992).

7. Robin F. A. Fabel, *The Economy of British West Florida, 1763–1783* (Tuscaloosa: University of Alabama Press, 1988), 75; Narrett, *Adventurism and Empire*, 35–36; Cronon, *Nature's Metropolis*, 312.

8. John G. Clark, *New Orleans, 1718–1812: An Economic History* (Baton Rouge: Louisiana State University Press, 1970), 167–69.

9. Dawdy, *Building the Devil's Empire*, 224–26; Frances Kolb, "The New Orleans Revolt of 1768: Uniting against Real and Perceived Threats of Empire," *Louisiana History* 59 (Winter 2018): 5–39. The two most significant full studies of the Revolt of 1768 remain John Preston Moore, *Revolt in Louisiana: The Spanish Occupation, 1766–1770* (Baton Rouge: Louisiana State University Press, 1976), and Carl A. Brasseaux, *Denis-Nicolas Foucault and the New Orleans Rebellion of 1768* (Ruston, La.: McGinty, 1987).

10. For a discussion of trade during the French period, see Dawdy, *Building the Devil's Empire*, 106–20.

11. O'Reilly to Arriaga, New Orleans, October 17, 1769, in *Spain in the Mississippi Valley, 1765–94: Translations from the Spanish Archives in the Bancroft Library*, 3 vols., trans. and ed. Lawrence G. Kinnaird (Washington, D.C.: American Historical Association, 1949), 1:104–5 (hereafter *SPMV*); O'Reilly, February 15, 1770, Parsons Collection, box 3E482, folder 46, Dolph Briscoe Center for American History, University of Texas, Austin; New Orleans Merchants to the Superior Council, September 8, 1766, C13A, reel 46, 298–99, Archives Coloniales, Center for Louisiana Studies, Edith Garland Dupre Library, University of Louisiana Lafayette.

12. Manchac of the 1700s had a different location than the town of Manchac today.

13. Clark, *New Orleans*, 162–63.

14. Colten, *Southern Waters*, 21.

15. George Morgan, Letterbook 1766–1767, December 15, 1766, Historical Society of Pennsylvania, Philadelphia (hereafter HSP).

16. Robert W. Hastings, *The Lakes of Pontchartrain: Their History and Environments* (Jackson: University Press of Mississippi, 2009), 6–10, 40–45.

17. Johnstone to Pownall, West Florida, February 19, 1765, in *Mississippi Provincial Archives: English Dominion, 1763–1766*, ed. Dunbar Rowland (Nashville, Tenn.: Brandon, 1911), 273. For more detailed discussion of these engineering projects, see also Hastings, *Lakes of Pontchartrain*, 41–42; Narrett, *Adventurism and Empire*, 36–39.

18. Thomas Hutchins, *An Historical Narrative and Topographical Description of Louisiana and West-Florida* (Gainesville: University Press of Florida, 1968), 43.

19. Fitzpatrick to Arthur Strother, Mobile, November 7, 1769, *Merchant of Manchac: The Letterbooks of John Fitzpatrick, 1768–1790*, ed. Margaret Fisher Dalrymple (Baton Rouge: Louisiana State University Press, 1978), 77 (hereafter *MM*).

20. O'Reilly to Hernandez, New Orleans, February 15, 1770, Parsons Collection; O'Reilly to Arriaga, New Orleans, October 17, 1769, in *SPMV*, 1:97, 103; Clark, *New Orleans*, 175.

21. Clark, *New Orleans*, 175; Robert P. Swierenga, *The Forerunners: Dutch Jewry in the North American Diaspora* (Detroit: Wayne State University Press, 1994), 209–10. The Monsantos were Sephardic Jews. Isaac was born at the Hague, his father David Rodriguez Monsanto at Amsterdam. Isaac appears to have been the leader among his brothers and sisters and the engine in getting most of the family to New Orleans. The Brittos, Fastios, and Monsantos had done business together out of Curaçao at least from 1757 to 1763, and then again at New Orleans. Bertram Wallace Korn traces the Monsanto family, including brothers Manuel, Jacob, and Benjamin, and sisters Gracia, Angelica, and Eleanora, in *The Early Jews of New Orleans* (Waltham, Mass.: American Jewish Historical Society, 1969), 10–73.

22. Fitzpatrick to Thomas James, Manchac, October 20, 1773, 162; Fitzpatrick to Miller and Swanson, Manchac, December 26, 1773, 166–67; Fitzpatrick to Isaac Johnson, December 27, 1774, Manchac, 180; and Fitzpatrick to Captain Wm. McIntosh, Manchac, June 11, 1780, 347–51, all in *MM*.

23. Fitzpatrick to Miller, Swanson and Co., Manchac, May 8, 1773, 146–47; Fitzpatrick to Miller, Swanson and Co., Manchac, September 14, 1773, 160; and Fitzpatrick to Miller, Swanson and Company, Manchac, October 22, 1773, 163, all in *MM*.

24. Descoudreaux, Manchac, September 20, 1772, legajo 189A, ff. 615–16, Papeles Procedentes de Cuba, Special Collections, Edith Garland Dupré Library, University of Louisiana Lafayette (hereafter PPC); Land Grant, February 3, 1773, reel 7, 191, West Florida Papers, David Library of the American Revolution (hereafter WFLP). It is noted in William Wilton's petition for land near Pointe Coupée that it is the same land "whereon one Hamilton resided some time ago without leave and is since gone over to the Spanish Side of the River Mississippi."

25. Clark, *New Orleans*, 200; "Procédure contre Jacob Monsanto," Natchitoches, March 27, 1773, in Inventory of the Notary Since 1732, PPC, legajo 198, f. 546. Also Fitzpatrick to McGillivray and Struthers, Manchac, May 31, 1770, *MM*, 86–89; Fitzpatrick to McGillivray and Struthers, Manchac, June 4, 1770, *MM*, 90; Fitzpatrick to Philip Livingston, New Orleans, March 9, 1772, *MM*, 116; Fuselier de la Clair to Unzaga, Opelousas, February 16, 1773, PPC, legajo 189A, f. 42; Fuselier de la Clair to Unzaga, March 1, 1773, PPC, legajo 189A, f. 45.

26. Fitzpatrick to McGillivray and Struthers, Manchac, May 31, 1770, *MM*, 86–89; Fitzpatrick to McGillivray and Struthers, Manchac, June 4, 1770, *MM*, 90; Fitzpatrick to McGillivray and Struthers, Manchac, July 23, 1770, *MM*, 90–91; Fitzpatrick to McGillivray and Struthers, Manchac, September 12, 1773, *MM*, 94–95; Fitzpatrick to Peter Swanson,

Manchac, August 30, 1770, *MM*, 159–60; Fitzpatrick to Peter Swanson, Manchac, October 31, 1770, *MM*, 97–98; Fitzpatrick to Peter Swanson, Manchac, January 21, 1771, Manchac, 98–99, *MM*; Fitzpatrick to John Ritson, Manchac, April 20, 1771, *MM*, 105; Fitzpatrick to Philip Livingston Jr., New Orleans, March 9, 1772, *MM*, 156; Fitzpatrick to Jean Lafitte, New Orleans, July 20, 1773, *MM*, 133–35; Fitzpatrick to John Stephenson, August 28, 1772, Manchac, *MM*, 127; "Santiago Lorrains, called Tarascon vs. Santiago Philip Jacquelin Durey," April 25, 1775, trans. Laura Porteous, *Louisiana Historical Quarterly* 11 (1928): 163. Louis Ranson, who served as *síndico procurador general* (public advocate) to the cabildo in 1770, also did business with British merchants. Fitzpatrick used Ritson's plantation below New Orleans to trade Louisiana produce to other British merchants. The merchant Jean Lafitte was a different person from the now well-known pirate.

27. Light T. Cummins, "Oliver Pollock: An Early Anglo Landowner on the Lower Mississippi, 1769–1824," *Louisiana History* 29 (Winter 1988): 37, 42; Land Grant to Oliver Pollock, December 2, 1772, WFLP, reel 6, 61; "Estevan Barre vs. Santiago Laffont," August 18, 1780, trans. Laura Porteous, *Louisiana Historical Quarterly* 14 (1931): 627.

28. Gage to Haldimand, New York, April 26, 1767, Haldimand Papers, reel 2, 26–30, David Library of the American Revolution, Washington Crossing, Pa. (hereafter Haldimand Papers); Haldimand to Gage, Pensacola, August 5, 1767, Haldimand Papers, reel 2, 100; Aubry, New Orleans, June 30, 1766, PPC, legajo 109, f. 25; Loyola to Ulloa, July 2, 1766, PPC, legajo 109, ff. 23–24; Land Grant, November 2, 1772, WFLP, reel 6, 48; Land Grant, January 10, 1773, WFLP, reel 7, 187; Land Grant, December 2, 1772, WFLP, reel 6, 60; Land Grant, August 25, 1773, WFLP, reel 7, 91; "Patrick Morgan and Santiago Mather vs. Juan Bautista Bienvenu as bondsman for the late Nicolas Lamother," May 3, 1779, trans. Laura Porteous, *Louisiana Historical Quarterly* 13 (1930): 686–93; Fabel, *Economy of British West Florida*, 92, 97, 106–7, 217.

29. "Declaration of Stephen Shakespeare, his ship Rebecca" and Willing to Galvez, March 24, 1778, in *SPMV*, 1:276, 263; Fabel, *Economy of British West Florida*, 31, 97, 108; Clark, *New Orleans*, 164–65.

30. Fabel, *Economy of British West Florida*, 31; "Declaration of Stephen Shakespeare, his ship Rebecca," May 1778, in *SPMV*, 1:273–75.

31. O'Reilly to Unzaga, Havana, April 3, 1770, in *SPMV*, 1:165.

32. Judice to Unzaga, Lafourch, January 23, 1773, PPC, legajo 189A, ff. 470–71. Longfellow based Gabriel on the myth of Pierre Louis Arceneaux and Emmaline Labiche, who were separated in the Grand Dérangement. Arceneaux, like many other Acadians, settled in Spanish Louisiana and entered promptly into commercial cooperation with his legendary British foe. See also Carl A. Brasseaux, *In Search of Evangeline: Birth and Evolution of the Evangeline Myth* (Thibodeaux, La.: Blue Herron, 1988).

33. Carl A. Brasseaux, *The Founding of New Acadia: The Beginnings of Acadian Life in Louisiana, 1765–1803* (Baton Rouge: Louisiana State University Press, 1987), 131.

34. Unzaga to Verret, New Orleans, August 11, 1770, in Carl A. Brasseaux, ed. and trans., "Official Correspondence of Spanish Louisiana, 1770–1803," *Louisiana Review* 7 (1978): 172–73.

35. Piernas to Dustiné, New Orleans, August 11, 1770, PPC, legajo 195, f. 422. "On experimente a cette capital un grand manque de ris et mahis, parce que les habitants ne veulent pas descendre pour les vendre, et cela pour ne pas voulir les donner aux prix du tariff, mais bien aux anglais, l'excuse d'être occupé a leur récolte."

36. Unzaga to Verret, August 11, 1770, 173–74.

37. For a recent treatment of the *petites nations*, see Elizabeth Ellis, "Petite Nation with Powerful Networks: The Tunicas in the Eighteenth Century," *Louisiana History* 58 (2017): 133–78.

38. Usner, *Indians, Settlers, and Slaves*, 130.

39. Fitzpatrick to Charles Stuart, Manchac, November 9, 1772, *MM*, 137–38. By this time, the Mobilians were a very small nation. The census of Rapides in 1773 has only this to say about them: "they numbered 7 men, 6 women, and 4 children." Winston De Ville, *Rapides Post on Red River: Census and Military Documents for Central Louisiana, 1769–1800* (Ville Platte, La.: Provincial, 2003), 20; Descoudreaux to Unzaga, April 23, 1772, Manchac, PPC, legajo 189A, f. 596.

40. *Petites nations* Indians balanced relations with larger Indian groups besides alliances with empires. The early 1770s saw increased tension among Indian groups in the Lower Mississippi because of the Creek-Choctaw War.

41. Descoudreaux to Unzaga, Manchac, March 20, 1772, PPC, legajo 189A, ff. 585–86.

42. Council Chamber, Pensacola, April 7, 1772, WFLP, reel 2, 55–67.

43. Descoudreaux to Unzaga, Manchac, March 20, 1772, PPC, legajo 189A, ff. 585–86; Descoudreaux to Unzaga, Manchac, May 7, 1772, PPC, legajo 189A, ff. 603–4; Descoudreaux to Unzaga, Manchac, April 23, 1772, PPC, legajo 189A, f. 596.

44. Descoudreaux to Unzaga, Manchac, February 16, 1773, PPC, legajo 189A, ff. 634–36; Fuselier de la Clair to Unzaga, March 31, 1773, PPC, legajo 189A, ff. 46–47; De Ville, *Rapides Post on Red River*, 20.

45. Descoudreaux to Unzaga, no date but follows document dated April 23, 1772, Manchac, PPC, legajo 189A, f. 599; Descoudreaux to Unzaga, Manchac, February 27, 1772, PPC, legajo 189A, f. 531; Robert R. Rea, "Redcoats and Redskins on the Lower Mississippi, 1763–1776: The Career of Lt. John Thomas," *Louisiana History* 11 (Winter 1970): 16, 28; Agreement of Several Tonica Chiefs, Headmen, Warriors, and Women and John Thomas, April 29, 1775, WFLP, reel 19, 136–38.

46. Descoudreaux to Unzaga, Manchac, March 20, 1772, PPC, legajo 189A, ff. 585–86.

47. Descoudreaux to Unzaga, Manchac, February 27, 1772, PPC, legajo 189A, f. 531.

48. Descoudreaux to Unzaga, Manchac, March 20, 1772, PPC, legajo 189A, ff. 585–86.

49. Descoudreaux to Unzaga, Manchac, March 10, 1772, PPC, legajo 189A, f. 583; Descoudreaux to Unzaga, Manchac, n.d., PPC, legajo 189A, f. 599; Descoudreaux to Unzaga, Manchac, February 27, 1772, PPC, legajo 189A, f. 531; Rea, "Redcoats and Redskins," 16, 28; Agreement of Several Tonica Chiefs.

50. Descoudreaux to Unzaga, Manchac, March 20, 1772, PPC, legajo 189A, ff. 585–86.

51. Descoudreaux to Unzaga, Manchac, February 27, 1772, PPC, legajo 189A, f. 531; Descoudreaux to Unzaga, Manchac, March 10, 1772, PPC, legajo 189A, f. 583.

52. Fitzpatrick to Miller, Swanson and Co., Manchac, May 8, 1773, 146–47; Fitzpatrick to Miller, Swanson and Co., Manchac, September 14, 1773, 160; Fitzpatrick to Miller, Swanson and Company, Manchac, October 22, 1773, 163, all in *MM*.

53. Descoudreaux to Unzaga, Manchac, May 7, 1772, PPC, legajo 189A, ff. 603–4; Descoudreaux to Unzaga, Manchac, April 23, 1772, PPC, legajo 189A, f. 596; Fitzpatrick to Charles Stuart, Manchac, November 9, 1772, *MM*, 137–38; Council Chamber, Pensacola, April 7, 1772, WFLP, reel 2, 55–67; Descoudreaux to Unzaga, Manchac, March 20, 1772, PPC, legajo 189A, ff. 585–86; Descoudreaux to Unzaga, Manchac, n.d., PPC, legajo 189A, f.

599; Descoudreaux to Unzaga, Manchac, February 27, 1772, PPC, legajo 189A, f. 531; Rea, "Redcoats and Redskins," 16, 28; Agreement of Several Tonica Chiefs.

54. James Hunter to Oliver Pollock, Saint Kitts, August 19, 1767, Oliver Pollock Papers, Hill Memorial Library, LSU (hereafter OPP); Cummins, "Oliver Pollock," 38–41; Cummins, "Anglo Merchants and Capital Migration in Spanish Colonial New Orleans," in *New Orleans and Urban Louisiana, Part A. Settlement to 1860*, ed. Samuel C. Shepherd Jr., Louisiana Purchase Bicentennial Series 14 (Lafayette: Center for Louisiana Studies, University of Louisiana at Lafayette, 2005), 251.

55. Clark, *New Orleans*, 174; Fabel, *Economy of British West Florida*, 36; Richard Harrison to Oliver Pollock, New Orleans, July 7, 1778, in *SPMV*, 1:294–95; James A. James, "Oliver Pollock, Financier of the Revolution in the West," *Mississippi Valley Historical Review* 16 (1929): 69; Cummins, "Anglo Merchants and Capital Migration," 251; Charles Rappleye, *Robert Morris: Financier of the American Revolution* (New York: Simon & Schuster, 2010), 23–24.

56. James, "Oliver Pollock," 68–69; Cummins, "Oliver Pollock," 38–41; Power of Attorney, WFLP, reel 17, 356–58.

57. "CUSTOM HOUSE, Philadelphia, INWARD ENTRIES, Cleared at the Customs House," December 20, 1770, June 13, 1771, June 27, 1771, December 5, 1771, December 12, 1771, all in *Pennsylvania Gazette*.

58. Morgan, Fort Chartres, December 11, 1767, George Morgan Letterbook, 1766–68, HSP.

59. Morgan, October 27, 1767, and Morgan to Partners, Fort Chartres, December 2, 1767, George Morgan Letterbook, 1766–68, HSP.

60. Macnamara to BW&M, New Orleans, September 6, 1767, Baynton, Wharton, and Morgan Papers, David Library of the American Revolution, Washington Crossing, Pa. (hereafter BWM), roll 4, 999–1002; Morgan to Macnamara, Fort Chartres, December 20, 1767, George Morgan Letterbook, 1766–68, HSP; Macnamara to BW&M, New Orleans, July 28, 1767, BWM, roll 4: 996–98; Morgan to Fitzpatrick at New Orleans, October 25, 1769, BWM, roll 1, 398–99; Morgan to Fitzpatrick, Manchac, April 10, 1771, BWM, roll 5, 914; BW&M to John Fitzpatrick at Manchac, Philadelphia, March 19, 1772, BWM, roll 1, 316; Morgan to Pollock, Philadelphia, June 22, 1771, BWM, roll 1, 476; Morgan to Pollock, Philadelphia, September 12, 1772, BWM, roll 1, 482; Skins from Illinois to New Orleans, BWM, roll 1, 314–15.

61. William Pencak, "Jews and Anti-Semitism in Early Pennsylvania," *Pennsylvania Magazine of History and Biography*, July 2002, 369–70.

62. Fitzpatrick to Van Horn, Manchac, November 23, 1776, *MM*, 215; William Dunbar, May 27, 1776; February 9, 1777; September 4, 1777; December 12, 1777; December 21, 1777; and January 4, 1778, in William Dunbar, *Life, Letters and Papers of William Dunbar*, ed. Eron Rowland (Jackson: Press of the Mississippi Historical Society, 1930), 23, 44, 50, 55, 56, 57; Act of Sale, David Ross to James Smith, Pintado Papers, reel 4, container 5, Alexander Herd Library, Vanderbilt University, Nashville.

63. Fabel, *Economy of British West Florida*, 33, 105; Unzaga to de la Torre, New Orleans, February 27, 1772, PPC, legajo 1145, ff. 52–53.

64. Gwendolyn Midlo Hall, *Africans in Colonial Louisiana: The Development of Afro-Creole Culture in the Eighteenth Century* (Baton Rouge: Louisiana State University Press, 1995), 280; Fabel, *Economy of British West Florida*, 106; Act of Sale, Petro Lartigue to

William Dunbar, July 28, 1787, WFLP, reel 1, 142; Act of Sale John Fitzpatrick to Hubert Rowell, July 14, 1787, WFLP, reel 1, 218; and Inventory of Jacob Nash, December 23, 1789, WFLP, reel 1, 462.

65. Jean-Pierre Leglaunec, "Slave Migrations in Spanish and Early American Louisiana: New Sources and New Estimates," *Louisiana History* 46 (Spring 2005): 188, 191; Leglaunec, "A Directory of Ships with Slave Cargoes, Louisiana, 1772–1808," *Louisiana History* 46 (Spring 2005): 214–15.

66. —— to Willing and Morris, London, December 12, 1775, Robert Morris Papers, HSP, Folder 5: Willing-Morris Correspondence; in OPP, see Comyn to Pollock, Manchac, January 21, 1775; Phillip Francis (Richmond) to Pollock (New Orleans), February 10, 1775; John Hodge (Pensacola) to Pollock (New Orleans), February 14, 1775. Charles was the brother of Thomas and James Willing.

67. See Hall, *Africans in Colonial Louisiana*, 275–315.

68. See William S. Coker and Thomas D. Watson, *Indian Traders of the Southeastern Spanish Borderlands: Panton, Leslie and Company and John Forbes and Company, 1783–1847* (Pensacola: University of West Florida Press, 1986).

69. For a recent study of conflict on the Gulf Coast during the American Revolution, see Kathleen DuVal, *Independence Lost: Lives on the Edge of the American Revolution* (New York: Random House, 2015).

70. Light T. Cummins, *Spanish Observers in the American Revolution, 1775–1783* (Baton Rouge: Louisiana State University Press, 1992); Narrett, *Adventurism and Empire*, 88; Peggy K. Liss, *Atlantic Empires: The Network of Trade and Revolution, 1713–1826* (Baltimore: Johns Hopkins University Press, 1983), 114–16.

71. J. Barton Starr, *Tories, Dons, and Rebels: The American Revolution in British West Florida* (Gainesville: University Press of Florida, 1976), 81–83. Morris's actions were not approved by the committee but represented his efforts to back Revolutionary War efforts in the South and his appreciation for the importance of French and Spanish aid to the success of the patriot cause. Rappleye, *Robert Morris*, 141; The Commercial Committee to Edward Hand, November 21, 1777, York in Pennsylvania, in *Letters of Members of the Continental Congress*, ed. Edmund C. Burnett (Washington, D.C.: Carnegie Institute of Washington, 1902), 2:565.

72. Starr, *Tories, Dons, and Rebels*, 84–85; J. Leitch Wright, *Florida in the American Revolution* (Gainesville: University Press of Florida, 1975), 46–47.

73. Narrett, *Adventurism and Empire*, 79–88; Starr, *Tories, Dons, and Rebels*, 81–92.

PART IV   *Empire and Expertise*

Spanish and Indigenous Influences on Virginian Tobacco Cultivation

MELISSA N. MORRIS

In a 1651 book on the New World, George Gardyner wrote of Virginia: "Their onely commodity is Tobacco, which I think to be more naturall to the Countrey then any other thing. The best sort is the sweet scented, which is not inferiour to the Spanish."[1] Gardyner's description obscured the origins of Virginia's tobacco in the first sentence, only to reveal it again in the second. In the 1650s Virginia and tobacco were synonymous, with the colony exporting more than a million pounds of tobacco annually. Its cultivation had spread from the earliest English settlements near Jamestown to most of the colonial Chesapeake. Yet the tobacco grown throughout the region was not native. Like both the Africans who increasingly tended it and the English who owned and worked on the plantations, *Nicotiana tabacum* was a newcomer. The plant came from the south—from the Spanish Empire. The story of how so-called Spanish tobacco came to Virginia takes us to times and places usually considered outside the scope of early American history. It is a story worth telling, if we seek to understand how tobacco cultivation dominated the Chesapeake colonies during the colonial period.

The Spanish founded their empire on the great riches of preexisting civilizations in Mexico and South America and the early discovery of mineral wealth. Northern European colonial enthusiasts of the sixteenth century articulated visions of their own empires modeled on Spanish precedents.[2] The English, French, and Dutch not only hoped to find precious metals like the Spanish did, but they initially looked for it in places near Spanish and Portuguese colonies. Piracy and illicit trade in the Caribbean comprised the first phase of their colonial activity. Attempts to colonize the circum-Caribbean soon followed.

These experiences informed English colonization in Virginia. Before "Spanish tobacco" found a home in the Chesapeake, the English and others traded, grew, and smoked it elsewhere. Commercial experience in the wider Atlantic inspired the English to transport the crop to Virginia, supplanting local tobacco species. Uncovering how this introduced species of tobacco became Virginian reveals unexpected English connections with the Spanish Empire. Comparative histories of the Spanish and English Empires have emphasized the ways the Spanish provided the inspiration and framework for northern Europeans in the Americas, and they also detail the ways the English (and others) departed from the Spanish model.[3] Recent scholarship has urged us to move away from straightforward comparisons and to instead see empires as interdependent entities. For scholars of the English in the Americas, opportunities remain to explore the ways in which they engaged with the Spanish and how such interactions advanced imperial goals.[4]

The earliest phase of northern European colonization demonstrates that the English had a wide range of interactions with Spanish colonists and the Indigenous and African peoples they claimed as subjects.[5] The transmission of agricultural knowledge is one way to see how northern Europeans interacted with and relied on these groups. South American cultivators influenced their Virginian and Caribbean counterparts. The English took note of and introduced Spanish America's plants and agricultural practices to their own colonies.

Uncovering tobacco's origins requires attention to these agricultural practices. Sugar has dominated studies of agriculture in the early modern Atlantic. Producers needed specialized equipment in order to make granulated crystals from sugarcane juice. From the seventeenth century, Europeans made a series of improvements to production, rewarding farmers for adopting new technology. Because of this, historians have inferred that the spread of sugar cultivation in the Atlantic world required a transfer of knowledge. The physical evidence for this knowledge transfer included equipment and written instructions among European planters.[6] Historians have more easily found and traced this process because there is more evidence for the explicit transfer of technological innovation.[7]

Scholars interested in African influence on American agriculture have turned especially to tracing rice cultivation in early South Carolina and Georgia. These works have demonstrated that enslaved Africans introduced not just rice itself but also agricultural know-how. For example, Carolina planters increasingly sought Africans from ethnic groups that already farmed rice, which was becoming the colony's staple commodity. The work of Judith A. Carney and others has sought to expand the way scholars think about the introduction of new crops, urging them to consider the intellectual transfers that necessarily accompanied botanical exchanges, an antidote to a scholarly obsession with technology.[8]

Sugar and the varieties of rice that came to dominate Atlantic markets were each brought to the Americas. Common sense might suggest that Indigenous agricultural products were easier for Europeans to learn to grow, since they were already present in the places they colonized. This presumption is supported by a disdain for Indigenous agriculture that stretches back to the early Spanish conquests. Europeans found crops growing together, in a way that looked untidy to them. They offered it as evidence that Natives did not properly use the land and that it could thus be appropriated. The corrective offered for colonizers' scorn has been to argue for the effortless efficiency of pre-Columbian farming.[9] Both positions obscure agricultural skills that Indigenous peoples throughout the Americas possessed. Alfred W. Crosby's concept of the Columbian exchange decouples botanical goods from the way they are grown, consumed, and used. This disjunction contributes to the notion that crops from the Americas quickly dispersed throughout the globe, which suggests either its effortlessness or inevitability.[10]

Contemporaries, however, were quite aware that growing crops required expertise. They sought information in the form of written instructions, European authorities, and, above all, experienced cultivators. Rather than a straightforward transmission of skills, these tutors often altered how goods were grown for emergent transatlantic markets. Agricultural practices reveal the centrality of Indigenous, African, and Iberian knowledge networks to the early colonization efforts of northern Europeans. For the English growing tobacco in Virginia, such connections were numerous. The crop that developed was a product both of decades of experience in the Atlantic world and of environmental and cultural conditions unique to the Chesapeake.[11]

By the end of the sixteenth century, English readers interested in the exploits of the Spanish in the Americas could choose from an abundance of books in their own language. The first major account of Spanish exploits to appear in English was Richard Eden's *The Decades of the newe world or west India*.[12] Published first in 1555, it was a compilation of several translated works, chiefly Peter Martyr d'Anghiera's *De orbe novo*.[13] Importantly, Eden's edition includes only the first three decades, with the result that the narrative focused largely on the discovery and conquest of the Caribbean, ending in 1516, even though Martyr himself continued the work through 1524, to cover the conquest of Mexico.[14] Eden also included excerpts from Gonzalo Fernández de Oviedo y Valdés's history of the West Indies. Fernández de Oviedo provided his readers with information on the plants and animals, climate, resources, and peoples, particularly those of his home, Santo Domingo. Eden also added excerpts from the papal bull that granted Spain most of the Americas, treatises on navigation, works on mines, and a chapter on Christopher Columbus. This haphazard compilation consequently emphasized the Caribbean phase of the conquest and the environment. Eden's volume was the preeminent English work on Spanish America for the next quarter century.[15]

In the late sixteenth century, new English editions of works on Spanish America abounded. In 1577 John Frampton's translation of Seville physician Nicolás Monardes's treatise on the plants of the Americas, titled *Joyfull newes out of the new founde worlde*, appeared. This very popular work was reprinted several times.[16] Rather than covering the exploits of conquistadors, Monardes extolled the virtues of the New World's plants. Monardes included a lengthy treatise on tobacco, to which Frampton appended additional information about the plant. Like many plants introduced to Europe in this period, tobacco was initially judged for its medicinal merits. According to the text, tobacco was good for headaches, stomach pains, and healing wounds, among other things.

English readers of this period may also have encountered the 1578 translation of Francisco López de Gómara's account of Cortés's conquest of Mexico, or a 1581 translation of Agustín de Zárate's history of Peru. Two years later, Bartolomé de Las Casas's work on the West Indies first appeared in English.[17] In 1589 Richard Hakluyt published the first volume of his *Principall Navigations*.[18] Frequent republishing suggests that these works were popular. Passengers traveling to the Americas also probably took them on board their ships. Hakluyt himself advised that "the books of the discoveries of the west Indies and the conquestes of the same" would "kepe men occupied from worse cogitations, and . . . raise their myndes to courage and highe enterprizes."[19]

Works on the Spanish Empire emphasized its most famous theaters of conquest: the Caribbean (at least initially), Peru, and Mexico. Even today, we call to mind the very same places when discussing the sixteenth-century Spanish Empire. This sampling of the most widely read accounts, however, shows that English readers might also have read about the environment, and about places on the margins of the empire. Works on the exploits of English privateers, in particular John Hawkins or Francis Drake, also offered glimpses of different places in the Americas.[20]

The economy of the Spanish-American Empire was more diverse than its image in Europe. Far from the silver mines of Potosí and the ruins of the glittering Aztec Empire, colonists increasingly engaged in agriculture. Spanish colonists initially experimented with growing familiar European crops, particularly wheat and barley, and when these attempts failed, that came to rely on indigenous foods and supplies from Spain. Dominican friars on Hispaniola led the next concerted efforts at finding viable crops. These friars thought agriculture would bring stability to the island after most of the island's gold deposits dried up. The end of the mining economy also led to the establishment of sugar plantations on Hispaniola.[21] By the late sixteenth century, Spanish colonists using enslaved laborers started cultivating tropical crops: cacao in Mexico and Guatemala, indigo in Central America.[22] Around the same time, colonists in eastern Venezuela and northern Hispaniola started producing tobacco for illicit trade. In general, the late sixteenth-century Spanish Empire was not devoted to agricultural production. The Spanish, however, did turn to plantations in some places, foreshadowing the subsequent practice of the northern Europeans.[23]

Decades before the English established their first permanent colony, they were already familiar with parts of the Americas, especially the Spanish Caribbean. When Arthur Barlowe condensed his ship's log to provide a summary of a trip to Virginia for Walter Ralegh, he skipped over their visit to the Caribbean. "These Islands, with the rest adioyning, are so well knowen to your selfe, and to many others, as I will not trouble you, with the remembrance of them."[24] Until they established their own colonies in the Caribbean in the 1620s, English ships on their way to Virginia came via the Spanish West Indies. Archaeologists at Jamestown unearthed several Spanish olive jars, used all over the world to store and transport all manner of goods, including wine, olive oil, and honey. Such jars provide physical reminders of complicated interactions that English and Spanish had in the Americas.[25]

Efforts to colonize Virginia in the 1580s provided a chance to test out the imperial plans the English had developed both from their own experiences in the Americas and from what they had learned about the Spanish Empire. Colonizers expected to find mines, a northwest passage, and other spectacular things, yet they also were interested in learning about the area's useful flora. Rather than understanding Virginia as an entirely distinct, North American space, the English reckoned it would produce the same kinds of things that the Spanish American colonies did.

Contemporary maps and geographic descriptions supported the notion that colonists could easily transport the people and plants of the Spanish Empire to Virginia. Early visual and written depictions of Virginia placed it closer to Florida, and thus to the rest of the Spanish Empire. The 1599 map that appeared in the second volume of Hakluyt's *Principall Navigations* has "La Florida" confined to the peninsula alone, while "Virginia" takes up the rest of the Southeast.[26] Jodocus Hondius's 1623 map, like other maps of the period, depicted a foreshortened East Coast, which brought Virginia southward. Based on a 1607 engraving, the map does not detail much of the Chesapeake, but rather the "Virginia" of the Roanoke settlers, in present-day North Carolina. This map also brings Virginia and Florida together culturally: it shows a dugout canoe and claims that Native peoples of both places used it. European powers and Indigenous polities contested where exactly "Virginia" began and "Florida" ended, but these depictions gave the impression that the places the English had colonized were closer to Florida than they actually were. It was only over the course of the seventeenth century, when Europeans explored, colonized, and named the places in between, that the perceived distance between "Virginia" and "Florida" increased.

As they endeavored to learn about the plants of Virginia, the English took their cues from Caribbean precedents. They saw Virginia's environment as an extension of the places to the south that they knew better. To that end, colonists collected native plants and those introduced by the Spaniards, especially sugar, to cultivate in Virginia. On his way to establishing a colony at Roanoke, Richard Grenville and his men made several stops in the Caribbean, including Puerto Rico and Santo Domingo. These English colonists obtained livestock, sugarcane, and other tropical plants to attempt to grow in Virginia. A Spanish witness reported the group "took away with them many banana plants and other fruit-trees which they found along the shore, and made drawings of fruits and trees."[27] Thomas Hariot recorded the subsequent agricultural results: "We carried thither Suger canes to plant which beeing not so well preserued as was requisit, & besides the time of the yere being past for their setting when we arriued, wee could not make that proofe of them as wee desired. Notwithstanding, seeing that they grow in the same climate, in the South part of Spaine and in Barbary, our hope in reason may yet côtinue."[28] Relying on contemporary understanding of climate, Hariot expected that Virginia would produce the same agricultural crops as the Caribbean, South America, or Mexico, or as places in Eurasia of the same latitude.[29]

The English did not know that Virginia's soil and climate were unsuitable for sugar, but they did recognize that successful agriculture required expert cultivators. In his "Discourse of Western Planting," written two years before, Richard Hakluyt suggested voyages set out with "suger cane planters wth the plantes." In 1585 the elder Hakluyt wrote a pamphlet for Virginia that recommended the colony procure "Men bred in the Shroffe in South Spaine, for discerning how Olive tree may be planted there."[30] One place to find such people was Spanish America.

Not long after Grenville took plants from the Indies, Francis Drake raided it for colonists. In 1586, after sacking the city, Drake recruited enslaved Africans to join his fleet. A letter written from Havana in June to Philip II reported that next Drake "took 300 Indians from Cartagena, mostly women, 200 negroes, Turks and Moors, who do menial service, and he carries them along though they are not useful in his country." But Drake had no intention of taking them back to England. He planned instead to leave these captives at Roanoke, where their skills would indeed be useful. Drake next pillaged Saint Augustine, where he collected more essentials. A second letter from Cuba recorded that "he has taken with him everything required, by land or sea, to establish a settlement, including even negroes which he seized at Santo Domingo and Cartagena."[31] When Drake arrived in Virginia, he instead helped the English evacuate the settlement. The first attempt at colonizing Virginia had already failed in large part due to conflicts with the Indigenous peoples.[32]

Despite this quick collapse, Sir Walter Ralegh immediately became determined to attempt to colonize Virginia again, learning from the first group's mistakes. Under the leadership of John White, the colony would be composed of "citizen-planters." When establishing the colony, White turned to the Caribbean for plants, much as colonists did in the earlier attempt at Roanoke. When the English set out for Virginia in 1587, they intended "to gather yong plants of Oringes, Pines [pineapples], Mameas [mamey], and Plantonos [plantains] to set at Virginia," but their pilot refused to take them to the place where White and others knew these plants grew.[33]

The early Virginia enterprises, however, failed to realize an English empire. Meanwhile, English ships continued to visit the Caribbean islands and the northern coast of South America. Much of this experience was a continuation of previous raiding and trading, but between the years 1585 and 1607 a new trade good emerged: tobacco. Obtaining it was the objective of many English activities in the Americas. The rise of tobacco cultivation and exportation to European markets further suggests that botanical and agricultural products became central to new colonial projects.

Tobacco is indigenous to the New World and grew in many parts of both North and South America at the time of European contact. Beginning with Columbus, Europeans observed tobacco use but only slowly adopted it themselves. Europeans incorporated tobacco into their pharmacopeia from the mid-sixteenth century. Over the following decades, they also increased their recreational consumption.[34] The English were particularly fond of it. Paul Hentzner, a German traveling in England in 1598, wrote that "everywhere . . . the English are constantly smoking Tobacco."[35] As the European market for tobacco expanded, so did its cultivation in the Americas.

By the late sixteenth century, impoverished Spanish colonists throughout the Caribbean had started growing tobacco. Cultivators grew some for local use, employed tobacco as a currency, and even used it to pay tithes. In some places, locals sold it to passing ships. Tobacco became "an important vehicle of incursions on Spanish colonial territory."[36] On Hispaniola's fertile north coast, an ethnically diverse array of cultivators started a trade in tobacco that attracted Dutch and French privateers.

Along the Venezuelan coast and across it on the island of Trinidad, another lively illicit trade developed that attracted more English ships. There, two small Spanish outposts grew tobacco expressly to sell to foreigners. The settlements, one on Trinidad and another on the mainland along the Orinoco River, produced enough tobacco by 1607 to merit the attention (and disapproval) of the nearby governor of Cumaná. He warned Philip III of Spain that "English and

Dutch ships are never lacking there."[37] In 1608 the governor of Bogotá also wrote to the king to complain that these settlements had become "the chosen resort of secular criminals, irregular priests, and apostate friars and in general a seminary of rascals." Indeed, the "chief attraction is the trade with the pirate enemies."[38] English sources corroborate the governors' claims that the settlements were routinely visited by foreign ships.

In February 1611 English trader Thomas Roe observed that he had just been to "Port d'espagne in the Island of Trinidad where are 15 sayles of ships freighting Smoke: English, French, Dutch." Roe highlighted Spain's inability to control the area. The Spanish colony, he warned, would "be turned all to Smoke" because the government there "hath more skill in planting Tobacco and selling yt, then in erecting Colonyes, or marching of armyes."[39] Even as Roe and others relied on these Spanish settlements for tobacco, they were thinking of ways to undermine them.

This trade led English voyagers to develop a greater familiarity with the peripheral Spanish settlements near Trinidad and Venezuela and the area to the southeast, the present-day Guianas. This region lay between the farthest outposts of Spanish and Portuguese colonization and thus attracted the interest of northern Europeans. English efforts in this area are most famously associated with Walter Ralegh's sometimes fantastic descriptions and his failed search for El Dorado, laid out in his 1596 *The Discoverie of the Large, Rich, and Bewtiful Empyre of Guiana*. Reappraisals of Ralegh have emphasized that, rather than being pure imagination, his narrative demonstrates that he was a careful student of the region. He collected much of his lore from Indigenous and Spanish informants.[40] Nor was Ralegh only looking for gold. Ralegh, an avid smoker, was interested in tobacco's commercial potential. He wrote of Guiana as a place where "those that love *Tobacco*" could "smoke themselves tyll they become bacon," a line excised from the final version of the *Discoverie*.[41] Ralegh's concurrent interest in both Virginia and Guiana reflects a broader trend: the English pursued colonial projects throughout the Americas, not just in the North.

When foreign traders came for tobacco, many of them also explored the nearby coasts. It was common for ships coming from Europe to first head south along the coast of Africa, cross the Atlantic where winds were most favorable, and then sail west along northeastern South America before arriving at Trinidad. Many ships took the opportunity to trade with Indigenous groups along the way and to chart the rivers they found. The aforementioned Thomas Roe sailed northwest along the South American coast before arriving at Trinidad to trade tobacco. Writing to the Earl of Salisbury, Roe claimed to "have seene more of this coast rivers and inland from the Great River of the Amazones under the line [the equator] to Orenoque in 8 degrees, then any Englishman now alive."[42] Dutch and English explorers recorded their voyages to this area graphically. The maps they made and circulated expanded knowledge of the region in their home countries.

It was along this stretch of land and into the interior that small groups of northern Europeans established colonies between around 1600 and the 1630s. These colonies varied dramatically. Some collapsed almost immediately, while others continued for years, and a few led to permanent colonies. Several colonies were intentionally situated close to the Spanish, to antagonize them, trade with them, or both. Others were deliberately a safer distance away.

These colonists also aimed to acquire tropical commodities. Initially, they bartered with Indigenous allies for trading goods. In every colony that endured for more than a few weeks, however, the colonists soon turned to agriculture, and chiefly tobacco. Colonists perhaps realized that it was in high demand and short supply. Tobacco, which does not require special equipment and has a wide cultivation range, was also a logical choice for small colonies in search of profitable agricultural goods. Most importantly, Indigenous peoples in Guiana and the Amazon region had experience growing tobacco and provided the European outposts with knowledge and labor.

The English learned about tobacco cultivation and production from the colonies on Trinidad and along the Orinoco River. The Spanish in the region had made innovations to tobacco processing, such as curing, and had developed the type of tobacco that became most popular in Europe. Robert Harcourt, a longtime supporter of South American colonies, held out great hopes for tobacco, which could be "planted, gathered, seasoned, and made up fit for the Merchant in short time, and with easie labour." He added that "when we first arrived in those parts, wee altogether wanted the true skill and knowledge how to order it, which now of late wee happily have learned of the Spaniards themselves."[43] These lessons made their way to the fledgling English colonies of Guiana.

The English Guiana projects relied on both Indigenous and Spanish practices to grow tobacco. Because the colonies were small and the English were novices in tobacco cultivation, Indigenous favor, labor, and knowledge were crucial. Charles Leigh, the leader of the first colony, was "promised Indians," presumably by a local leader, to help him "build and to plant."[44] A 1613 Spanish report alleged the English had colonized on the mainland near Margarita Island, just west of Trinidad, "with the favour of the Caribs, with the intention of cultivating tobacco."[45] The threat of the more numerous Spanish perhaps convinced Indigenous people to form alliances with English colonists.

English cultivators were also implementing new changes to tobacco production. An account of Phillip Purcell's colony recalled that "they gave the Indians glass beads and other things, teaching them how to produce large quantities of tobacco, because the Indians only knew how to do it in their own uncouth fashion, and not with the perfection which this Captain Porcel saw it done in the Orenoco." Whether the tobacco was indeed desirable or just able to fetch a good price due to market conditions, the plantations had some success. A 1617 letter to Thomas Roe related that some of Purcell's colonists who had recently returned to England came back "ryche" because they "brought with them so muche Tobacco."[46]

Like the early attempts to colonize Virginia, these South American projects failed. The Roanoke ventures, however, are often seen by historians as a precursor to Jamestown, while the South American colonies are largely overlooked. They should all be understood as part of the same project. Both North and South American endeavors were planned for spaces just beyond Spanish control. As colonization efforts in Virginia gained traction, they also built on decades of experience in the Caribbean. To contemporaries, the colonization of Virginia was not the break with previous experiences that it might seem to us.[47]

Lessons the English learned from Spanish-American endeavors are most evident in the continued efforts to force Virginia's environment into the mold of Spanish America. Virginia lacked fruit trees and sugarcane, but it did have tobacco. Thomas Hariot had noted in 1588 that the Roanoke people had "an herbe which is sowed apart by it self & is call by the inhabitants *uppówoc*. . . . The Spaniardes generally call it Tobacco." The Roanoke colonists arrived just as tobacco was becoming more popular, so none of them seem to have noted what the 1607 colonists did: Virginia's local tobacco was not "Spanish." The species native to South America was *Nicotiana tabacum*, a plant with pink flowers and broad leaves. In much of North America, the native variety was *N. rustica*, a plant with yellow flowers and a higher nicotine content. Although tobacco was present in the Chesapeake, the colonists needed "Spanish tobacco" if they wanted to compete in European markets. The source of the tobacco they eventually grew has been typically traced to John Rolfe. He probably brought the seeds from Bermuda, where Spanish sailors who had stopped there in the past had probably left it.[48]

By the time the English colonized Jamestown in 1607, Europeans preferred Spanish tobacco. This is why Virginians decided to introduce *Nicotiana tabacum* from South America even though *Nicotiana rustica* grew all over eastern North America and was regularly smoked in religious and diplomatic contexts. Authors from the seventeenth century to the twenty-first have assumed that consumers favored *tabacum* because it was better. Just as rum has higher alcohol content than beer, *rustica* has higher nicotine content than *tabacum*. Both beer and *tabacum* are milder than their counterparts. But this alone does not explain the preference. Members of the Powhatan Confederacy, like Indigenous societies from Quebec to Mexico, liked *rustica* well enough. They perhaps even smoked it in greater quantities. George Percy, one of the colonists who traveled to Virginia in 1607, noted that the Powhatan pipes were much like their own, "but far bigger."[49]

Early European travelers to North America also readily smoked *rustica*. Thomas Hariot recalled that during the 1585 attempt to colonize Roanoke, "We ourselues during the time we were there vsed to suck it after their maner, as also since our returne, & haue found manie rare and wonderful experiments of the vertues thereof."[50] John Brereton, who penned a 1602 account of a voyage to New England, described the tobacco there as "very strong and pleasant, and much better than any I have tasted in England."[51]

Some of the Jamestown colonists were dedicated smokers. They arrived, in fact, with *N. tabacum* acquired from Indigenous cultivators on Dominica in tow.[52] A familiarity with *N. tabacum* induced William Strachey to finally report that Virginia tobacco "is not of the best kynd yt is but poore and weake and of a byting tast." All the same, scores of pipes left behind in Jamestown before 1614 suggest that colonists made do with *rustica*. The English who developed the first tobacco plantations in Virginia arrived with ideas about the plant from their wider experiences. Yet, because tobacco was a native crop, Powhatan practices also came to influence cultivation. The English altered the environment to suit their own purposes, but they did it under conditions that were at once Atlantic and local, bringing together experiences with Spanish America and the Powhatan.

The mere transplantation of nonnative tobacco was insufficient. Virginia colonists also needed assistance in learning to grow and cure it. Rolfe himself wrote in 1616 that Jamestown tobacco indeed showed great promise but needed "a little more trial, and experience in the curing thereof," after which it would "compare with the best in the *West Indies*."[53] In their quest to grow tobacco better, Virginians consciously modeled themselves after exemplary cultivators of all backgrounds from the Spanish Empire. Ralph Hamor defended Virginia's fledgling tobacco industry by claiming it was as good as any from "west-Indie Trinidado or Cracus [Caracas]."[54] Virginia Company records likewise refer to "the ffarming [*sic*] of the Spanish tobacco."[55] A 1620 treatise suggested that cultivators were still learning to imitate the Spanish: "there is some as good Tobacco brought from *Virginia* and the *Summer Islands*, as the first Tobaccos were that we had out of *Spaine*. And no doubt, but as they [the Spanish] discovering further into the Land, found better grounds for Tobacco: so will our people doe also as they goe further."[56] Virginians still had much to learn about their "Spanish tobacco."

John Rolfe named his farm and his tobacco "Varina" after a Venezuelan town, Barinas. Virginians named another strain "Orinoco" after the

Venezuelan River where the English carried on illicit trade. Such branding was novel, and Virginia cultivators were innovative in this regard. Yet the brands were imitative, too. Rather than staking out Virginia's product as distinctive, cultivators were claiming it was similar to Spanish tobacco. Its allure persisted long after Chesapeake tobacco dominated the market in London. In 1682 an account of Carolina stated, "*Tobacco* grows very well; and they have of an excellent sort, mistaken by some of our *English* Smoakers for *Spanish* Tobacco, and valued from 5 to 8*s*. the Pound; but finding a great deal of trouble in the Planting and Cure of it, and the great Quantities which *Virginia*, and other of His Majesties Plantations make, rendring it a Drug over all *Europe*; they do not much regard or encourage its Planting."[57] Even though the Chesapeake colonies were making enough tobacco to discourage Carolinians from doing so, the standard against which any tobacco was measured was still Spanish.

Contemporaries were aware that tobacco was a plant of local origin, and that in consuming and growing it the English were following both Indigenous and Spanish customs. Critics of tobacco argued that by adopting the habit, the English were imitating heathen savages. In *A Counterblaste to Tobacco* James I asked how far tobacco users might go in following Indigenous customs: "Shall we, I say, without blushing, abase our selves so farre, as to imitate these beastly *Indians*, slaves to the *Spaniards*, refuse to the world, and as yet aliens from the holy Covenant of God? Why doe we not as well imitate them in walking naked as they doe? in preferring glasses, feathers, and such toyes, to golde and precious stones, as they do? yea why do we not denie God and adore the Devill, as they doe?"[58] Although consumption was the graver mistake, cultivation was also targeted because colonists who devoted land and labor to tobacco were neglecting an opportunity to develop commodities that might be of more use to England.

Those who were knowledgeable about cultivation methods and favorable to tobacco argued just the opposite: English cultivators should adopt Indigenous practices and avoid Spanish innovations, which tainted the natural product. The author of *An Advice How to Plant Tobacco in England* spoke out against the illicit trade the English conducted off the coast of Venezuela, because it had helped keep the Spanish colony afloat. Worse still, the author warned, the Spanish tainted their tobacco to disguise its defects. Writing in 1615, the author also maligned tobacco from Virginia and Bermuda, where they had not learned how to properly prune the leaves and, he feared, "imitate the Spanish in juicing it."[59]

The English did indeed adopt Indigenous practices. Europeans preferred *N. tabacum*, but they differed in how they smoked it. In much of South America, tobacco was smoked in cigars, by wrapping dried tobacco leaves up in one large leaf. Cigars consequently became the preferred mode of consumption in Iberia, too. Pipes were the dominant means of smoking tobacco among the Indigenous societies of North America's East Coast. A 1573 text describes "the taking-in of the smoke of the Indian herbe called 'Tobaco' by an instrument formed like a little ladell."[60] When the first group of English colonists came to Roanoke, they adopted not cigars but pipes, after the method of the Roanokes. According to the botanist Carolus Clusius, when they returned to England they "brought with them similar pipes for taking tobacco smoke. Thereupon the use of tobacco spread even throughout the whole of England, especially among the courtiers with the result that they saw to the manufacture of many similar pipes for the inhalation of tobacco smoke."[61] Pipe smoking thus prevailed in England rather than cigar smoking. Hariot returned from Roanoke a dedicated pipe smoker, eventually dying of nose cancer. The 1608 arrival of Robert Cotton, "tobacco-pipe-maker," in Jamestown underscored English colonists' devotion to consuming tobacco this way.[62] Pipes continued to be so thoroughly dominant that an English traveler to Costa Rica in 1735 had to describe just what "seegars" were for his reader.[63]

Although the Powhatan were a different political and cultural group than the Roanoke, they shared much in terms of culture with their Eastern Algonquian neighbors to the south, including the use of pipes. As the colonizers lived longer among Indigenous peoples in Virginia, they learned even more about tobacco agriculture. Although the plant itself came from the Spanish, Virginians had to do more than merely plant it. Tobacco is a fickle plant, requiring careful attention. Aspects of its cultivation among the Powhatan conformed to English expectations about agriculture, which probably facilitated their education. In Virginia, as elsewhere, tobacco was probably cultivated in a separate plot rather than using intertillage—where multiple crops were grown on the same ground—which looked messy to Europeans.[64] Unlike other crops, which women mostly grew, men cultivated tobacco. This fact made tobacco agriculture more familiar to the English and likely also caused them to pay more attention to it than other crops. While the English had more contact with Indigenous women than has been previously recognized, seventeenth-century chroniclers typically failed to document much about their lives. As Helen C. Rountree notes, "English observers learned little about Powhatan uses for wild plants," a body of knowledge maintained by women.[65] A final reason that made tobacco a more prominent crop to the English in Virginia was that the Powhatan integrated tobacco use into their political ceremonies. Tobacco was only used by those eligible to participate in these rituals: married men. Since the English encountered the Powhatan as a foreign nation, they, too, were regularly welcomed with tobacco.

Tobacco had to be cured to ship across the Atlantic because fresh leaves would rot. For many medicinal uses, fresh leaves were required, but smoking also requires dried leaves. Not all Indigenous groups cured tobacco, but the Powhatan did. Strachey recorded that they "dry the leaves . . . over the fire and sometimes in the sun, and crumble it into powder—stalks, leaves, and all." The English had to adopt further innovations to the process to match European expectations, but living among a group who already practiced rudimentary curing helped. Works on tobacco before 1615 that discuss cultivation did not explain how it might be cured. The English who arrived in Virginia likely needed instruction in this task.[66]

Colonists also adopted other Indigenous cultivation techniques. The Powhatan cleared new land by girding trees to kill them and then burning the underbrush. They then grew crops among the stumps and dead trees. The English adopted this method to save themselves the time and intense labor of cutting down trees and clearing the stumps. The colonists also initially planted their tobacco in hills as the Powhatan did.

Ironically, the Virginians' adoption of an Indigenous crop, which they likely grew with some Powhatan tutelage, spelled disaster for the two groups' relationship. Because tobacco exhausts the soil, Virginia's planters always needed to acquire more land. The need to keep pushing into the interior meant that colonists took up far more land than they might otherwise need. Poor relations between the Powhatan and the English were perhaps inevitable, but expanded tobacco cultivation exacerbated existing conflict. The English visually recorded the violent intrusion into Indigenous space quite early. A 1636 map of Virginia shows Indigenous men shooting the English hogs that roamed freely, destroying their own crops.[67]

The adoption of tobacco in Virginia was always contested. Critics of tobacco from James I onward urged Virginians to produce something more useful. Tobacco monoculture regularly led to economic crises in Virginia, so these criticisms seem rather apt. These critics, however, continued to insist that Virginians should grow things that the environment could not produce, such as mulberries for silkworms and grapes for wine. In doing so, they continued the tradition begun in the decades before the English had permanent colonies, when their American endeavors were based largely on conjecture and fantasy.

Early English colonial promoters and investors saw in Virginia a chance to replicate at least some of the successes of the Spanish Empire. In their efforts to emulate the Spanish, they resorted to a vision of Virginia that was based more on fantasy than fact. Virginia did not have mines, or tribute-extracting empires, or millions of potential laborers. One could not grow the banana plant of Puerto Rico or the brazilwood of Brazil, nor introduce sugar that took so readily to the tropical soils of Cuba or Hispaniola. For all of these projects, the environment of Virginia was unsuitable. But there was one plant native to the southern Americas and introduced from the Spanish Empire that would flourish. Tobacco remade the Virginia landscape, ensured the stability of the English colony, and set the stage for conflict with the Indigenous peoples. Ultimately, the English appropriated this maligned weed, not golden cities or tropical riches, from South America's Indigenous peoples and Spanish colonists.

NOTES

1. George Gardyner, *A Description of the New World* (London, 1651), 99.

2. For works that discuss both the convergences and divergences between Spanish and English ideas of empire, see Anthony Pagden, *Lords of All the Worlds: Ideologies of Empire in Spain, Britain and France, c. 1500–c. 1800* (New Haven, Conn.: Yale University Press, 1995); Patricia Seed, *Ceremonies of Possession in Europe's Conquest of the New World, 1492–1640* (New York: Cambridge University Press, 1995); Jorge Cañizares-Esguerra, *Puritan Conquistadors: Iberianizing the Atlantic, 1550–1700* (Stanford, Calif.: Stanford University Press, 2006).

3. The classic comparative work of the Spanish and English is J. H. Elliott, *Empires of the Atlantic World: Britain and Spain in America, 1492–1830* (New Haven, Conn.: Yale University Press, 2006). See also the various essays in Jack P. Greene and Philip D. Morgan, eds., *Atlantic History: A Critical Appraisal* (New York: Oxford University Press, 2009), and Nicholas Canny and Philip Morgan, eds., *The Oxford Handbook of the Atlantic World* (New York: Oxford University Press, 2011).

4. Eliga H. Gould, "Entangled Histories, Entangled Worlds: The English-Speaking Atlantic as a Spanish Periphery," *American Historical Review* 112, no. 3 (2007): 764–86; Christopher Heaney, "A Peru of Their Own: English Grave-Opening and Indian Sovereignty in Early America," *William and Mary Quarterly* 73, no. 4 (2016): 609–46; Jorge Cañizares-Esguerra, ed., *Entangled Empires: The Anglo-Iberian Atlantic, 1500–1830* (Philadelphia: University of Pennsylvania Press, 2018).

5. For a take on entanglement that is focused more on Native contributions, see Ralph Bauer and Marcy Norton, "Introduction: Entangled Trajectories: Indigenous and European Histories," *Colonial Latin American Review* 26, no. 1 (2017): 1–17, along with the essays that follow.

6. John T. Crowley, "Sugar Machines: Picturing Industrialized Slavery," *American Historical Review* 121, no. 2 (2016): 403–36. See also J. H. Galloway, "Tradition and Innovation in the American Sugar Industry, c. 1500–1800: An Explanation," *Annals of the Association of American Geographers* 75, no. 3 (September 1985): 334–51; J. H. Galloway, *The Sugar Cane Industry: A Historical Geography from Its Origins to 1914* (New York: Cambridge University Press, 1989), esp. chaps. 4–7.

7. B. W. Higman, "The Sugar Revolution," *Economic History Review*, n.s., 53, no. 2 (May 2000): 213–36; Stuart B. Schwartz, ed., *Tropical Babylons: Sugar and the Making of the Atlantic World, 1450–1680* (Chapel Hill: University of North Carolina Press, 2003).

8. Judith A. Carney, *Black Rice: The Origins of Rice Cultivation in the Americas* (Cambridge, Mass.: Harvard University Press, 2002); Peter H. Wood, *Black Majority: Negroes in*

Colonial South Carolina from 1670 through the Stono Rebellion (New York: W. W. Norton, 1974); Daniel C. Littlefield, *Rice and Slaves: Ethnicity and the Slave Trade in Colonial South Carolina* (Baton Rouge: Louisiana State University Press, 1981); S. Max Edelson, *Plantation Enterprise in Colonial South Carolina* (Cambridge, Mass.: Harvard University Press, 2006).

9. Shepard Krech III, *The Ecological Indian: Myth and History* (New York: W. W. Norton, 1999); Michael E. Harkin and David Rich Lewis, eds., *Native Americans and the Environment: Perspectives on the Ecological Indian* (Lincoln: University of Nebraska Press, 2007). Also see Hayley Negrin, "Native Women Work the Ground: Enslavement and Civility in the Early American Southeast," in this volume.

10. Alfred W. Crosby, *The Columbian Exchange: Biological and Cultural Consequences of 1492*, 30th anniv. ed. (Westport, Conn.: Praeger, 2003).

11. For an example of Indigenous knowledge and labor in an early English colonial context, see D. Andrew Johnson, "Enslaved Native Americans and the Making of South Carolina, 1659–1739" (PhD diss., Rice University, 2018), chap. 6.

12. *The Decades of the newe worlde or west India . . . Wrytten in the Latine tounge by Peter Martyr . . . and translated into Englysshe by Richard Eden* (London, 1555).

13. Peter Martyr d'Anghiera, *De orbe novo* (Alcalá de Henares, 1530).

14. John Parker, *Books to Build an Empire: A Bibliographical History of English Overseas Interests to 1620* (Amsterdam: N. Israel, 1965), 44–46.

15. Eden's translation, done during the reign of Mary, also elides differences between England and Spain. See Andrew Hadfield, "Peter Martyr, Richard Eden, and the New World: Reading, Experience, and Translation," *Connotations* 5, no. 1 (1995–96): 1–22; Barbara Fuchs, "Religion and National Distinction in the Early Modern Atlantic," in *Empires of God: Religious Encounters in the Early Modern Atlantic*, ed. Linda Gregerson and Susan Juster (Philadelphia: University of Pennsylvania Press, 2011), esp. 59–62.

16. Nicolás Monardes, *Joyfull newes out of the new founde worlde*, trans. John Frampton (London, 1577). Frampton's edition was reprinted twice in 1577, and once each in 1580 and 1596. Parker, *Books to Build an Empire*, 76.

17. Bartolomé de Las Casas, *The Spanish colonie, or Briefe chronicle of the acts and gestes of the Spaniards in the West Indies, called the newe World* (London, 1583).

18. Richard Hakluyt, ed., *The principall navigations, voiages and discoveries of the English nation, made by sea or over land* (London, 1589).

19. *The Writings and Correspondence of the Two Richard Hakluyts*, ed. E. G. R. Taylor, Works Issued by the Hakluyt Society, no. 76 (London, 1935; reprint, Nendeln/Liechtenstein: Kraus, 1967), 325. The quote is from "Discourse of Western Planting." Taylor (325n1) suggests that Hakluyt probably had in mind Gómara, Zarate, and Richard Willes's 1577 *History of Travayle*, which was an update of Eden that included the later *Decades* of Peter Martyr d'Anghiera.

20. Raids on Spanish colonies focused on the circum-Caribbean, places that were accessible and sometimes poorly defended.

21. James Lockhart and Stuart B. Schwartz, *Early Latin America: A History of Colonial Spanish America and Brazil* (Cambridge: Cambridge University Press, 1983), 75.

22. Robin Blackburn, *The Making of New World Slavery: From the Baroque to the Modern, 1492–1800* (London: Verso, 1997), 148; Murdo J. McLeod, *Spanish Central America: A Socioeconomic History* (Berkeley: University of California Press, 1973).

23. David Watts, "Early Hispanic New World Agriculture, 1492–1509," in *Caribbean Slavery in the Atlantic World: A Student Reader*, ed. Verene Shepherd and Hilary McD.

Beckles (Princeton, N.J.: Marcus Wiener, 2000), 136–52; Paula De Vos, "The Science of Spices: Empiricism and Economic Botany in the Early Spanish Empire," *Journal of World History* 17, no. 4 (2006): 399–427; Antonio Gutiérrez Escudero, "Hispaniola's Turn to Tobacco: Products from Santo Domingo in Atlantic Commerce," in *Global Goods and the Spanish Empire, 1492–1824: Circulation, Resistance and Diversity*, ed. Bethany Aram and Bartolomé Yun-Castillo (New York: Palgrave Macmillan, 2014), 216–29.

24. David Beers Quinn, ed., *The Roanoke Voyages, 1584–1590*, 2 vols., Works Issued by the Hakluyt Society, no. 104 (Cambridge: Cambridge University Press, 1952), 1:93.

25. William M. Kelso, Nicholas M. Luccketti, and Beverly A. Straube, *Jamestown Rediscovery V* (Richmond: Association for the Preservation of Virginia Antiquities, 1999), 36–42.

26. William P. Cumming, *The Southeast in Early Maps*, 3rd ed., revised and enlarged by Louis De Vorsey Jr. (Chapel Hill: University of North Carolina Press, 1998), esp. 130–31.

27. Quinn, *Roanoke Voyages*, 1:187, 219, 2:742. The artist was John White, who produced drawings of bananas.

28. Thomas Hariot, *A Briefe and True Report of the New Found Land of Virginia* (London, 1588), 15.

29. For early modern Europeans, climate was latitude. See Sean Morey Smith, "Differentiating Hot Climates in the Anglo-American Colonial Experience," in this volume. See also Karen Kupperman, "The Puzzle of the American Climate in the Early Colonial Period," *American Historical Review* 87, no. 5 (December 1982): 1262–89; Sam White, "Unpuzzling American Climate: New World Experience and the Foundations of a New Science," *Isis* 106 (2015): 544–66; Anya Zilberstein, *A Temperate Empire: Making Climate Change in Early America* (New York: Oxford University Press, 2016).

30. Taylor, *Writings and Correspondence*, 321, 336.

31. Irene Wright, ed., *Further English Voyages to Spanish America, 1583–1594*, Works Issued by the Hakluyt Society, no. 99 (London, 1951), 173, 185.

32. The fate of the hundreds of African and Indigenous passengers is a mystery. For speculation on their possible fates, see David Beers Quinn, ed. *The Roanoke Voyages, 1584–1590: Documents to Illustrate the English Voyages to North America Under the Patent Granted to Walter Raleigh in 1584*, Hakluyt Society Second Series No. 54 (London, 1955), 1:254–55.

33. Ibid., 2:520–21. This comes from the account of John White, who was at odds with the pilot, Simon Fernandes. See 2:517n3.

34. Marcy Norton cautions that, with respect to trade, the connection between tobacco as medicine and tobacco as recreational drug is tenuous. Although tobacco was used medicinally before it was smoked, it was applied topically using fresh tobacco grown locally (i.e., in Europe). Medicinal tobacco was not acquired through transatlantic trade. See Marcy Norton, *Sacred Gifts, Profane Pleasures: A History of Tobacco and Chocolate in the Atlantic World* (Ithaca, N.Y.: Cornell University Press, 2008), 142–44.

35. Paul Hentzner, *Travels in England during the Reign of Queen Elizabeth* (London: Cassell, 1901), 42.

36. Michiel Baud, "A Colonial Counter Economy: Tobacco Production on Española, 1500–1870," *Nieuwe West-Indische Gids/New West India Guide* 65, nos. 1/2 (1991): 31.

37. British Library Add. MSS 36319, f. 149, "Pedro Suarez Coronel to Philip III," December 18, 1607.

38. *British Guiana Boundary Arbitration with the United State of Venezuela: Appendix to the Counter Case on behalf of the government of Her Britannic Majesty* (London, 1898), no. 2, "Don Juan de Borja, Governor of Santa Fé, to the King of Spain," Santa Fé, June 20, 1608.

The Santa Fé referred to here is actually Bogotá, the official name of which is Santa Fé de Bogotá.

39. "Sir Thomas Roe to Salisbury," Port d'Espaigne, Trinidad, February 28, 1611, National Archives, United Kingdom, C.O. 1/1, no. 25.

40. Walter Ralegh, *The Discoverie of the Large, Rich, and Bewtiful Empyre of Guiana*, transcribed, annotated, and introduced by Neil L. Whitehead (Norman: University of Oklahoma Press, 1997).

41. Walter Ralegh, *Sir Walter Ralegh's Discoverie of Guiana*, ed. Joyce Lorimer, Works Issued for the Hakluyt Society, 3rd ser., no. 15 (London: Ashgate, 2005), 206. This edition is of a manuscript version of *The Discoverie*, held at Lambeth Palace Library, rather than the published version.

42. "Sir Thomas Roe to Salisbury."

43. Robert Harcourt, *A Voyage to Guiana*, ed. C. A. Harris, Works Issued for the Hakluyt Society, no. 60 (London, 1927), 105.

44. Samuel Purchas, ed., "Captaine Charles Leighs Letter to Sir Olave Leigh his brother," in *Purchas His Pilgrims* (London: William Stensby, 1625), 16:317.

45. *British Guiana Boundary Arbitration*, appendix I, no. 14, p. 35.

46. Joyce Lorimer, ed., *English and Irish Settlement on the River Amazon, 1550–1646*, Works Issued by the Hakluyt Society, no. 171 (London, 1989), 157, 187.

47. Philip D. Morgan, "Virginia's Other Prototype," in *The Atlantic World and Virginia, 1550–1624*, ed. Peter Mancall (Chapel Hill: Omohundro Institute of Early American History and Culture and University of North Carolina Press, 2007), 342–80.

48. Karen Ordahl Kupperman, *The Jamestown Project* (Cambridge, Mass.: Belknap Press of Harvard University Press, 2007), 279–80. Also see Keith D. Pluymers, "Environmental Knowledge, Expertise, and the Development of Slavery in Bermuda," in this volume. I am indebted to conversations I had with Dave Givens at Jamestown Rediscovery for his insights into tobacco on Bermuda.

49. Edward Wright Haile, ed., *Jamestown Narratives: Eyewitness Accounts of the Virginia Colony, 1607–1617* (Camplain, Va.: Roundhouse, 1998), 92.

50. Hariot, *Briefe and True Report*.

51. John Brereton, *A briefe and true relation of the discoverie of the north part of Virginia* (London, 1602), 6.

52. Haile, *Jamestown Narratives*, 86.

53. John Rolfe, *A true relation of the State of Virginia lefte by Sir Thomas Dale, knight, in May last 1616* (New Haven, Conn.: Yale University Press, 1951), 35–36.

54. Ralph Hamor, *A True Discourse of the Present State of Virginia* (London, 1615).

55. Susan Myra Kingsbury, ed., *The Records of the Virginia Company of London* (Washington, D.C.: Government Printing Office, 1905), 2:420.

56. Edward Bennett, *A Treatise devided into three parts, touching the inconveniences, that the Importation of Tobacco out of Spaine, hath brought into this Land* (London, 1620).

57. T. A., *Carolina, or, A description of the present state of that country and the natural excellencies thereof* (London, 1682), 15–16.

58. James I, *A Counterblaste to Tobacco* (London, 1604).

59. C. T., *An Advice How to Plant Tobacco in England* (London, 1615).

60. William Harrison, "Great Chronologie," 1593, as quoted in Adrian Oswald, *Clay Pipes for the Archaeologist* (Oxford: British Archaeological Reports, 1975), 3. This entry was recorded for the year 1573.

61. Carolus Clusius, *Exoticorum Libri Decem*, quoted in Oswald, *Clay Pipes*, 4.

62. John Smith, *Travels and Works of Captain John Smith, President of Virginia and Admiral of New England, 1580–1631*, 3 vols., ed. Philip Barbour (Chapel Hill: University of North Carolina Press, 1986), 1:223, 2:162. Cotton was thus among the settlement's first craftsmen.

63. John Cockburn, *A journey over land from the Gulf of Honduras to the great South-Sea* (London, 1735).

64. Helen C. Rountree, *The Powhatan Indians of Virginia: Their Traditional Culture* (Norman: University of Oklahoma Press, 1989), 47.

65. Ibid., 44. Although women were the primary plant foragers, men collected medicinal plants.

66. The colonists eventually would adopt air-curing, but they would have done well to continue fire-curing as the Powhatan did, since it preserves the leaf better. Fire-curing made a comeback in the nineteenth century.

67. For more on how hogs offer particular insight into English-Native relations in North America, see Virginia DeJohn Anderson, "King Philip's Herds: Indians, Colonists, and the Problem of Livestock in Early New England," *William and Mary Quarterly* 51, no. 4 (October 1994): 601–24.

Environmental Knowledge, Expertise, and the Development of Slavery in Bermuda

KEITH PLUYMERS

In 1616, according to Nathaniel Butler, Bermuda's governor from 1619 to 1622, the ship *Edwin* landed with "plantains, Sugar-Canes, Figs, Pines, and the like, all of which were presently replanted and are since increased into great numbers especially the plantains and figs, very infinitely: she brought with her also one Indian and a Negro (the first these Islands ever had)."[1] Amid this list of imported plants lies the first recorded instance of a person of African descent brought to labor in an English colony.

Slavery has been one of the most important and well-studied topics in North American and Atlantic history. Despite Bermuda's place at the beginning of the history of forced African migration and labor in the English Atlantic, histories of Atlantic slavery tend to treat it as an outlier. The two most prominent historians of early modern Bermuda emphasize the atypical character of slavery there—seeing legal ambiguities, the relatively late development of fixed ideas of race, and unique conditions of labor that resulted from the islands' predominantly maritime economy.[2] Nonetheless, the comparatively well-documented history of people of African descent in Bermuda makes it a critical case for understanding unfree labor in the early English Atlantic. Historian Abigail L. Swingen has argued that ideas about labor, population, and political economy—"visions of empire"—led British imperial officials and colonists to prefer enslaved African laborers in the colonies. In historian John C. Coombs's revised chronology of Virginia slavery, competing ideas about empire played a critical role in the significant differences between the black populations of Bermuda and Virginia. For Coombs, debates on the character of empire were a contest between the Earl of Warwick's desire for a religiously motivated privateering campaign against Spain and Edwin Sandys's aversion to such efforts.[3] But tolerance for privateering and eschatological conflicts with Catholic Spain were not the only factors that brought people of African descent to Bermuda. Instead, conflicting visions for the islands' economy and environment shaped English decisions to bring people of African descent to Bermuda and the policies that governed the lives of Afro-Bermudians after they arrived.

Early colonists and adventurers crafted their visions for labor and economic activity in response to their understandings of Bermuda's environment. They believed that the archipelago's environment closely resembled that of Spain's American colonies, particularly those of the Spanish Caribbean. Colonists and adventurers in England sought to import plants and people that would enable them to achieve the riches of the Spanish world. Some colonists attempted agricultural experiments with these imported plant species, but several early Bermudian investors and governors believed that English colonists lacked the skills and knowledge to do so. Thus, they looked for experts, some of whom were people of African descent with experience in the Spanish Empire. Yet within the next five years, the rise of a new governor—Nathaniel Butler—occasioned conflict over the productive capacity of Bermuda's land and waters. This conflict would result in the call for dramatic shifts in the treatment and status of people of African descent. Chronicling these disputes allows us to see how political ecology—the differing visions for the exploitation and regulation of the physical environment—led to shifts in ideas about African and Afro-Bermudian labor.

Colonists, governors, and adventurers disagreed about the validity of expertise and the potential for the commercial exploitation of the islands' environment. Historian Eric Ash has shown that during the reign of Elizabeth I, experts took on an increasingly important role for governors and investors, but that expertise was always fraught and subject to negotiation. Backers of different projects and proposals each marshaled their own experts. Investors consistently questioned the experts they had retained and sought to assert managerial dominance despite their profound ignorance about the technical and practical processes involved in the endeavors they funded.[4] Similar conflicts about expertise, ignorance, and the sources of knowledge about Bermuda's environment shaped discussions about the roles of people of African descent in the colony.

Although Bermuda is a small archipelago at the margins of many Atlantic histories, the relationship among English political ecology, conceptions of African and Afro-Caribbean expertise, and the development of slavery in Bermuda suggests broader connections between environmental ideas and coerced labor in the English Atlantic. Judith Carney, Peter H. Wood, and Daniel C. Littlefield have made a compelling case that West African environmental knowledge and skill were the foundation for South Carolina rice cultivation and that existing evidence suggests that English colonists sought out African expertise to grow the grain and did so increasingly over time.[5] Bermuda's history demonstrates that attempts to exploit the skills and expertise of Africans and Atlantic Creoles was not a unique characteristic of rice cultivation, nor solely an eighteenth-century phenomenon. Instead, desire for

African agricultural expertise defined English plans to exploit African labor from the outset.[6]

ↀ

Bermuda lies roughly 650 miles off the coast of present-day North Carolina. It consists of a series of discrete islands formed slowly as wind-blown sediments settled into layers of limestone atop a submerged volcano. As open-ocean islands in the midst of the Gulf Stream, Bermuda occupies a unique ecological niche. Ocean currents, seabirds, and winds bathed the islands in a wide range of species, only some of which successfully gained a foothold. Among those that became established were corals, mangroves, seagrasses, and species associated with their ecosystems that are characteristic of the Caribbean. The presence of these characteristic plants and animals has led some modern scientists to classify it as part of a "Greater Caribbean" ecoregion. Yet Bermuda lies at the northern edge of this region, and the communities of terrestrial and marine species reflect the islands' isolation and climate. As a result, the World Wildlife Fund classifies Bermuda as a distinctive ecoregion because the islands' "flora and fauna [are] quite distinctive from any continental area or from Neotropical islands to the south."[7] Attempts to reconcile similarities and differences between Bermuda and Caribbean islands were at the heart of English thinking about the colony in its earliest years.

Descriptions of Bermuda's environment and climate were crucial to early colonial plans. Accounts of climate, flora, and fauna in early modern natural histories and promotional tracts reflected both beliefs about the relationship between latitude and climate and the political and economic visions of the authors.[8] The first English colonists to land in Bermuda arrived in a fortuitous accident. In 1609 their ship, the *Sea Venture*, was caught in a violent storm and managed to run aground in Bermuda, enabling the crew to survive. Nonetheless, the first crew reports from the islands to circulate in England described the landscape, seascape, and climate in terms that conveyed the potential profitability and healthfulness.

William Strachey, whose account of the *Sea Venture*'s fortuitous survival circulated in London, sought to convey Bermuda's value through claims that the islands shared characteristics with Spain's Caribbean and American colonies. Strachey drew on Spanish accounts and natural histories in his account of Bermuda's environment. He quoted at length from Gonzalo Fernández de Oviedo's *Sumario de historia natural o De la natural Historia de las Indias* (1526), which he cited as "*The Summary or Abridgment of His General History of the West Indies*, written to the Emperor Charles the Fifth." Likewise, he referenced the Italian theologian and Spanish court scholar Peter Martyr d'Anghiera's

Decades of the New World, which had been translated into English in multiple editions during the 1560s.[9]

Beyond these explicit citations, general references to Spanish American and Caribbean colonies occurred repeatedly in Strachey's account. Strachey described the Bermuda palmetto (*Sabal bermudana*) through a comparison to palms found in the Spanish Caribbean. He complained that the Bermudian trees were "not the right Indian palms such as in San Juan, Puerto Rico are called cocos and are there full of small fruits like almonds (of the bigness of the grains in pomegranates), nor of those kind of palms which bear dates, but a kind of simerons or wild palms, in growth, fashion, leaves, and branches resembling those true palms." He compared his experience eating the flesh of sea turtles to "the manatee at Santo Domingo, which made the Spanish friars (at their first arrival) make some scruple to eat them on a Friday, because in color and taste the flesh is like to morsels of veal." Most strikingly for English readers hoping for reports of valuable commodities, he reported that Bermuda was home to pearl fisheries "which some say, and I believe well, is as good there as in any of their other Indian islands, and whereof we had some trial."[10] Strachey's comparisons to Puerto Rico and Santo Domingo suggested that even if Bermuda was not quite identical to Spain's Caribbean colonies, it was nonetheless comparable.

At times, Strachey stretched his source material to connect Bermuda to the Spanish colonies. In additional description of Bermuda's palmettos, he referenced the rich red dyestuffs of colonial Mexico obtained from cochineal. Among the leaves of Bermuda's palmettos, Strachey claimed, "We oftentimes found growing to these leaves many silkworms involved therein, like those small worms which Acosta writeth of, which grew in the leaves of the tuna tree, of which, being dried, the Indians make their cochineal, so precious and merchantable." Strachey's description borrowed from José de Acosta, the sixteenth-century Spanish Jesuit who had published about the New World. Acosta had described cochineal, a small, scaled insect, as worms and recorded that they preyed on the prickly pear cactus.[11] Strachey's odd assemblage of palmettos, silkworms, and cochineal departed from the conventions of early English travel writing and from his Spanish source material. Early modern English writers valued silk and did not generally connect it to cochineal or to palm trees. Thomas Hariot's *Briefe and True Report* (1590) claimed that English colonists needed to plant "mulberry trees and others fit for [silkworms] in commodious places." Acosta likewise connected silkworms to mulberries, writing that colonial sericulture had only emerged after the trees were brought from Spain. Silvester Jourdain's 1610 account of Bermuda described the abundance of silkworms on the mulberries he claimed existed in "great plenty" on the islands.[12]

Strachey, in his quest to convey Bermuda's value, blurred the lines between palms, mulberries, and cacti and between silkworms and cochineal.

Strachey's consistent references to Spanish authors and flora and fauna from the Spanish Caribbean, including his rhetorical excesses, were critical to his argument for English permanent colonization. Fears of devils and harsh oceanic conditions, he claimed, had scared Spanish colonists away from the islands. This was fortuitous for the English because the islands were "as habitable and commodious as most countries of the same climate and situation." Bermuda's northerly latitude might have given some contemporaries pause, but Strachey argued that the islands shared a climate with profitable Spanish possessions through regular references to Spanish authors and his assurance that "the commodities of the other western islands would prosper there, as vines, lemons, oranges, and sugarcanes." Superstition may have deterred earlier Spanish colonization, but the time for a permanent English colony was limited. "Well may the Spaniards and these Biscayan pilots, with all their traders into the Indies, pass by these islands, as afraid (either bound out or homewards) of their very meridian," he hoped. For if they landed and found it unoccupied, they would quickly assimilate the familiar and valuable islands into their Atlantic empire.[13]

Strachey explicitly framed his account for Bermuda around Spanish natural histories and his assumptions about Spanish political ambitions. Strachey's shipmate, Silvester Jourdain, likewise appeared to draw on Spanish sources. Jourdain's pamphlet *A Discovery of the Bermudas* (1610) described the wreck of the *Sea Venture* and the actions of the crew but also sought to convey Bermuda's rich potential. Jourdain described the islands as "never inhabited by any Christian or heathen people but ever esteemed and reputed a most prodigious and enchanted place," but without any reference to the source for these purportedly long-standing opinions. His description of Bermuda's natural resources largely echoed Strachey but without any explicit reference to Spanish sources. Jourdain's account presented a conventional association between silkworms and mulberries rather than Strachey's muddled description that included palmettos, prickly pears, and cochineal. Jourdain also avoided any speculation on the islands' ability to support imported plants or animals, focusing instead on the wealth of edible fish, birds, and turtles, and a list of commodities already present.[14]

The Virginia Company's *True Declaration of the Estate of the Colonie in Virginia* (1610) appeared to discount Spanish sources of information. The pamphlet contained a single reference to Acosta in its brief description of Bermuda. According to the Company, Acosta had claimed that "there was not one hoof" in the islands of the Caribbean; therefore, "it increaseth the wonder, how our people in the *Bermudos* found such an abundance of hogs." The Company went on to describe *Sea Venture*'s miraculous landing and the presence of sufficient hogs, birds, and fish to sustain the crew and enough trees to build new vessels as examples of divine favor analogous to biblical blessings dispensed to the Israelites during their decades of wandering. This passage treated Bermuda as a place similar to Caribbean islands but simultaneously hinted that Spanish accounts of their nature should be read skeptically since English colonists benefited from "the direct line of God's providence."[15]

Claims about Bermuda's environment in promotional literature shaped instructions for early colonists. The 1612 commission issued to Bermuda's first governor, Richard Moore, reflected this optimistic assessment of the islands' environment. It contained instructions for collecting immediately profitable commodities, particularly ambergris—a waxy discharge from sperm whales used as a stabilizer in perfumes and in medicines. It also called for colonists to ship back "commodities that are to be raised there by the Industry of your Company, either by planting vines, Sugar Canes, or any such like." A report later printed as an addendum to Jourdain's narrative buttressed this optimism, arguing that Bermuda's soil was "the richest ground to bear forth fruit (whatsoever one shall lay into it)."[16] The first orders for colonists and reports on the islands cast them as an environment immune to limits of climate or soil fertility. Only sufficient labor was necessary to develop a range of valuable commodities. In subsequent years colonists struggled to produce these goods, but this assessment of Bermuda's marine and terrestrial environments persisted. As a result, colonial governors, Company leaders, and English investors looked to reform labor and find experts to unlock the islands' potential.

Early attempts to create pearl fisheries in Bermuda reveal issues of conflict over environmental knowledge, expertise, and labor. A 1612 letter from the Earl of Northampton to the king echoed Strachey's language about the failure of Spain to harvest a rich store of pearls. "From this Island of Devils," he gloated, "our men have sent some Amber [ambergris] and some seed pearls for an assay which the Devils of the Bermudas love not better to retain then the Angeles of Castile do to recover." The founding charters from both 1612 and 1615 set rules governing forthcoming profits from pearls.[17] In response to early accounts of the islands, adventurers in England anticipated rich returns.

Establishing pearl fisheries proved more difficult. The Company also sent along Richard Norwood, the islands' eventual surveyor, to set up the pearl fisheries, citing his experience diving elsewhere. In a 1639 journal recounting his 1613 arrival in Bermuda and his experiences on the islands until 1614, Norwood reported that Bermuda was unsuited to commercial pearl fisheries. Nearshore oyster beds yielded only valueless pearls. The enterprising Norwood planned to "make trial in very deep water . . . [using] some provision against the aforesaid pressure of the air." But he worried that because Bermudian pearls from the shallows were unmarketable, deepwater pearls would not justify the cost of the more difficult dives required to obtain them.[18]

Evaluating the quality of pearls required skill and judgment, qualities strained by distance and the necessity for trust in colonial contexts. Pearls, according to historian Molly A. Warsh, have "slippery material qualities" because their value depends on assessments of shape, color, and luster, rather than simply size or weight. In her study of Spanish colonial pearl fisheries, Warsh argues that these characteristics frustrated systems of regulation and assessment crafted around gold and silver.[19] Adventurers invested in Bermuda faced a difficult choice. They could trust Norwood's judgment and abandon one of their most heralded potential commodities, or they could persist, risking money, time, and labor in the hopes that other evaluators would find the pearls valuable.

The adventurers chose to persist. In 1614 Governor Moore claimed to agree with Norwood's initial assessment but urged him to try diving anyway. The effort apparently failed to yield results. Two years later, the Company issued orders outlining rules for managing oyster beds, prohibiting trawling and dredging lest the oysters "forsake the coast." Instead, "the best approved course is diving and drawing them up in baskets." The Company's instructions implicitly discounted the validity of Norwood's assessment of Bermuda's pearl fishery. Instead, they attributed the failure of the oyster beds to English incompetence and destructive harvesting practices. The next instruction reinforced the Company's implication that labor, not environmental conditions, was to blame for the state of the pearl fisheries. The Company warned Governor Daniel Tucker to "be very careful in your choice of honest men" in the pearl fisheries to avoid anyone who "may privilie do us wrong."[20]

When the Company's experts failed to provide the valuable pearls promised in early descriptions of the islands, they did not reassess the feasibility of pearl fisheries—they sought out new experts. In the same document in which the Company condemned colonists' purportedly careless practices, they endorsed a voyage to the Savage Islands, a set of small islands located off the coast of modern Venezuela, to trade for cattle, cassava, sugarcane, and "negroes to dive for pearls."[21] As historian Kevin Dawson has shown, swimming and diving were crucial skills enslaved Africans carried across the ocean that shaped recreation, labor, and the cultures and practices of slavery around the Atlantic world. Spanish colonists along Venezuela's Pearl Coast sought to exploit these skills alongside those of Native laborers, both enslaved and free, over the course of the sixteenth and seventeenth centuries. As Dawson notes, the English seaman Sir Richard Hawkins remarked on the skill of African divers in the sixteenth century.[22] In response to the failure of their own expertise, the

Bermuda adventurers sought out skilled laborers from the Spanish Caribbean whose skills were crucial in a successful pearl fishery. It was likely this search for experienced pearl divers that brought the unnamed "Indian and a Negro" mentioned in Butler's history.[23]

Bermudians quickly sought to exploit African and Afro-Caribbean expertise in agricultural as well as maritime endeavors. Butler noted that the *Edwin* carried plantains, sugarcane, pineapples, and figs along with the expert divers. He claimed that the plants "were presently replanted and are since increased into great numbers especially the plantains and figs, very infinitely."[24] Butler's claim suggested that the plants flourished without significant skill or effort, echoing the promise in earlier published accounts. But correspondence from colonists indicates that introducing these Caribbean plants to Bermuda was more difficult than Butler implied. Colonists sought outside expertise and, as was the case with pearls, looked, in part, to people of African descent to provide it.

The decision to seek this expertise from people enslaved in the Spanish Caribbean likely reflected both practical concerns with distance and a desire to exploit particular skills associated with peoples already enslaved in the Caribbean. As Warsh described, the Spanish pearl fisheries were "a jumble, with indiscriminate mixing of people and pearls." Spanish sources sometimes articulated preferences for people from particular regions in West Africa, but it was the mixing of Africans and Native peoples from the Caribbean and Brazil on the Pearl Coast that produced a distinctive set of practices and knowledge. The region and its divers were renowned in written and visual sources across the European continent. Similarly, people of African descent acquired diverse skills as rural laborers, something recognized by both Spanish and other European observers. People of African descent functioned as "a surrogate peasantry" in the Spanish Caribbean, responsible for raising animals and cultivating food crops specific to the region and imported from both Europe and Africa. In doing so, enslaved rural laborers developed diverse skills in the production of cash crops such as tobacco, sugar, and ginger as well as the production of food crops.[25]

In the 1610s governors and colonists experimented with diverse plants and animals to see what would thrive in Bermuda. Adventurers in London displayed a thirst for detailed knowledge about Bermuda's environment. Daniel Tucker, who served as governor from 1616 to 1619, tested numerous crops on his personal land and reported on his results to the Company. According to Tucker, vines, pineapples, plantains, and sugarcane all thrived in the islands. Cane had fared so well, he claimed, that he would have sufficient seed to supply other colonists. But, Tucker warned, sugarcane could only thrive with abundant water. The islands' limited supplies of water meant that adventurers who wished to grow sugar needed to acquire shares of land amply served by wells.

Despite Tucker's warning, Robert Rich, the agent for the Earl of Warwick and for Sir Nathaniel Rich, planted sugarcane alongside his plantains on a tract of land that Tucker had claimed was unsuitable. Rich wrote that the crops did "greatly fructify." Like Tucker, Rich experimented with diverse crops. In 1618 he asked for currant vines to be sent over from a Levant merchant in London, claiming that Bermuda's climate would suit this Middle Eastern fruit. In the same year, he asked Warwick to hire a ship to scour the West Indies for "endy [West Indian] plants, goats and salt, whereof we here stand in great need."[26]

In addition to conducting experiments on their own land, colonists sought out expert advice. The Somers Isles Company's 1616 commission listed the plants the Company sent to Bermuda along with instructions for their cultivation. The Company sent vines both whole and in cuttings. It included aniseeds, seeds for mulberry trees, "sweet fennel seeds, commine seeds, Marjoram, Basil and Onion seeds . . . orange seeds, lemon, and citron." The Company ordered colonists to use this stock of seeds to create a self-sustaining crop, sending some seeds and produce back to England each year while retaining enough store to sow the following year. They also sought to improve tobacco cultivation and trade by contracting with Mr. Tickner, "a skilfull planter & curer of tobacco," to teach the settlers his method. The Company contracted with a Mr. Wilmot to bring plants from other Caribbean islands for trial in Bermuda.[27] At the same time that Robert Rich sought out plants from the West Indies, he requested a vigneron and gardener from England to improve his vineyard and garden.[28]

Rich also sought expertise among Afro-Bermudians.[29] He moved one of his servants and an unnamed Afro-Bermudian man to two shares occupied by Goodman Wethersby. The lone description Rich used for these shares was "barrenness," and he suggested that English agricultural methods had failed to yield any produce. In response, Rich wrote, "I would have them well followed by the negres planting of west endy [West Indian] plants, wherein he hath good skill."[30] Rich's writings suggest he felt that people of African descent, likely those who had been born or enslaved in the Spanish Caribbean, could transform barren lands into productive shares through their skill in cultivating Caribbean plants.

Rich and Tucker attempted to introduce diverse plants on their holdings and sought skilled individuals from Europe and the Spanish Caribbean to help them do so. But other colonial residents in Bermuda offered a different perspective on the islands' economic potential. In *A letter, sent into England from the Summer Ilands* (1615), Lewes Hughes, Bermuda's minister, hinted at doubts about the pursuit of diverse agricultural products. "There is great hope," he wrote, that settlers might "live very comfortably here and grow rich if they will provide seeds of Indico, &c, and plants of currants, figges, raisons, mulberry-trees for the silk-worms, & vines." Hughes's list did not include sugarcane or the other plants grown in the West Indies. Moreover, he seemed to put little stock in the immediate realization of the commodities he did list: "For the present, Tobacco is the best commodity."[31]

Afro-Bermudians played a crucial role in early tobacco cultivation. In addition to seeking the services of an English expert in curing tobacco, Robert Rich also looked to Bermuda's increasingly large Afro-Bermudian population for skill with tobacco.[32] As was the case with pearl fishing and the "West Indian" plants, colonists sought Afro-Caribbean skills because tobacco had succeeded in Spain's Atlantic colonies. Rich noted in 1618 that tobacco cultivation involved the same experimental practices that he and Tucker had used for other plants. "This last summer," he wrote, "we have made trial of divers and sundry kinds of plants of the principal whereof, having had through [thorough] experience, we have reserved the seed, which generally of all the Islands is noted."[33] After experimenting with multiple varieties, Rich settled on tobacco, which he associated with the Caribbean.

Rich made it clear that Afro-Bermudians were heavily involved in these experiments. He complained that he would have shipped more tobacco back to England but "my neager in trial spoiled it." This alleged spoiling, however, did not shake Rich's faith in the expertise of all Afro-Bermudians. In the same letter, he asked Sir Nathaniel Rich to procure Francisco, a man owned by another colonist, whose "judgment in the curing of tobacco" made him more valuable to Rich than any other Afro-Bermudians. Rich must have gotten his wish fairly quickly. Francisco appeared on a list of people resident in Southampton Tribe from March 1618, one month after Rich sent his letter.[34]

Rich's search for a skilled tobacco curer reveals several aspects of early Bermudian views of agricultural skill and expertise among Afro-Bermudians. Both the plans to procure pearl divers from the Spanish Caribbean and Rich's attempts to marshal the agricultural skills of Afro-Bermudians suggest that some colonists associated particular expertise with African and Afro-Caribbean people. But Rich's letters indicate that he saw skill as an individual characteristic rather than a collective attribute. Rich used his shares and his relatives' land to engage in trials of different plants and different soils, and he looked to skilled individuals to engage in those exercises. These endeavors suggest that colonists and Company leaders believed Bermuda was capable of supporting plants and enterprises found in the Spanish Caribbean but that laborers with knowledge and expertise were crucial to realizing this vision.

In late 1619 new governor Nathaniel Butler arrived in the islands and began to question the forms of land use, agriculture, and sources of environmental knowledge of his predecessor. In his correspondence with Nathaniel Rich and Warwick, Butler bluntly dismissed all the commercial crops that settlers and adventurers had written about so enthusiastically in 1618. He characterized Daniel Tucker's enthusiastic plans for sugar as "vain and impossible ones and so known by himself, and therefore assuredly disguised in their ends." In a calmer missive from November, Butler wrote that sugarcane, even if profitable, would take up too much space. Bermudians had no land "to spare from our necessary food, the rather by reason that most of it consists of bread and loblolly, both which are made of corn." Vines, too, he claimed, "must necessarily take up too much room for us to rest in any ease." Only mulberry trees for silk production and olive trees should be grown. Trees "being planted for fences, will require no more ground than we allow the unprofitable Palmetto for the same end." According to Butler, anything that took up space that could be devoted to corn or tobacco was a waste. Butler disparaged searches for diverse crops and natural philosophical pursuits as the actions of corrupt Bermudian officials or naive English adventurers. "Thousands of your discursative Courts in England," he wrote to Warwick, will yield less "true understanding . . . [than] six months sight and experience here." English adventurers, he suggested, might play with transported plants, but the hard truth was, "there will be never found any true ground of hope of any commodity growing here any way half so beneficial as Tobacco."[35]

For Butler, so-called experts were often charlatans exploiting credulous investors seeking magical solutions rather than steady commodities. This attitude is captured in his account of an experiment in which Governor Tucker attempted to profit from Bermuda's endemic mangroves. According to Butler, who despised Tucker and opposed his vision for the agricultural life of the colony, Tucker had ordered "a trial to be made for the tanning of the raw hides with the bark of a mangrove tree and to that end framed divers cisterns of cedar and appointed one or two of the Colony people (who professed most for themselves and their skills, that way, to take that charge in hand)." The results were disastrous: "Not only the labor but many of the hides were utterly lost and spoiled to the extreme enraging of the Governor and the punishment of some of the boasting tanners."[36] Butler condemned Tucker as a schemer easily taken in by unscrupulous men brandishing questionable expertise and dedicated to impossible ploys to plant sugar. Any attempt to profit from mangroves, Butler suggested, was equally ill informed and foolish.[37]

Butler, despite his disregard for Tucker's agricultural experiments, saw some utility in Bermuda's native plants. He lamented that in 1614 colonists had cleared away the palmettos from Saint George's seeking food. Doing so led to "such a disabling of the place for Tobacco (which is as yet the staple commodity) as that not only to this day, but for many years to come, it must needs feel the weight of that stroke." Butler understood that palmettos were essential to agriculture in Bermuda because the islands were subjected to "huge, great winds and thereby frequent blasts." "For remedy to hope in fences," he warned Sir Nathaniel Rich, "is to lean on a broken reed, for the best fences, we find, will not sufficiently safe guard our Tobacco." But palmettos could serve as windbreaks. The issue, however, lay in the plant's profitability. In a 1620 letter to Nathaniel Rich, Butler made it clear, with his characteristic bluntness, that the purpose of the colony was profit and that profits required the transformation of the landscape. "Assure yourself," he cautioned, "that if you place your hopes of these Islands only or chiefly upon the expectation of in-bred commodities you will find yourselves deceived and abused."[38]

Butler's anxieties about deceit and abuse stemmed from issues he faced shortly after arriving in Bermuda. In January 1620 he wrote, "At the present, we labor under the want of bread." He argued that wasteful overconsumption, an influx of new, undersupplied colonists and fourteen people of African descent, and harvest failure due to destructive winds had left the colony in a precarious position. Under his predecessor, colonists took to "ravenous devouring in mighty bowls of Loblolly [corn porridge], and huge and monstrous puddings, everyone striving to have the biggest." In addition to this gluttony, he accused colonists of sheer negligence that cost two hundred thousand ears of corn "with the treading of it under feet at their doors and casting [it] to hogs." To prevent future dearth, Butler set out to reform the morals of Bermudian colonists and, more immediately, to cause "more acres, by thousand and a half, to be set with corn this year than (as they say) were evergreen to be, at one time in this [sic] Islands."[39]

Butler distrusted imported experts and saw agricultural experiments and "discursative courts" as pointless wastes of money and time. He repeatedly expressed anxieties about Bermuda's natural limits and the need to produce commodities in large enough quantities to offset the high transportation costs of transatlantic trade. For Butler, the primary issue facing the islands was labor, not expertise. Butler's views on economic and environmental limits in Bermuda shaped his attitudes toward Afro-Bermudians. In 1622 Butler wrote, "Slaves are the most proper and cheap instruments for this plantation that can be"—though, he added, only the governor could be trusted to handle them. "Another thing I find would be very useful in these parts," he added in the next line, "is the labor of Asses."[40] As Virginia Bernhard has noted, Butler's remark on "proper and cheap instruments" was "the first specific application of the term [slaves] to blacks."[41]

Bernhard argued that Butler may have used the word "slaves" in a "figurative sense," but even if the legal status of Afro-Bermudians remained ambiguous, Butler's remarks represented a departure from earlier attitudes toward African expertise.[42] Formerly, colonists sought people of African descent from the Spanish Caribbean for their special skills as pearl divers and cultivators of West Indian plants. Nathaniel Rich learned Francisco's name and valued his skill at curing tobacco. In contrast, Butler emphasized labor as muscle power or energy, a point reinforced by his call for draft animals immediately after his remarks on slaves.

Other colonists seem to have also become increasingly concerned with labor. In January 1620 Thomas Durham wrote Sir Nathaniel Rich with a frank assessment of his estates. John Day and John Williams, who occupied Rich shares in Southampton Tribe, "planted little Corn and potatoes, but never cared for raising any profit [or] planting tobacco more than for their own use." Cooke and Creswell, two servants, "made away" for want of victuals. The tenants on shares at Heron Bay included "Edward Athens [Athen] and Thomas Turner, politike fellows." Athen in particular drew Durham's ire as "a famous man and a great practitioner in phisicke and all not worthy a straw but flattering and dissimulation." Mr. Needham "intendeth to plant corn and potatoes upon [his shares at Brackish Pond, Devonshire] to raise no profit out of them planting tobacco." The Riches' most "painful [painstaking]" and "lusty" tenants had not yet reached their productive potential. But they could, Durham wrote, "raise great profit" if only they had a "boy" or two to labor in the fields. The only group Durham wrote had actually produced anything were Afro-Bermudians, who had harvested 1,350 pounds of tobacco.[43]

Durham emphasized labor in his assessment of the tenants. He had noted that Afro-Bermudians produced more tobacco than English colonists, but he made no mention of skill to explain the difference. Instead, he praised the most productive English tenants for their willingness to work hard. Marmaduke Dando was "a painfull man as breathes." Cooke and Creswell "being two lusty fellowes may raise much profitt as any in the land."[44] Tobacco production, according to Durham's assessment, depended on the character of the laborers and the supply of labor. Improving yields required increases in quantity of effort, not new techniques for cultivation.

In addition to his desire for more labor, Butler's call for slaves in Bermuda reflected his concerns with discipline and surveillance. Butler's government and those that followed his departure in 1622 passed numerous measures to impose discipline on laborers, servants, and other poor Bermudians. These measures included new restrictions on Afro-Bermudians. Bernhard has shown that Francisco and many of the first Afro-Bermudians lived independently with their families near other white tenants free from significant surveillance, but this began to change in 1621 as the Company replaced bailiffs with "overseers."

Fearing that masters and landowners failed to monitor their tenants and servants, Butler attempted to create government officers who would conduct surveys and maintain records for how much each person planted and haul anyone suspected of sloth or pilfering before the assizes. In 1623 Bermuda's General Assembly passed a law specifically cracking down on Afro-Bermudians that prohibited them from carrying weapons, keeping certain animals, and moving about without permission at night.[45]

This concern for disciplining laborers, curtailing their free movement, and increasing the control of the governor and assembly also shaped policies to regulate Bermuda's environment. In 1620 the Assembly sought to protect sea turtles against the depredations of hungry Bermudians. "In their continual goings out to sea for fish," the assembly complained, settlers "do upon all occasions, and at all times as they can meet with them, snatch & catch up indifferently all kinds of Tortoises both young & old, little and great and so kill, carry away and devour them." This indifferent harvesting risked "scaring off them from of our shores and the danger of an utter destroying and loss of them."[46] The assembly's act to preserve sea turtles came as part of a broader set of actions to increase and regulate corn production and control laborers. Acts set out regulations for the movement and behavior of servants and enslaved people, set planting requirements for corn, required turkeys and other fowl to be kept inside at harvest time, and called for stronger enclosures. The act to preserve sea turtles was explicitly written to protect pregnant females and young turtles to attempt to ensure that the animals would not disappear.[47] It also, however, allowed the governor and the assembly to exert greater control over a potential food source. Limiting access to sea turtles had the potential to also force Bermudians to labor in cornfields for their food instead of simply turning to the sea.

Butler acknowledged that attempts to regulate colonists' animals were controversial. In a 1620 postscript, he informed Sir Nathaniel Rich that he had paused plans to dramatically reduce the number of turkeys around the town of Saint George's by culling them or shipping them to "islands uninhabited." Butler worried that he "might be censured for it in your Courts at home as if I had committed some waste that way." Yet he immediately followed this complaint with another postscript asking for partridges and pheasants. "These are excellent Islands for them," he wrote, "and besides they will profit us much in killing up our Ants and worms, which annoy us sore."[48] In 1623, again citing the depredations of worms and caterpillars, the assembly reversed its position on turkeys and set out punishments for anyone poisoning the birds.[49] A consistent theme animated these vacillations over fowl: Butler and the assembly wanted to ensure that nothing threatened agricultural production.

Within a few years the desires to control the poorest Bermudians and to protect agriculture merged. In 1627 the assembly shifted its focus from destructive animals to the status of their owners. "Divers apprentices, servants and artificers and other People who have either none or but small store of land," they complained, "bring up great numbers of Turkeys to the great damage of their neighbors upon whose land they both breed and feed." In response, the assembly prohibited anyone living on fewer than eight acres from having more than two turkeys. It followed this prohibition with another injunction against "some Indulgent masters who give leave unto their apprentices and hired servants to keep hog (or swine) under them which do oftentimes great damage to their said masters and their neighbors by breaking loose."[50] The government took these acts seriously. Shortly after their passage in 1627, four men were presented to grand juries for keeping turkeys without sufficient land "by which means the Country is greatly oppressed by destroying every man's corn in general," marking another person's turkeys, and "keeping a hog of a Negro."[51] These actions, while justified as protections against marauding beasts, reduced the ability of poor European servants and captive Africans to cultivate their own sources of food or income. Rather than treat Afro-Bermudians as skilled, independent experts who would increase agricultural yields and cultivate foreign plants, these rules envisioned them as threats to agriculture.

&

The set of restrictions on keeping and hunting animals and the emphasis on producing corn in significant quantities represented a shift in English attitudes toward Bermuda's environment. Strachey's letter describing the islands had emphasized their possibilities as places capable of producing the riches of the Spanish Empire. In the first years of English colonization, Europeans sought expertise, including from people of African descent who could dive for pearls and cultivate unfamiliar plants. Beginning under Butler's governorship, however, colonial authorities became increasingly concerned with the production of corn and tobacco, and Butler and other colonists cast doubt on experimental activities. Instead, Butler, the Assembly, and the Company leadership began to emphasize natural limits of animal populations, pests, winds, and land. This view of the natural world did not require expertise—it required discipline.

In response to these conditions, several English colonists elected to leave the colony to live on the Somers Isles Company's land in Virginia.[52] In a 1623 letter to John Ferrar, Miles Kendall complained that his tenants "have not land sufficient to employ themselves on and that which they have is not worth anything but for provision." He recommended that Ferrar "transport as many as were willing to Virginia." Several settlers heeded Kendall's call and wrote

Ferrar demanding that he ship them a substantial store of provisions to emigrate. "I know what belongs to a plantation," one wrote, "and a man that works hard must not want victuals." "It is well known," another complained, "to all that are acquainted with your land that it will not yield tobacco neither find them provision that live upon it."[53] Bermudians craved laborers to intensify production but struggled to keep colonists, who lamented that their land yielded neither salable tobacco nor sufficient food to survive. In contrast, Afro-Bermudians were unable to leave. English belief in the fantastic possibilities of Bermuda's terrestrial and maritime environments to yield riches and sustain Caribbean plants had first brought people of African descent to the islands. Anxieties about natural limits on the productive capacity of the land led colonists to rely on Afro-Bermudians after this initial wonder began to fade.

NOTES

1. Nathaniel Butler, "History of the Bermudas," folder 42 ["f." = folio here, not folder, to reflect the dual and inconsistent pagination of the manuscript], p. 76, Sloane 750, British Library, London.

2. Virginia Bernhard, "Beyond the Chesapeake: The Contrasting Status of Blacks in Bermuda, 1616–1663," *Journal of Southern History* 54 (November 1988): 545–64; Bernhard, *Slaves and Slaveholders in Bermuda, 1616–1782* (Columbia: University of Missouri Press, 1999); Michael J. Jarvis, *In the Eye of All Trade : Bermuda, Bermudians, and the Maritime Atlantic World, 1680–1783* (Chapel Hill: University of North Carolina Press, 2010), 29–32; Jarvis, "Maritime Masters and Seafaring Slaves in Bermuda, 1680–1783," *William and Mary Quarterly* 59 (July 2002): 585–622.

3. Abigail L. Swingen, *Competing Visions of Empire: Labor, Slavery, and the Origins of the British Atlantic Empire* (New Haven, Conn.: Yale University Press, 2015); John C. Coombs, "The Phases of Conversion: A New Chronology for the Rise of Slavery in Early Virginia," *William and Mary Quarterly* 68 (July 2011): 340–41.

4. Eric H. Ash, *Power, Knowledge, and Expertise in Elizabethan England* (Baltimore: Johns Hopkins University Press, 2004).

5. Judith A. Carney, *Black Rice: The African Origins of Rice Cultivation in the Americas* (Cambridge, Mass.: Harvard University Press, 2001), 80–90; Daniel C. Littlefield, *Rice and Slaves: Ethnicity and the Slave Trade in Colonial South Carolina* (Urbana: University of Illinois Press, 1991), 76–77, 102–3; Peter H. Wood, *Black Majority: Negroes in Colonial South Carolina from 1670 through the Stono Rebellion* (New York: Alfred A. Knopf, 1974), 56–62.

6. Ira Berlin, "From Creole to African: Atlantic Creoles and the Origins of African-American Society in Mainland North America," *William and Mary Quarterly* 53, no. 2 (1996): 251–58.

7. Martin Lewis Hall Thomas, *The Natural History of Bermuda* (Bermuda: Bermuda Zoological Society, 2004). On Bermuda's geology, see 18, 26–32. On Bermuda's plant and animal communities, see 30–36, as well as Joanna C. Ellison, "Pollen Evidence of Late Holocene Mangrove Development in Bermuda," *Global Ecology and Biogeography Letters* 5 (November 1996): 315–26; D. Ross Robertson and Katie L. Cramer, "Defining and Dividing the Greater Caribbean: Insights from the Biogeography of Shorefishes," *PLoS ONE*

9 (July 2014), https://doi.org/10.1371/journal.pone.0102918; Eugenio Santiago-Valentin and Richard G. Olmstead, "Historical Biogeography of Caribbean Plants: Introduction to Current Knowledge and Possibilities from a Phylogenetic Perspective," *Taxon* 53 (May 2004), https://doi.org/10.2307/4135610: 299–319; Lisa Mastny, "Bermuda," *World Wildlife Fund*, http://www.worldwildlife.org/ecoregions/na0301, accessed May 3, 2019.

8. Karen Ordahl Kupperman, "The Puzzle of the American Climate in the Early Colonial Period," *American Historical Review* 87, no. 5 (December 1982): 1262–89; Keith Pluymers, "Taming the Wilderness in Sixteenth- and Seventeenth-Century Ireland and Virginia," *Environmental History* 16 (October 2011): 610–32; Nicolás Wey Gómez, *The Tropics of Empire: Why Columbus Sailed South to the Indies* (Cambridge, Mass.: MIT Press, 2008), 399–400; Anya Zilberstein, *A Temperate Empire: Making Climate Change in Early America* (New York: Oxford University Press, 2016), 19–52; Sean Morey Smith, "Differentiating Hot Climates in the Anglo-American Colonial Experience," in this volume.

9. William Strachey and Silvester Jourdain, *A Voyage to Virginia in 1609: Two Narratives, Strachey's "True Reportory" and Jourdain's Discovery of the Bermudas*, ed. Louis B. Wright (Charlottesville: University of Virginia Press, 2013), 21, 23, 26; Peter Martyr, *The Decades of the Newe Worlde or West India Conteynyng the Nauigations and Conquestes of the Spanyardes*, trans. Richard Eden (London, 1555).

10. Strachey and Jourdain, *Voyage to Virginia in 1609*, 22–23, 26.

11. Ibid., 23; José de Acosta, *Natural and Moral History of the Indies*, ed. Jane E. Mangan (Durham, N.C.: Duke University Press, 2002), 212–13.

12. Thomas Hariot, *A Briefe and True Report of the New Found Land of Virginia* (Frankfurt, 1590), 7–8; Acosta, *Natural and Moral History*, 229; Strachey and Jourdain, *Voyage to Virginia in 1609*, 57.

13. Strachey and Jourdain, *Voyage to Virginia in 1609*, 21–23.

14. Ibid., 55–58.

15. Councell for Virginia, "A True Declaration of the Estate of the Colonie in Virginia (1610)," in *Tracts and Other Papers Relating Principally to the Origin, Settlement, and Progress of the Colonies in North America: From the Discovery of the Country to the Year 1776*, ed. Peter Force, vol. 3 (Washington, D.C.: William Q. Force, 1844), 10–11.

16. J. H. Lefroy, *Memorials of the Discovery and Early Settlement of the Bermudas or Somers Islands, 1515–1685*, vol. 1 (London: Longmans, Green, 1877), 60, 69.

17. Lefroy, *Memorials*, 1:65 (quotation), 58–60; "Bermudas Charter," June 29, 1615, Records of the Colonial Office, National Archives (U.K.), CO 38/1 f. 1.

18. Richard Norwood, *The Journal of Richard Norwood, Surveyor of Bermuda*, ed. Wesley Frank Craven and Walter Brownell Hayward (New York: Bermuda Historical Monuments Trust, 1945), 52.

19. Molly A. Warsh, "A Political Ecology in the Early Spanish Caribbean," *William and Mary Quarterly* 71 (October 2014): 519. For more on pearls in the early modern world, see Warsh, *American Baroque: Pearls and the Nature of Empire, 1492–1700* (Chapel Hill: Omohundro Institute of Early American History and Culture and University of North Carolina Press, 2018).

20. Significant disputes over dredges had already occurred in the Spanish Atlantic. See Warsh, *American Baroque*, 63–71; Norwood, *Journal of Richard Norwood*, 52; Lefroy, *Memorials*, 1:110–11.

21. Lefroy, *Memorials*, 1:115–16.

22. Kevin Dawson, "Enslaved Swimmers and Divers in the Atlantic World," *Journal of American History* 92 (March 2006): 1348–50. For more on the Pearl Coast see Warsh, "Political Ecology."

23. Butler, "History of the Bermudas"; Bernhard, *Slaves and Slaveholders in Bermuda*, 18–19.

24. Butler, "History of the Bermudas."

25. Warsh, *American Baroque*, 95 (quotation), 91–95, 104–15; David Wheat, *Atlantic Africa and the Spanish Caribbean, 1570–1640* (Chapel Hill: University of North Carolina Press, 2016), 186 (quotation), 186–97.

26. Vernon Ives, ed., *The Rich Papers: Letters from Bermuda, 1615–1646, Eyewitness Accounts Sent by the Early Colonists to Sir Nathaniel Rich* (Toronto: University of Toronto Press, 1984), 98–99, 50, 54, 56, 70.

27. Lefroy, *Memorials*, 1:116–17.

28. Ives, *Rich Papers*, 55.

29. As this essay indicates, many of the first people of African descent brought to Bermuda were likely born or had spent significant portions of their lives in the Caribbean. Others may have been more recently transported from Africa in the transatlantic slave trade. To avoid unwieldy phrases such as "African and Creole people from the Caribbean of African descent," I have opted for the simplified but inexact term "Afro-Bermudian."

30. Ives, *Rich Papers*, 59.

31. Lewes Hughes, *A Letter, Sent into England from the Summer Ilands* (London, 1615), Bv-B2r.

32. Bernhard, *Slaves and Slaveholders in Bermuda*, 17–19. Bernhard notes that, although there is no evidence for exact population statistics, there were Afro-Bermudians working on the Company's general land as well as for individual colonists. Bernhard, citing the Rich correspondence, argues that Robert Rich believed the Afro-Bermudians' skill with tobacco would lead to a profitable harvest.

33. Ives, *Rich Papers*, 58.

34. Ibid., 59, 81.

35. Ibid., 189, 222–23, 186, 180.

36. Butler, "History of the Bermudas," Sloane 750 ff. 48v–49r, British Library, London.

37. Ives, *Rich Papers*, 189. Butler railed against Tucker throughout his history of Bermuda accusing him of failing at sugar cultivation, supporting pirates, and plotting at meetings of the Somers Isles Company in England to reintroduce sugar cultivation and undermine Butler's plans. See Sloane 750 ff. 49r, 69–70, 104v.

38. Ives, *Rich Papers*, 180; Sloane 750 ff. 10r; 19r–v.

39. Ives, *Rich Papers*, 155, 157.

40. Ibid., 229–30.

41. Bernhard, *Slaves and Slaveholders in Bermuda*, 29.

42. Ibid., 30.

43. Ives, *Rich Papers*, 171–73, 176. This rate of production was significantly higher than usual in Bermuda and comparable to rates of production in seventeenth-century Virginia. See Bernhard, *Slaves and Slaveholders in Bermuda*, 24.

44. *Ives, Rich Papers*, 173.

45. See, for example, the 1620 act of the Bermuda House of Assembly "concerning vagabonds and the entertaining of other men's servants." Lefroy, *Memorials*, 1:173; Bernhard,

Slaves and Slaveholders in Bermuda, 25, 29–32; A. C. Hollis Hallett, ed., *Bermuda under the Sommer Islands Company, 1612–1684: Civil Records*, 3 vols. (Hamilton, Bermuda: Juniper-hill, 2005), 1:13.

46. Lefroy, *Memorials*, 1:172–73.

47. Ibid., 173–76.

48. Ives, *Rich Papers*, 181.

49. Lefroy, *Memorials*, 1:302–4.

50. Ibid., 452–53.

51. Hallett, *Bermuda*, 1:103.

52. For a note on this land, see Hallett, *Bermuda*, 2:583.

53. "Miles Kendall to John Ferrar," April 15, 1623, Ferrar Papers (FP) 467; "Thomas Day to John Ferrar," March 17, 1623, FP 457; "Edward Healing to John Ferrar," March 31, 1623, FP 362; "David Lewis to John Ferrar," April 7, 1623, FP 466; "Richard Smith to John Ferrar," March 20, 1623, FP 460, Old Library, Magdalene College, Cambridge.

The Nature of William Bartram's *Travels*

PETER C. MESSER

In 1773 William Bartram left Philadelphia for the southeastern corner of Great Britain's mainland North American colonies in search of useful and interesting plants and other products of nature for his English patron, John Fothergill. For the next four years, Bartram traveled through Georgia, East and West Florida, and the Native American territories that now form parts of the states of Alabama, Louisiana, Mississippi, and Tennessee. On his return, he reintegrated himself into the horticultural and botanical community of eastern Pennsylvania and over the course of two decades transformed the notes and reports he had compiled during his time in the Southeast into *Travels*, which he published in 1791. *Travels* provided a wealth of description of this corner of North America that Bartram hoped would edify and inform his readers in both Europe and America. The edification that Bartram offered spoke directly to a series of national—securing the economic, intellectual, and, indirectly, political credibility of the newly created United States—and personal concerns—crafting a way for Americans to reform themselves and their nation. To convey these messages Bartram embraced the role of a pilgrim whose travels and consequent interactions with the land and its productions offered insights into how people understood and used nature with profound implications for his fellow citizens, the nation, and the natural world he described. The resulting narrative offered a potent critique of contemporary scientific practice and aesthetic theory.

Bartram's critical perspective on science and aesthetics appears most clearly when *Travels* is read in an Atlantic context, that is to say, as a work written to reflect the intellectual and material connections of the author, and the region and nation, to the broader Atlantic world. Most of the scholarly work on Bartram has acknowledged his various debts to European authors and thinkers but has portrayed these connections largely as his application of the existing discourses to uncover stable foundations for the new republic. Those works that have emphasized his distinct perspective on these subjects have generally focused on the way they anticipated subsequent literary genres, and not on their critical implications for contemporaries. More recent scholarship has highlighted Bartram's use of nature and the relationship he saw in it to a wider Atlantic world to grapple with questions of empire, but these authors have stopped short of considering the implications for science and aesthetics and how they complicate those questions.[1] Inserting Bartram's ideas into a broader Atlantic context allows us to see both the author and his vision of the Southeast in a slightly different light: one that is more rooted in contemporary debates and is ultimately more critical of his contemporaries, in both Europe and America, than previously assumed.

In the broadest sense, Bartram wrote in the language of eighteenth-century natural history. He published his work to offer "useful observations on the different productions," or "various works of Nature," that he hoped would "contribute to our existence" and "promote the happiness and convenience of mankind." Bartram conspicuously included in this project illustrating the "glorious display of the Almighty hand" apparent in "the vegetable world," and the "almighty power, wisdom, and beneficence of the Supreme Creator and Sovereign Lord of the universe" observable in "animal creation." Finally, he hoped his efforts would convince the government to send "men of ability and virtue" among the Indians so that they might devise "a judicious plan for their civilization and union with us."[2] Bartram presented these aspirations for his book in a relatively straightforward manner; they represented, however, a subtle but clear argument in an ongoing debate, on both sides of the Atlantic, about how to know nature and practice natural history. In the process, Bartram did not simply take sides but attempted to craft a distinctive perspective that criticized certain common assumptions and offered alternatives in their place—alternatives that embraced the intellectual and material connections that put both him and his subject in a broader Atlantic world.

With regard to the overarching purpose of studying plants and nature, Bartram embraced a decidedly contemplative and philosophical perspective. He summed the matter up succinctly in a letter to Henry Muhlenberg, explaining that he derived "happiness and permanent advantage from the Study and contemplation of Nature" because it enabled him to "behold with inexpressibly pleasing awe, & veneration, The Majesty, Power, and Goodness of God the Creator thereof."[3] As William Cahill observed, this perspective placed Bartram at odds with many contemporaries in both England and America whose vision of natural history focused mostly on taxonomy—identifying species of plants and animals through a limited number of distinguishing features.[4] Bartram's declaration, both to Muhlenberg and in *Travels*, that he saw natural history as intended to provoke contemplation and philosophy represented more than a passive assertion of interest; it was a reflection of his belief in the inadequacy of taxonomy as a way of knowing nature. When discussing the prospect of Benjamin Smith Barton's foray into natural-history writing with Muhlenberg, Bartram found Barton to be "well acquainted with the Linn. System," but he stressed that this knowledge in and of itself was insufficient: "it absolutely requires time experimental knowledge, great erudition, & even much Travelling & researches to be able to publish to the World. A Faithful & accurate Essay towards the Nat. history."[5] Bartram's own descriptions of plants reflected this more expansive vision of the way knowledge might be accumulated and diffused, combining, as Christophe Irmscher has observed, "taxonomic classification, botanical description, ethnographic field note, narrative report, or lyrical vignette."[6] Bartram's discussion of plants and animals in *Travels*, in other words, placed him in a broader Atlantic conversation about how to know nature and communicate that knowledge to the reading public, and, by an extension, provided an illustration of how these things should be known and discussed.[7]

Bartram's invocation of a more contemplative and philosophical vision of natural history, one intended to awaken in readers a sense of the power of the divine and the sublime, introduced aesthetics into his account of the plants, animals, and landscapes of the Southeast. Authors who sought, in William Smellie's words, to go beyond the "bare enumeration of facts, or descriptions of the dimensions, figure, and colour of animals" and embrace "philosophy and argument require" needed to embrace "a higher and more figurative" style of writing, one that "addresses to passions, and the finer feelings of men," giving "full scope to the exercise of genius and taste."[8] In eighteenth-century aesthetic discourse these passions and finer feelings were addressed through the sublime and the beautiful. The sublime, as Edmund Burke explained, invoked "ideas of pain, and danger" in an observer in order to excite "the strongest emotion which the mind is capable of feeling," which, by overwhelming reason, would lead the observer "into the counsels of the Almighty by a consideration of his works."[9] Beauty, *The Spectator* explained, "delights Soul" as images "paint themselves on the Fancy, with very little Attention of Thought or Application of the Mind on the Beholder" as the beholder "immediately assent[s] to the Beauty of an Object, without inquiring into the particular Causes and Occasions of it."[10] Neither the utility of aesthetic discourse in natural-history writing nor these specific interpretations of the sublime and beautiful would have been unfamiliar to Bartram, who owned a copy of Smellie's work and, by all accounts, was well versed in contemporary aesthetic theory.[11] Consequently, in reading *Travels* we should keep in mind not simply Bartram's invocation of aesthetic discourse but the probability that he did so with the intent of complementing or enhancing his more scientific descriptions of plants and animals.

Bartram's relatively novel approach to scientific description and the important role that aesthetics would play in his account become more noteworthy in light of his belief in the need to reconsider, and perhaps revise, the accepted truths that governed scientific practice. Bartram believed that "the Universe may act & operate by established Order & system" and that every human "Soul" had on it "impressed or inscribed, the primordial arrangement of Ideas, or Intellectual System of the Human Understanding," an arrangement that was "of such a fas[h]ion & quality as to receive new or Aditional Archetypes when ever the Almighty sees fit."[12] *Travels*, in other words, should also be read as a book written by an author who believed that in searching for the divine in nature the "Almighty" might reveal new ways of understanding the broader world in which it was part. One such insight, in all probability, revolved around the relationship between humans and the animal and vegetable kingdoms, and the lessons that they might offer humanity. In an unpublished essay "On the Dignity of Human Nature," Bartram condemned the systems for studying nature and its productions devised by Linnaeus and the Comte de Buffon because they created an artificial separation between humans and animals; Bartram found particular fault with their implicit argument that humans were superior to plants and animals and had a unique perspective on the divine.[13] Contrary to this assumption, Bartram believed that humanity could uncover "myny useful hints . . . from studying & observing a sort of moral system or regulation of Maners and conduct" among animals. With regard to plants, he insisted that they were "Animated, organical active Beings" that manifested "the Power, Wisdom, and beneficence of the Almighty" and were "equally useful & necessary" to understand nature and the divine principles it revealed.[14]

Bartram was less explicit about insights the Almighty might reveal to him, and his readers, when it came to aesthetics and the ways in which the sublime and beautiful worked to edify those who experienced them. His views of human nature, and the role of passion and reason in directing it, however, suggest that he would have paid particular attention to how he deployed aesthetic discourse in service of knowing nature and the divine. Though not always evident in *Travels*, according to Laurel Ode-Schneider, Bartram held a remarkably dark view of human nature and believed that humanity's tendency toward hubris and avarice had led to "a universe in disarray, spinning out of control." This view lay behind Bartram's belief that humans and animals had more in common than the former wanted to believe, but also behind his conviction that one of humanity's greatest shortcomings lay in the tendency to allow "The Mind" to be "seduced by the interposition of Our Passions & affections by which means, we can't sufficiently attend to & obey the dictates of Reason."[15] This suspicion of the excessive influence of the passions raised obvious problems for any attempt to invoke either the sublime or the beautiful in an exploration of natural history, as both of these aesthetic tropes presumed that feelings would replace reason as the means through which the individual received knowledge.

Bartram, consequently, would have to fashion a way of writing natural history that tapped into the potential of aesthetic discourse to encourage contemplation and philosophical reflection without overwhelming the dictates of reason, which should also accompany their views of nature and the wider world.

Bartram's contribution to contemporary debates about science and aesthetics appears primarily in moments in which the encounters between humans and their environment in the Southeast revealed the inherent limitations of those systems of thought. In the most straightforward sense this process appeared in Bartram's combination of his American experiences with European scientific practice and aesthetic categories to create an Atlantic way of knowing that balanced scientific reasoning with the contemplation of aesthetics, and the passion of aesthetics with the reason of science.[16]

Bartram's journey across East Florida to the Seminole town in Cuscowilla illustrated how sublimity could provide a useful complement to the conventional scientific practice that he found lacking in contemplation and erudition. As he traveled west through a series of plains and savannahs, Bartram, over four pages, noted the soil's "strength" and "fertility" as revealed in the "great variety of grasses, herbage and remarkably low shrubs" that grew there. He provided descriptions of the leaves, flowers, and fruits to justify the Linnaean names Bartram gave to those plants that were "new" to him, the identifying nomenclature for several different species of birds, and a narrative description of the scorpion lizard. He interspersed these descriptions with observations on the peculiar features of the landscape; a new species of plant whose fruit was a "delicious, wholesome food"; "curious and beautiful" shrubs, including several "depressed and degraded" magnolia trees created by "the ravages of fire" set by the Native Americans. As his traveling party continued, Bartram simply took to listing the Latin names of the "varieties of trees and shrubs" they passed, culminating with his party ascending a hill "ornamented with a variety and profusion of herbaceous plants and grasses, particularly amaryllis atamasco, clithroia, phlox, iopmea, convolvulvus, verbena corymbosa, ruellia viola &c."[17]

From the perspective of the botanist, or colonizer, this section of *Travels* has provided a great deal of information. Bartram described new species, identified familiar ones, documented curious and interesting features, and even, in passing, taught readers something of the manners of the Indigenous inhabitants. From Bartram's perspective, however, it seems that too much information had been presented too quickly, because as the party left the plains, they, and the reader, were ushered out of the world of science and curiosity and into that of the sublime. The party entered a "magnificent grove of stately pines, succeeding to the expansive wild plains we had a long time traversed, had a pleasing effect, rousing the faculties of the mind, awakening the imagination by its sublimity, and arresting every active inquisitive idea, by the variety of the scenery, and the solemn, symphony of the steady Western breezes, playing incessantly, rising and falling through the thick wavy foliage."[18] Framed in this manner the American experience of nature illustrated how the sublime could function as an antidote to taxonomic and scientific inquisitiveness run amok, or at least wild, by refocusing the mind away from mere observation and into the realm of contemplation.

The beautiful could play a similar role. On his travels to the Cherokee villages in western Georgia, for example, Bartram found himself seated in the moss surrounding an idyllic pool and his attention drawn to the "vegetable beauties" surrounding him, which he proceeded to identify. They included the "Magnolia auriculata, Rhodedendron Ferrugineum, Kalmoia latofolia, Robina montana, Azelea flammula, Rosa paniculata, Calycanthus Floridus," and at least sixteen others. The dense text of Linnaean nomenclature provided readers with a clear image of what plants might be found in the mountains of Georgia, as well as a sense of sociability and connection among botanists in both Europe and America, an essential component of what Bartram viewed as the purpose of natural history.[19] What was left unsaid was the exact nature of the sociability that he had established, a point that could not necessarily be taken for granted. Bartram's long conversation with Muhlenberg, for example, highlights the former's interest in natural history as a means of contemplation and the latter's near single-minded focus on taxonomic identification.[20] Bartram attempted to ensure that readers would not neglect the contemplative aspect of natural history by quickly transitioning from the language of taxonomy to that of aesthetics. He described how "these roving beauties stroll over the mossy, shelving human rocks, or from off the expansive wavy boughs of trees, bending over the floods, salute their delusive shape, playing on the surface; some plunge their perfumed heads and bathe their flexile limbs in the silver stream; whilst others by the mountain breezes are tossed about, their blooming tufts bespangled with pearly and chrystiline dew drops, collected from the falling mists, glistening in the rainbow arch."[21] Taxonomy was useful, Bartram seemed to remind readers, as a way of fostering connections among a diverse array of botanists, but they should aspire to a more complete connection to each other, one grounded on the contemplative understanding of plants and their significance produced by this beautiful American scene.

Bartram also used his experiences to illustrate how the rational order provided by taxonomy could check the excesses of sublimity and beauty found in the Southeast. As he paddled up the Saint Johns River, for example, the forests "wore a grand and sublime appearance; the earth rising gradually from the river westward, by easy swelling ridges, behind one another, lifting the distant groves up into the skies." He immediately described the trees as being "the grand laurel magnolia, palma elata, liquidambar styraciflua, fagus sylvatica, querci, juglans hickory, fraxinus, and others." At the other extreme as he moved up the Pearl River he declared, "What a sylvan scene is here! The pompous Magnolia reigns sovereign of the forests; how sweet the aromatic Illicium groves! How gaily flutter the radiated wins of the Magnolia auriculata, each branch supporting an expanded umbrella, superbly created with a silver plume, fragrant blossom, or crimson studded strobili and fruits. I recline on the verdant bank, and view the beauties of the grieves, Æsculus pavia, Prunus nemoralis, floribus racemosis, foliis sempervirentibus, nitidis, Æsculus alba, Hydrangia quercifolia, Cassine, Magnolia pyrmidata, foliis ovatis, oblongis, acumminatis, basi auriculatis, [and] strobilo oblong ovato," among many others.[22] In both cases, the reader is initially drawn in to a view of nature in North America that points toward the larger aesthetic and emotional experiences that Bartram sought to encourage; the majesty of the landscape and the gaiety and fragrance of the flowers both implicitly remind the reader of the omnipotence and omnipresence of the Creator. With the hint provided, however, Bartram quickly returned to his reader a sense of order and regularity in the world revealed by his ability to reduce the scenes of sublimity and beauty to a string of Latin botanical names. The process, as one critic has observed, disrupted the narrative of *Travels* and made it difficult to read, but it also ensured that the reader did not get lost along the way.[23]

Bartram's peregrinations also provided the occasion for a more substantive critique of both taxonomical science and aesthetics by illustrating how the experience of nature in the southeastern corner of North America revealed the weaknesses in both systems. With regard to science, Bartram's travels allowed him, according to literary scholar Christophe Irmscher, to write "accident and luck," two aspects of botanizing usually edited out of natural histories, into the process of discovering and identifying a unique species.[24] The proper identification of a plant required the botanist to describe leaves, flowers, and fruit, which, of course, made successful botanizing contingent on when the naturalist passed by the plant. Bartram's inability to find botanicals was a repeated theme in *Travels*. He could not identify "a species of Æsculus or Pavia" because he "could find none of the fruit and but a few flowers." Another nondescribed plant remained so because "not having time to examine the fructification, or collect good specimens, I am ignorant of what order or genus it belongs to." Finally, he came across "an arborescent aromatic vine" with "long oblong leaves . . . on opposite branches," but because "its season of flowering past, and the seed scattered," he was "entirely ignorant to what genus it belongs."[25] In the case of the *Franklinia alatamaha*, Irmscher contends, this misfortune had led to its misidentification as a species of *Gordonia*, which Bartram set out to correct in *Travels*.[26] In isolation, the error may appear to be insignificant. In light of Bartram's repeated invocations of the contingent nature of botanical identification, his correction of the botanical record suggested something more. However useful taxonomical categories may be as a way of organizing nature, when viewed through the lens of the actual experience of botanizing in America, they appeared more contingent than definitive, as a useful tool but not an unfailing final word. Bartram captured this sentiment in his observation to Muhlenberg that "there still remains much confusion & error . . . owing to the ignorance & carelessness of the compilers of the numerous Nomenclatures without sufficient descriptions."[27]

Bartram also highlighted how relying on taxonomy to know a place and the plants in it masked interesting and important information. As he described traveling through the hills outside of Augusta, he paused amid one of his long list of botanical names to observe, "who would have expected to see the Dirca palustris and Dodecatheon maedea grow in abundance in this hot climate," where "they attain to a degree of magnitude and splendor never seen in Pennsylvania." Similarly, when traveling through the mountains in Georgia, Bartram found "many trees and plants common" to the north, "but what seems remarkable, the yellow Jessamine (bigonia sempervirens), which is killed by a very slight frost in the open air in Pennsylvania, here, on the summits of the Cherokee mountains associates with the Canadian vegetables, and appears roving with them in perfect bloom and gaiety."[28] Taxonomy had been developed in large part to impose order on nature, by providing a systematic, portable, and convenient way of describing and distinguishing among plants and animals, yet as experienced on Bartram's travels it seemed to undermine that goal.[29] The contrast between the Latinate names that supposedly made the plants recognizable and knowable, and the real evidence of living plants' unrecognizable behavior struck at the heart of what taxonomy was intended to provide: order.

Bartram approached aesthetics from the same Atlantic perspective he applied to taxonomy, merging local experiences with broadly understood principles to highlight the limits of the latter and craft a better way of knowing nature.[30] Beauty, for example, had become increasingly suspect in English intellectual circles and, largely through Edmund Burke's influence, associated with a feminine love of luxury and ease that threatened to corrupt the manly vigor on which these authors believed society depended.[31] Taken too far, Burke warned, the "relaxed state of the body" associated with beauty led to "melancholy, dejection, despair, and often self-murder."[32] Bartram's experiences, however, suggested otherwise, reminding readers of the utility that authors such as those of *The Spectator* found in beauty. Beauty occasionally distracted Bartram, as when in Augusta he found the feminized local "vegetation, in perfection," appearing "with all her attractive charms, breathing fragrance" enticing him to stay, but his restlessness and "curiosity" always kept him moving. Occasionally, beauty even played a role in forwarding Bartram's ambitions. As he descended the Saint Johns River, he found himself "induced by the beautiful appearance of the green meadows" and delayed his journey to botanize and explore an "Elysium" on the east bank of the river; after having "diverted away the intolerable heats" in the "fruitful fragrant groves, with renewed vigour," he resumed his "sylvan pilgrimage."[33] Bartram's travels through the Southeast, in other words, served as a reminder to readers of the limits of the emerging Burkean view of beauty: in the American forests beauty was no threat, and it may even be particularly useful to the traveler.

At the same time Bartram defended the integrity and utility of the beautiful, he highlighted the limitations of the sublime. As Burke explained, sublimity presumed that experiencing "pain and terror" would have a transcendent effect on the observer (or readers) as reason was suspended and the individual was ushered into the corridors of the divine.[34] Bartram's experience, however, suggested that sublimity did not always lead to enlightenment, and sometimes seemed to have the opposite effect. For example, "raging storms" were, according to both Burke and *The Spectator*, among the most sublime things in nature and figured prominently in *Travels*.[35] Yet Bartram rarely allowed them to convey real sublimity. On his journey from Philadelphia to Charleston at the beginning of the book, Bartram found himself in a storm in which "powerful winds . . . rushing forth from their secret abodes suddenly spread terror and devastation; and the wide ocean, which, a few moments before, was gentle and placid, is now thrown into disorder, and heaped into mountains, whose white curling creates seems to sweep the skies!" Similarly, on his journey to Overhill towns of the Cherokee, he passed through "a charming vale amidst sublimely high forests, awful shades! Darkness gathers around; far distant thunder rolls over the trembling hills: the black clouds with august majesty and power, move slowly forwards, shading regions of towering hills, and threatening all the destruction of a thunder storm." When the storm erupted "the mountains tremble and seem to reel about, and the ancient hills to be shaken to their foundations: the furious storm sweeps along. . . . The face of the earth is obscured by the din of thunder." Both cases offer powerfully sublime images—thunder, wind, ocean waves—that are presented in an active voice that attempts to convey the author's real terror to the reader, and yet neither encounter sees Bartram or the reader get beyond terror into awe or understanding of the Almighty. In the first, Bartram simply reported that the storm "continued near two days and nights" and "not a little damaged our sails, cabin-furniture, and staterooms, besides retarding our passage." In the second case, he was "deafened by the din" and the "tempestuous scene damps my spirits . . . as I hasten on the plain" to find refuge in an Indigenous hunting cabin.[36] Ironically, the resignation that characterized Bartram's reaction to his encounter with these raging storms reflected the sense of "melancholy, dejection, [and] despair" that Burke associated with the polar aesthetic opposite of the sublime: beauty.[37]

Taken together, these repeated illustrations of the shortcomings of conventional scientific practice and Burkean aesthetic discourse led Bartram to fashion for his readers new ways of seeing and understanding the world. The best illustration of this attempt to synthesize a new way of thinking involved Bartram's descriptions of plants and animals that involved the subject in the creation of human knowledge about it. With regard to plants, conventional Linnaean description revolved around distinctive but arbitrarily determined features of the plant—flower, fruit, and leaves—that might easily be removed, preserved, and entered into a catalog.[38] Even Mark Catesby's more expansive descriptions of plants revolved around categories defined and imposed by humans.[39] Bartram's descriptions, on the other hand, moved the scientific process away from the observer imposing order on the subject and to the subject revealing order to the observer, offering descriptions in which plants' seemingly willful behavior framed the way in which people should know them.

Bartram's description of the *Gordonia lasianthus*, for example, begins with a modified Linnaean description, adding color and scent to his description of leaf shape, position, and flower morphology, but then concentrates on the way in which the living plant shaped his knowledge of it. The flowers appear "in such incredible profusion, that the tree appears silvered over with them," all the while it "continually pushes forth new twigs," and in "the winter and spring, the third year's leaves . . . are gradually changing colour, from green to golden yellow, from that to scarlet, from scarlet to crimson; and lastly to brownish purple, and then fall to the ground." The "Gordonia Lasianthus," he continues, "may be said to change and renew its garments every morning throughout the year." He then turns his attention to the tree's "natural situation," emphasizing that it grew "nearest to the water of any other tree, so that in droughty seasons its long serpentine roots . . . may reach into the water."[40] Catesby had also noted that the tree "begins to blossom in May, and continues bringing forth its Flowers" through "the greatest part of the Summer" and that it "grows only in wet places, and usually in Water," so the information Bartram provided was not necessarily new.[41] But where Catesby placed himself in the position of reporting those features, Bartram places the plant itself in the central position, emphasizing an active process of growing that revealed to the observer the qualities that defined it. The tree was, thus, as Bartram wrote, one of the "Animated, organical active Beings" that manifested "the Power, Wisdom, and beneficence of the Almighty" by exciting "our admiration & attachments, by their excellent & elusive charms."[42]

Bartram's treatment of animals reflected a similar set of assumptions, though the natural historical systems he opposed were more diverse. Linnaean taxonomy offered a static system that classified and distinguished them according to an assemblage of parts more visible on a dissection table than in nature: heart, lungs, jaws, penis, sense organs, and motive organs.[43] The Comte de Buffon, on the other hand, classified animals according to a more complete vision of a living animal, describing its habitat, how it gave birth, and how it survived, though he, too, placed the animal on a dissection table so that he might observe its internal parts. The objective of this more complete image, however, remained very much understanding the animal in relation to humans, particularly how they might be useful to humans.[44] Bartram took issue with both of these interpretations by using his experiences to construct a way of knowing animals that focused on the living and active animals he wanted readers to see.

Bartram's discussions of the alligator and rattlesnake, which European authors, particularly Buffon, believed revealed the degenerated quality of nature in North America, highlight his alternative way of knowing animals.[45] Bartram's treatment of the alligator needs to be read in the context of the section that immediately precedes it: the well-known encounter with alligators on the Saint Johns River in which Bartram is attacked, almost pulled from his canoe, and then nearly dragged under the water as he stood unsuspecting on the shore. Bartram survived the encounter with the judicious use of a club, his ability to reason his way out of trouble, and the behavior of the alligators (notably, his attempt to deter the alligators by shooting them failed).[46] The section is significant because the manner in which the alligators assault Bartram exhibits the same behaviors that Buffon offered to illustrate the "natural terrors" the alligator spread and the "unceasing devastations" it caused in the "uninhabited regions of Africa and America." Buffon had used that information to segue into a second description, via dissection, of the animal's anatomy—its skeleton, cartilage, tail, jaw, and leg muscles—and how people successfully killed it.[47] The danger that the animals posed to humans, quite simply, led Buffon, under the guise of his scientific system, to reassert humanity's control over it by cutting the animal open, pulling it apart, and describing how it might be killed. More or less the same dangers, however, led Bartram in a very different direction. With danger averted by reasoned observation, his science allowed the alligator's behavior, rather than the scientist's knife or fears, to dictate what mattered about it.

Bartram noted many of the external observable qualities described by Buffon and prescribed by Linnaean taxonomy—where alligators laid their eggs, how they hatched, the animal's size, its strength, the location and size of its eyes and nostrils, the size of its head and movement of the jaw, and the nature of its skin. But rather than peel back the skin to examine its internal organs or skeleton, Bartram left the animal very much alive. He described how the female alligator "carefully watches her eggs" and is "assiduous and courageous in defending" the young alligators that are "continually whining and barking" around her; the "horny plates" covering the alligator are "impenetrable when on the body of a live animal"; and "when they clap their jaws together it causes a surprising noise." He explained that "what is yet more surprising to a stranger, is the incredible loud and terrifying roar" they make in "their breeding time" that "resembles very heavy distant thunder," and when "hundreds and thousands are roaring at the same time, you can scarcely be persuaded, but that the whole globe is violently and dangerously agitated." The description ends with an account of the mating ritual in which the alligator first "darts forth" to the center of the lake where the animal "swells himself" with "air and water," causing "a loud sonorous rattling in the throat" before being forced out "with a loud noise, brandishing his tail in the air, and the vapor ascending from his nostrils like smoke," before finally the animal, "swollen to an extent ready to burst," then "spins or twirls round the surface of the water."[48] What mattered to Bartram was not the structure of the animal's skeleton, or its internal organs, or even the way it related to humans, but particular behaviors that it exhibited as it lived on its own terms in the wild. Readers should know the alligator through the parental behavior of the mother, the loud roars that shook the forest at breeding time, and the sight of a twenty-foot animal spinning in the water surrounded by smokelike vapor, characteristics neither Buffon nor Linnaeus would have afforded much attention.

Bartram's description of the rattlesnake unfolded on similar terms, though it also offered a commentary on what people might learn had they been paying attention to the living animal. The rattlesnake occupied a distinctive place in the efforts of both Americans and Europeans to understand nature in North America, with the latter convinced that it offered proof of the continent's inferiority, while the former held a more ambivalent perspective.[49] Perhaps with this complicated history in mind, Bartram's description created possibly his most willful and humanlike animal. He described the snake as "a wonderful creature" whose bite could "not only . . . kill the largest animal in America, and that in a few minutes time, but . . . turn the whole body into corruption; but such is the nature of this dreadful reptile, that he cannot run or creep faster than a man or child can walk, and he is never known to strike until he is first assaulted or fears himself in danger, and even then always gives the earliest warning by the rattles at the extremity of the tail." He continued that in

PETER C. MESSER

his travels through "the Southern states" he had "stept unknowingly" near one that sat coiled and "ready for a blow," but "the generous," even "magnanimous creature" refrained.[50] All of these aspects of the snake's behavior would have been recognizable to readers as they all constituted staples of the existing description of the snake. A variant of Bartram's description of inadvertently stepping near a coiled snake had appeared in Pehr Kalm's description of the animal, though the Swedish naturalist was less generous than Bartram with regard to the snake, adding that "such indifference can not be relied upon, for there are times when he strikes without provocation."[51] If the snake's behavior was broadly familiar, however, the way the observer understood it was not. Bartram created an animal governed by a very human "nature" that explained its behavior in terms of fear, generosity, and magnanimity, and made the animal's actions, as understood on its own terms, essential for understanding its significance.

Bartram's readers may not have shared his anthropomorphized vision of the snake, which may explain the description's sudden switch from a report of the animal's behavior to an invocation of the sublime. If, despite the snake's passive nature, the observer pursued or threatened it, Bartram explained, the snake "throws himself into a spiral coil; his tail by the rapidity of its motion appears like a vapour . . . his whole body swells through rage, continually rising and falling as a bellows; his beautiful particoloured skin becomes speckled and rough by dilatation; his head and neck are flattened, his cheeks swollen and his lips constricted discovering his mortal fangs; his eyes red as burning coals, and his brandishing forked tongue of the colour of the hottest flame, continually menaces death and destruction, yet never strikes unless sure of his mark."[52] This description of a beautiful yet demonlike serpent whose rapidly moving tail, swelling body, transforming skin, mortal fangs, and flaming tongue presaging the demise of the transgressing human left the reader in terror of the snake but also in wonder of its power and restraint.[53] In keeping with Bartram's view of the alligator and even the *Gordonia*, the snake now set the terms on which people would know it, not by the ability of the observer to see and describe its actions but by the capacity of the serpent to provoke a response in the observer or reader. The now sublime rattlesnake, all of a sudden, became a poor illustration of the inferiority of the continent and its people, and a much more vivid illustration of the manifestation of the divine in it.

This changed perception of the snake set the stage for the lesson that followed. The qualities that the rattlesnake demonstrated, generosity and magnanimity, were virtues that Bartram found praiseworthy in humans, and the restraint that the snake showed despite its tremendous power was a quality not often found in humans.[54] As if to underscore the last point, Bartram's description of the snake was followed by a series of anecdotes in which Bartram and his traveling companions found themselves confronted by rattlesnakes and, in all but one case, being unable to restrain themselves from killing the animal.[55] Read in light of this behavior, Bartram's initial description of the snake becomes an instance of "myny useful hints" that people might learn "from studying & observing a sort of moral system or regulation of Maners and conduct" among animals.[56]

Bartram also encouraged his readers to apply aesthetics, particularly beauty, in conjunction with his more dynamic way of knowing plants to refute European critics of North America. Buffon included among his evidence of North America's inferiority the observation that it was "every where covered with trees, shrubs, and gross herbage," so that "Nature remains concealed under her old garments, and never exhibits herself in fresh attire."[57] Bartram used beauty to argue otherwise, transforming a dreary wilderness into further evidence of the "glorious display of the Almighty hand" that he believed abounded in North American nature. He described "beautiful palmated leaved convolvulus," a vine that "rambles over the shrubs, and strolls about on the ground; its leaves are elegantly sinuated, of a deep grass green, and sit on long petioles." Similarly, he reported that the new "Æsculus pavia" was a "conspicuously beautiful flowering shrub," with stems that "wreath about every way, after a very irregular and free order," with peculiar "heavy spikes of flowers" that when "charged with the morning dews, bend the slender lexile stems to the ground." He described a "species of Robina" as a "beautiful flowering tree" that possessed "a singular pleasing wildness and freedom in its manner of growth."[58] The almost willful irregular growth and conscious free movement that Bartram described in these plants constituted archetypal symbols of beauty, and they transformed Buffon's evidence of the weakness of North America into an illustration of its inherent civility and potential for refinement.[59]

Somewhat more unconventionally, Bartram also presented beauty as a source of strength. Early in the book, he "passed the utmost frontier of the white settlements" and found "the prospect around enchantingly varied and beautiful." Into this idyll "an Indian appeared" whose armed appearance frightened Bartram, who attempted to ride away unnoticed. When discovered Bartram "resolved to meet the dreaded foe with resolution and cheerful confidence," and when confronted by the "angry and fierce" Native man, Bartram "offered him my hand, hailing him, brother." Initially shocked, the man recovered and "spurred up to me, and with dignity in his look and action, gave me his hand," bringing the confrontation to an amiable, if tense, end.[60] Beauty not only did not represent a threat to Bartram, it became the natural context from which he drew the inspiration to stand up to and defuse a potentially deadly confrontation with the Native man. Bartram had, in other words, derived the sort of insight and courage from beauty usually reserved for the sublime.

This more invigorated beauty, combined with the problematic qualities of unchecked sublimity, led Bartram to offer his readers an aesthetic that combined beauty and sublimity. In Burke's formulation, not only did beauty represent the weaker and more dangerous of the two aesthetic qualities, it tended to be destroyed or overwhelmed when in the presence of sublimity.[61] While not all authors had found the two experiences as incompatible as Burke did, they tended to portray beauty as a complement to the sublimity that softened the latter into the picturesque.[62] Instead, Bartram presented beauty as neither overwhelmed nor as a moderating influence, but an equally powerful path to knowledge. Thus, while enjoying a meal on a small Georgia plantation, Bartram emphasized the simultaneous yet separate experience of both beauty and sublimity. He described sitting among the beauty evoked by "the lively salubrious breezes," the "music" of songbirds, and the sight of a "brilliant hummingbird" that "darted through the flowery groves" while experiencing "awfully great and sublime" scene created by the "beating surf" and "the dashing" of waves that "like mighty giants, in vain assail the skies" and then "fall prostrate upon the shores of the trembling island." Moreover, he often seemed to prioritize beauty over sublimity when deriving a lesson in the presence of both aesthetics. When the "peaceful" and "gentle" Altamaha River was "disfigured" by "furious winds and sweeping rains" that "bent the lofty groves" and "prostrated the quaking grass," it was only after "the beautiful river regained its native calmness" that he realized and imparted a larger message to his readers. The temporary disruption to his journey, he explained, was analogous to "the varied and mutable scenes of human events in the stream of life," in which too often the "painful feelings" provoked by "inferior passions" led people "to deviate from the admonitions and convictions of virtue." Thus, it was the beauty that followed the sublimity that led to the insight into the workings of the divine. When faced with obstacles people should "wait and rely on our God, who in due time will shine forth in brightness, dissipate the envious cloud, and reveal to us how finite and circumscribed is human power, when assuming to itself independent wisdom."[63]

The degree to which Bartram's presentation of sublimity and beauty represented a pointed contribution to contemporary debates about how to know nature and its meaning for the broader world appears most clearly when seen in light of the contemporary gendered dimensions of sublimity and beauty. Bartram's interpretation of aesthetic theory took a decidedly feminine quality and elevated it to a position on par with a masculine one. The change is worth noting, in part, because Burke found the feminine nature of beauty particularly troubling, and, in part, because Mary Wollstonecraft, as part of her larger critique of social mores and practice, argued for an aesthetics more attuned to the power of beauty.[64] It is difficult to say definitively that Bartram sided more with Wollstonecraft than Burke, but there is some suggestive evidence on the matter. Bartram made no attempt to create a hierarchy among the masculine and feminine virtues he identified in his essay on human dignity, suggesting he suffered from less anxiety on the subject than Burke. In a letter offering advice to his nephew, Bartram urged "Humility," one of his feminine virtues, to the young man, and it was this same virtue that Bartram identified as the lesson learned during his stormy encounter with sublimity and beauty on the Altamaha.[65] Thomas Hallock has also argued that Bartram's botanizing often took the form of a celebration of male friendship with distinct homoerotic undertones at odds with an increasingly heteronormative culture, suggesting Bartram's willingness to prod at emerging gender ideologies.[66] At least one of the reviews of *Travels* suggests that whatever Bartram's intentions, some readers found his elevation of beauty to be troubling; an anonymous author writing in the *Massachusetts Magazine* was generally receptive to the book but found Bartram's descriptions "rather too luxuriant and florid, to merit the palm of chastity and correctness."[67] Bartram's application of familiar European aesthetic categories to his experiences in the Southeast, in other words, appears to reflect an attempt to offer his own contribution to an evolving Atlantic discourse on gender and identity.

Reading *Travels* from an Atlantic perspective provides a valuable insight into the process of constructing knowledge about the environment at the close of the eighteenth century. In the broadest sense it highlights the contingent nature of that process. When seeing Bartram as an early romantic whose views anticipated the separation of aesthetics and science, we can too easily take that development for granted—an inevitability to be lamented or praised as suits our interests. When read as part of a vibrant transatlantic discussion, however, the contemporary stakes become more apparent as Bartram sought to steer his fellow natural historians toward a broader conception of the environment, the plants and animals within it, and their relationship to humans. In the process, it highlights how discussions of how to organize the natural world bleed over into conversations about organizing the human world, in this case the privileging of a consciously masculine view of science and nature at the expense of a feminine, or even queer, alternative. In the process, it encourages us to consider the assumptions behind our ways of knowing and communicating about the world in which we live. That self-awareness seems particularly important as we consider how to write histories that help readers engage with the crisis that is the Anthropocene and remind them of the need to affirm and defend useful ways of knowing, to think beyond the boundaries of country or region, and to appreciate the diversity of ways things might be known. Put another way, Bartram's *Travels* is important not because he understood anything that we do not, but because his problem—creating a world committed to devising a better and healthier way of knowing nature—is our problem, and the long-term viability of not just our community but the planet depend on figuring out how to solve it.

NOTES

1. When discussing Bartram's scientific methods, scholars have emphasized his use of conventional Linnaean classification, either as a means of underscoring the limits of a literary project to fashion an American style of writing or for its potential to reassure readers anxious over the discordant politics of the early American republic. See Pamela Regis, *Describing Early America: Bartram, Jefferson, Crèvecoeur, and the Influence of Natural History* (Philadelphia: University of Pennsylvania Press, 1999); Peter Fritzell, *Nature Writing and America* (Ames: Iowa State University Press, 1990); Christopher Looby, "The Constitution of Nature: Taxonomy as Politics in Jefferson, Peale, and Bartram," *Early American Literature* 22 (1987): 252–73; Thomas P. Slaughter, *The Natures of John and William Bartram* (New York: Vintage, 1996); Joyce Chaplin, "Nature and Nation: Natural History in Context," in *Stuffing Birds, Pressing Plants, Shaping Knowledge: Natural History in North America, 1730–1860*, ed. Sue Ann Prince (Philadelphia: American Philosophical Society, 2003), 75–95; John Gatta, *Making Nature Sacred: Literature, Religion, and Environment in America from the Puritans to the Present* (New York: Oxford University Press, 2004); Don Scheese, *Nature Writing: The Pastoral Impulse in America* (New York: Twayne, 1996); Thomas Hallock, *From the Fallen Tree: Frontier Narratives, Environmental Politics, and the Roots of a National Pastoral* (Chapel Hill: University of North Carolina Press, 2003); Christopher P. Iannini, *Fatal Revolutions: Natural History, West Indian Slavery, and the Routes of American Literature* (Chapel Hill: University of North Carolina Press, 2012).

2. William Bartram, *Travels through North and South Carolina, Georgia, East and West Florida, the Cherokee Country, the Extensive Territories of the Muscogulges or Creek Confederacy, and the Country of the Chactaws*, in *Bartram: Travels and Other Writings*, ed. Thomas P. Slaughter (New York: Literary Classics of the United States, 1996), 13, 19, 25.

3. William Bartram to Henry Muhlenberg, September 8, 1792, in William Cahill, "The Bartram-Muhlenberg Correspondence (1792, 1810)," in *William Bartram: The Search for Nature's Design*, ed. Thomas Hallock and Nancy E. Hoffman (Athens: University of Georgia Press, 2010), 399.

4. Cahill, introduction to "Bartram-Muhlenberg Correspondence," 383.

5. William Bartram to Henry Muhlenberg, November 29, 1792, in Cahill, "Bartram-Muhlenberg Correspondence," 414.

6. Christoph Irmscher, *The Poetics of Natural History: From John Bartram to William James* (New Brunswick, N.J.: Rutgers University Press, 1999), 38–39.

7. In this regard this essay takes issue with Kariann Yokota's argument that William Bartram operated in a postcolonial mindset in which his views about nature were largely directed by the imperatives of European scientific practice and institutions. Kariann Akemi

Yokota, *Unbecoming British: How Revolutionary America Became a Postcolonial Nation* (New York: Oxford University Press, 2011), 165–80.

8. William Smellie, "Introduction" to *Natural History General and Particular*, by the Count de Buffon (London: W. Strahan and T. Cadell; Edinburgh: W. Creech, 1781), 1:xx–xxi. While Smellie's views were not necessarily shared by the devotees of taxonomy, his invocation of passions and feeling as an essential part of scientific knowledge in general and natural history in particular were not uncommon in eighteenth-century scientific circles. See Andrew Ashfield and Peter de Bolla, Introduction to *The Sublime: A Reader in British Eighteenth-Century Aesthetic Theory*, ed. Andrew Ashfield and Peter de Bolla (Cambridge: Cambridge University Press, 1996), 6–7; Michael McKeon, "Mediation as Primal Word: The Arts, the Sciences, and the Origins of the Aesthetic," in *This Is Enlightenment*, ed. Clifford Siskin and William Warner (Chicago: University of Chicago Press, 2010), 384–412.

9. Edmund Burke, *A Philosophical Enquiry into the Origin of Our Ideas of the Sublime and Beautiful*, ed. J. T. Boulton (New York: Columbia University Press, 1958), 136, 53. On the effect of the sublime more generally, see Alan Richardson, *The Neural Sublime: Cognitive Theories and Romantic Texts* (Baltimore: Johns Hopkins University Press, 2010), 26–27, 35.

10. [Joseph Addison and Richard Steele], *The Spectator*, no. 411, Saturday, June 21 (London: J. and R. Tonson and S. Draper, 1747), 91.

11. See inscription on cover of Smellie's translation of *Natural History General and Particular*, Library Company of Philadelphia, Am 1781 Buf w22.245; L. Hugh Moore, "The Aesthetic Theory of William Bartram," *Essays in Arts and Sciences* 12, no. 1 (March 1983): 17–35; Regis, *Describing Early America*, 62–68; Slaughter, *Natures*, 190–94.

12. Bartram to A. Laribore, 1795, in Laurel Ode-Schneider, ed., "'The Dignity of Human Nature': William Bartram and the Great Chain of Being," in Hallock and Hoffman, *William Bartram*, 348.

13. Bartram, "The Dignity of Human Nature," in Ode-Schneider, "'Dignity of Human Nature,'" 352.

14. Bartram to Muhlenberg, November 29, 1792, 413.

15. Ode-Schneider, "'Dignity of Human Nature,'" 343; Bartram, "Dignity of Human Nature," 358.

16. It is this combination that makes Bartram distinct; Addison and Steele writing in *The Spectator*, for example, found much utility in aesthetics as a way of understanding nature and the divine, which they tended to place in opposition to reason and science: "We might here add, that the Pleasures of the Fancy are more conducive to Health, than those of the Understanding, which are worked out by Dint of Thinking, and attended with too violent a Labour of the Brain. Delightful scenes, where in Nature, painting, or Poetry, have a kindly Influence on the Body, as well as the Mind, and not only serve to clear and brighten the Imagination, but are able to disperse Grief and Melancholoy, and to set the Animal Spirits in pleasing and agreeable Motions." Addison and Steele, *The Spectator*, vol. 6, no. 411, 93–94.

17. Bartram, *Travels*, 153, 154, 155.

18. Ibid., 155.

19. Thomas Hallock, "Male Pleasure and the Genders of Eighteenth-Century Botanical Exchange," *William and Mary Quarterly* 62, no. 4 (October 2005): 697–718.

20. Cahill, introduction to "Bartram-Muhlenberg Correspondence," 383.

21. Bartram, *Travels*, 280.

22. Ibid., 93, 331.

23. Hoffman, "William Bartram's Draft Manuscript for *Travels*," 285, in Hallock and Hoffman, *William Bartram*, 289.

24. Irmscher, *Poetics of Natural History*, 38–39, 42.

25. Bartram, *Travels*, 322, 338, 352.

26. Irmscher, *Poetics of Natural History*, 38–39, 42, 44–45.

27. Bartram to Muhlenberg, September 8, 1792, in Cahill, "Bartram-Muhlenberg Correspondence," 399.

28. Bartram, *Travels*, 263, 277.

29. Harriet Ritvo, *The Platypus and the Mermaid and Other Figments of the Classifying Imagination* (Cambridge, Mass.: Harvard University Press, 1997), 15–16.

30. Most scholars interpret Bartram's aesthetics as the application of European principles to the American context. See, for example, Regis, *Describing Early America*, 64–66.

31. Philip Shaw, *The Sublime* (London: Routledge, 2006), 60–63; Tom Furniss, *Edmund Burke's Aesthetic Ideology*, Cambridge Studies in Romanticism (Cambridge: Cambridge University Press, 1993), 34–38.

32. Burke, *Philosophical Enquiry*, 135.

33. Bartram, *Travels*, 53, 137, 139.

34. Burke, *Philosophical Enquiry*, 136.

35. Ibid., 82. See also Richard Steele, *The Spectator*, 8 vols. (Glasgow: A. Duncan, 1767), 7:62; James Usher, "Clio: or a Discourse on Taste," in Ashfield and de Bolla, *Sublime: A Reader in British Eighteenth-Century Aesthetic Theory*, edited by Andrew Ashfield and Peter de Bolla (Cambridge, 1996), 47.

36. Bartram, *Travels*, 27, 281.

37. Burke, *Philosophical Enquiry*, 135.

38. Ritvo, *The Platypus and the Mermaid*, 15–16.

39. Joyce Chaplin, "Mark Catesby, a Skeptical Newtonian in America," in *Empire's Nature: Mark Catesby's New World Vision*, ed. Amy R. Meyers and Margaret Beck Pritchard (Chapel Hill: Omohundro Institute of Early American History and Culture and University of North Carolina Press, 1998), 52.

40. Bartram, *Travels*, 147.

41. Mark Catesby, *The Natural History of Carolina, Florida, and the Bahama Islands: Containing the Figures of Birds, Beasts, Fishes, Serpents, Insects, and Plants*, revised by Mr. Edwards of the Royal College of Physicians, 2 vols. (London: Benjamin White, 1771), 1:44.

42. Bartram to Muhlenberg, November 29, 1792, 413.

43. Carl von Linné, *The animal kingdom, or zoological system, of the celebrated Sir Charles Linnæus. Containing a complete systematic description, arrangement, and nomenclature, of all the known species and varieties of the mammalia, or animals which give suck to their young*, ed. Johann Friedrich Gmelin (London: W. Strahan and T. Cadell; Edinburgh: W. Creech, 1792), 30–31.

44. Peter Hanns Reill, *Vitalizing Nature in the Enlightenment* (Berkeley: University of California Press, 2005), 48–49, 53.

45. Jacques Roger, *Buffon: A Life in Natural History*, trans. Sarah Lucille Bonnefoi (Ithaca, N.Y.: Cornell University Press, 1997), 304; Georges Louis Leclerc, Comte de Buffon, *The Natural History of the Quadrapeds by the Count de Buffon, translated from the French with an account of the life of the author*, 3 vols. (Edinburgh: Peter Brown & Thomas Nelson, 1830), 2:40; Buffon, *Natural History of Birds, Fish, Insects, and Reptiles*, vol. 4 (London:

H. D. Symonds, 1798), 279; Buffon, *The Natural History of Oviparous Quadrupeds, and Serpents*, ed. Count de la Cepede, vol. 4 (Edinburgh: Smellie, 1802), 278.

46. Bartram, *Travels*, 115–16, 114–22.

47. Buffon, *Natural History of Birds*, 4:279–81, quotation on 279.

48. Bartram, *Travels*, 121, 122.

49. Irmscher, *Poetics of Natural History*, 177. On the particular fear Europeans had of rattlesnakes, see Philip Levy, *Fellow Travelers: Indians and Europeans Contesting the Early American Trail* (Gainesville: University Press of Florida, 2007), 84–85. On the widespread hostility among Americans to the snake, see Peter C. Messer, "Republican Animals: Politics, Science, and the Birth of Ecology," *Journal for Eighteenth-Century Studies* 33, no. 4 (2010): 599–613; *Virginia Gazette*, May 11, 1776, in "Trivia," *William and Mary Quarterly*, 3rd ser., 33, no. 3 (1976): 528. Slaughter provides a catalog of the stories that Americans told about snakes that probably set the context for Bartram's presentation of the animal in *Natures*, 132–54.

50. Bartram, *Travels*, 223.

51. John Hill, *An History of Animals. Containing Descriptions of Birds, Beasts, Fishes, and Insects of the several Parts of the World; and Including accounts of the several classes of Animalcules, visible only by the Assistance of Microscopes* (London: Thomas Osborne, 1752), 107; Catesby, *Natural History*, 2:41; Esther Louise Larsen, ed. and trans., "Pehr Kalm's Account of the North American Rattlesnake and the Medicines Used in the Treatment of Its Sting," *American Midland Naturalist* 57, no. 2 (1957): 502–11. Kalm's report on people being unharmed by snakes is on 506.

52. Bartram, *Travels*, 223.

53. The sublimity of these qualities was discussed by John Dennis, "The Grounds of Criticism in Poetry (1704)," in Ashfield and de Bolla, *Sublime*, 38.

54. Bartram, "Dignity of Human Nature," 350, 352–53.

55. Bartram, *Travels*, 224–27.

56. Bartram to Muhlenberg, November 29, 1792, 413.

57. Buffon, *Natural History of the Quadrupeds*, 2:40, 42, 43.

58. Bartram, *Travels*, 13, 105, 268, 273.

59. Burke, *Philosophical Enquiry*, 114–15.

60. Bartram, *Travels*, 42–43. A variation of the experience occurs as Bartram, fearful of "being murdered by the Chactaws," has the "reanimating" exposure to the "fragrance" of "the Illicium groves" restore his courage (356).

61. Burke, *Philosophical Enquiry*, 157.

62. Edward Cahill, *Liberty of the Imagination: Aesthetic Theory, Literary Form, and Politics in the Early United States* (Philadelphia: University of Pennsylvania Press, 2012), 148–49.

63. Bartram, *Travels*, 72, 65–66.

64. Furniss, *Edmund Burke's Aesthetic Ideology*, 39, 192.

65. Bartram, "Dignity of Human Nature," 350; Bartram to James Bartram, September 23, 1804, in Hallock, "Life in Letters," in Hallock and Hoffman, *William Bartram*, 212–14.

66. See Hallock, "Male Pleasure."

67. *Massachusetts Magazine, or Monthly Museum* 4, no. 11 (November 1792): 686.

AFTERWORD

"We are all Atlanticists now," declared David Armitage as he assessed the "explosion of interests in the Atlantic and the Atlantic world as subjects of study among historians of North and South America, the Caribbean, Africa and western Europe."[1] His often quoted and just as often contested assessment has no equivalent in environmental history. No bold pronouncement: "We are now all environmental historians" (or would it simply be environmentalists?) has galvanized this growing field.[2] Nevertheless, environmental history, much like Atlantic history, continues to grow both as a subject of study and a framework into the historical past. These two distinct disciplines come together in this collection of essays, which explores moments of intersection and overlap between Atlantic and environmental history, and moments in which neither Atlantic nor environmental history seem to speak to each other, but they are in fact greatly enhanced by teasing out the connections between the two.

Circum-Atlantic environmental history brings together disparate places, actors, and themes. The concerns that animate this anthology are as disparate as the fields they represent. Discussions about movement, labor, climate, landscape, pathogens, lived experience, slavery, transportation, empire, and control share the limelight. Approaching Atlantic history from environmental perspectives is not simply about adding another layer to the already extensive field of Atlantic studies or about casting the environment as yet another actor in the early Atlantic world. It is about deconstructing the core constituent forces: slavery and empire, as they both challenged and defined the Atlantic world. Though slavery and empire are staples of Atlantic historiography, they take on a new form in this anthology.

Framed through questions about landscape, drought, ocean currents, and mineral extraction, for example, the large and often elusive concepts of slavery and empire become grounded in the gritty, hot, and practically tangible lived experiences of the seventeenth- through nineteenth-century American South. But conversely, it is in these deeply rooted connections, where deforestation and soil quality are the focus, that the expansive reach and connective effect of slavery and empire becomes most visible. Because, as the essays in the collection incisively show, even there, in the focused and seemingly local discussions about the environment, the power of slavery and the rule (as well as the limits) of empire are so clearly visible.

As in other environmental history works, the authors of this volume wrestle with the question of human agency in and over the physical world. From human material interaction with the environment to the cultural, legal, political, economic, and scientific actions affecting the environment, this anthology examines how individuals as well as society acted, but also how they were acted on by physical, ecological, and environmental forces beyond their control. Recognizing the agency as well as the contingency of human actions is a crucible of environmental history, but a concern rarely raised in the Atlantic paradigm, which makes the confluence of Atlantic environmental histories in this collection all the more exciting and important.

The anthology begins at this intersection. It shows how an examination of the American South's climate can refocus ways to study Atlantic slavery. Sean Morey Smith's essay on hot climates explores how promoters, pamphleteers, colonists, and early scientists described the climate and nature of the Caribbean. Elaine LaFay's work pushes that conversation further in time, to the antebellum South, and discusses the impact of ventilation and "good/bad" air. Combining slavery and climate, Smith reexamines what, when, and how the Caribbean and the American South were connected. LaFay shows how those big connections also played out in personal, intimate ways. Their works show how an Atlantic environmental frame can help balance big questions about modernity and profit without losing sight of the individual, even bodily, experiences that defined slavery. LaFay concludes her work by detailing how enslaved peoples themselves used environmental concepts and constraints, such as ventilation, to both depict the abuses of slavery and resist their life in bondage.

The essays in the second section show how environmental pressures, though experienced by everyone, were not equally felt. In other words, environmental history puts into focus the natural world inhabited and manipulated by people; the focus on slavery shows how that natural world did not afford the same possibilities or challenges to everyone. Hayley Negrin both broadens and deepens the conversation by bringing gender to the foreground. She examines how Virginia and Carolina planters used Native women's bodies to assert control over both Native labor and land. By enslaving Native women, who were often the ones responsible for the cultivation of their lands, English planters reshaped the colonial landscape; they removed agricultural power from Native women and usurped their production by transforming them into masculine, colonial European property. While Negrin shows how control of gender reshaped the environment needed for plantation slavery to develop, Matthew Mulcahy examines the ecological pressures that threatened slavery, specifically drought.

Droughts, unlike earthquakes, hurricanes, and other environmental disasters, did not "affect structural elements of society." Its effects were slow and hard to measure. Droughts, however, directly affected slavery. Mulcahy argues for a correlation between droughts and slave rebellions, showing how limited rainfall and decreased access to food exacerbated the already horrific conditions of the enslaved.

The anthology's third section further develops these discussions about the environment and slavery by examining how these Atlantic connections functioned and faltered at the imperial level. Bradford Wood's essay discusses how the environment deeply affected the colonization of North Carolina, not least of which was shaping distance. Wood details an unforgiving ocean that did more to separate than to connect the North Carolina colonists to England and to other colonies. Frances Kolb's essay, though rooted in the Lower Mississippi Valley, rather than in North Carolina, also foregrounds the importance of access to the larger Atlantic world. Her essay shows how commercial networks, dominated by British traders, *petites nations*, and the coerced movement of enslaved Africans, helped shape imperial policies. Kolb traces the rapid transformation of the region's trade waterways from local avenues to important gateways to the Atlantic world during the 1760s and 1770s. For Kolb and Wood, the environment defined and defied distance and any sense of connection.

The theme of "environmental inequality" resurfaces in the fourth section. How different individuals experienced, understood, and even described the environment varied significantly, and the essays in this section focus on competing visions and forms of representation. Melissa Morris takes us to Virginia and the origins of tobacco. She focuses on the agricultural practices, rather than just on the technology of harvesting this crop, and shows how the development of the Virginia tobacco staple blended Indigenous and European traditions. As such, the story of tobacco in Virginia is as much grounded in local and Native American practices as it is connected by larger Atlantic ecological connections.

Keith Pluymers's work takes these conflicts to Bermuda. He examines how English colonists who sought to work the land clashed with early Bermudian investors and governors who believed that only enslaved Africans with experience in the Spanish Empire could make the island profitable. By centering the debates on the exploitation and regulation of the physical environment, Pluymers shows that political ecology informed how competing labor and imperial ideologies played out on the ground. Peter Messer takes those ideas further in his examination of William Bartram's writings. Messer embarks on a topographical analysis and argues that Bartram's writings offer a far more critical assessment of the contemporary languages of science and aesthetics. Bartram's topographical descriptions of the Southeast not only critique European practices but also show the inadequacies of practiced scientific and aesthetic discourse. Though rooted in the examples of specific travelers and writers, all three authors in this section push their analysis beyond individual descriptions of the natural world and examine how imperial agents developed environmental frameworks for documenting, justifying, and even working against empire.

This anthology balances big questions with local examples. In case studies of drought or deforestation, larger political, legal, cultural, and economic questions surface. How does the environment shape slavery? How does it intersect with gender? How does it affect imperial power? Emphasizing the environment helps refocus the lived experience of people in the Atlantic world: the connections and disconnections that bound their lives, the trade that defined borders and distance, the landscape that affected sex and gender, the heat and suffering; but an environmental lens also brings into focus the asymmetries of those experiences in the American South. Environmental history might be "a big tent," encompassing many topics and interests, but the essays in this collection show that as big as that tent is, it is not equal in space or frame.

The Atlantic environment detailed in this anthology does not homogenize its actors. On the contrary, it brings to the foreground differences of experience and power. This volume is a call both to think through what role the environment plays in other historical paradigms, such as settler colonialism, middle grounds, and borderlands, as well as to further examine the deep and wide reach of the environment in the Atlantic world. We might not all be Atlanticists. We might not all be environmental(ists). But the confluence of these two fields exposes new connections and questions, offering different ways of framing and understanding the American South in the early Atlantic world.

Alejandra Dubcovsky

NOTES

1. David Armitage, "Three Concepts of Atlantic History," in *The British Atlantic World, 1500–1800*, ed. David Armitage and Michael Braddick (New York: Palgrave Macmillan, 2002), 11.

2. Douglas R. Weiner, "A Death-Defying Attempt to Articulate a Coherent Definition of Environmental History," *Environmental History* 10 (July 2005): 415.

CONTRIBUTORS

ALEJANDRA DUBCOVSKY is an associate professor of history at the University of California, Riverside. Her first book, *Informed Power: Communication in the Early American South*, won the 2016 Michael V. R. Thomason Book Award from the Gulf South Historical Association. Her work has been featured in several journals, including *Ethnohistory*, *Early America Studies*, the *Journal of Southern History*, *Native South*, and the *William and Mary Quarterly*. Her research has been supported by fellowships from the Huntington Library, the John Carter Brown Library, and Mellon Advancing Intercultural Studies.

THOMAS BLAKE EARLE joined Texas A&M University at Galveston as an assistant professor of history in 2019. Previously he served as a postdoctoral fellow at the Center of Presidential History at Southern Methodist University. His research covers American foreign relations, the environment, and the maritime world and has been featured in the *Journal of the Early Republic* and *Environmental History*.

D. ANDREW JOHNSON received his PhD in history at Rice University in 2018. His research covers enslaved peoples in colonial South Carolina and the Atlantic. His scholarship has been supported by the American Society for Eighteenth-Century Studies, the Bartram Trail Conference, the Huntington Library, the Robert H. Smith International Center for Jefferson Studies, and the American Historical Association with the Library of Congress. His work has been featured in the *Journal of Southern History*, the *Journal of Early American History*, and the *South Carolina Historical Magazine*.

FRANCES KOLB is a historian of early America and the Atlantic world. She received her PhD in American history from Vanderbilt University. Fellowships from the Newberry Consortium on American Indian Studies, the Program in Early American Economy and Society, and the David Library of the American Revolution supported the research that appears in this volume and her dissertation, "Contesting Borderlands: Policy and Practice in Spanish Louisiana." She was a postdoctoral research scholar in legal history at Vanderbilt Law School. She currently lives in Nashville, Tennessee.

ELAINE LAFAY received her PhD in the history and sociology of science from the University of Pennsylvania in 2019. She researches widely on the history of health, environment, and society in the U.S. South. Her current book project explores the role of atmospheric and medical knowledge in American imperialism in the nineteenth century.

PETER C. MESSER is an associate professor of history at Mississippi State University. He studies the relationship between knowledge, identity, and power in eighteenth-century natural history. He is the author of *Stories of Independence: Identity, Ideology, and History in Eighteenth-Century America*.

MELISSA N. MORRIS is a historian of the seventeenth-century Atlantic world and an assistant professor at the University of Wyoming. Her current book project, "Cultivating Colonies: Tobacco and the Upstart Empires, 1580–1640," considers the role tobacco cultivation and trade played in the earliest efforts by the English, Dutch, and French to colonize the Americas. It looks at how that trade emerged from a prolonged engagement with both Indigenous societies and Spanish colonists.

MATTHEW MULCAHY is a professor of history at Loyola University Maryland. He is the author of *Hubs of Empire: The Southeastern Lowcountry and British Caribbean* and *Hurricanes and Society in the British Greater Caribbean, 1624–1783*. He is currently completing a larger, cowritten study of disasters in the early modern Caribbean.

HAYLEY NEGRIN is an assistant professor of history at the University of Illinois at Chicago. Her current book project investigates the transformation of Indigenous kinship ties and politics under English chattel slavery in early North America. Using a mix of colonial and ethnohistorical sources, she tracks how southeastern Native American women and children specifically were targeted and trafficked from their own sovereign borders into Carolina and Virginia plantations in the seventeenth century. She considers how they reimagined community, politics, and relationships to the natural world even while under the deep stress of bondage.

KEITH PLUYMERS is an assistant professor of history at Illinois State University. He completed his PhD in 2015 in history at the University of Southern California and was the Howard E. and Susanne C. Jessen Postdoctoral Instructor at Caltech from 2015 to 2018. His book project, "No Wood, No Kingdom: Political Ecology in the English Atlantic," is under contract with the University of Pennsylvania Press.

SEAN MOREY SMITH is a PhD candidate in history at Rice University. He is completing his dissertation, "Abolition and the Making of Scientific Racism in the Anglophone Atlantic," on medical and scientific theories of race in abolitionist discourse. He has been published in *Slavery & Abolition* and *Medical History*.

BRADFORD J. WOOD is a professor of history at Eastern Kentucky University. Wood is the author of *This Remote Part of the World: Regional Formation in Lower Cape Fear, North Carolina, 1725–1775* and the coeditor, with Michelle LeMaster, of *Creating and Contesting Carolina: Proprietary Era Histories*. He grew up in Charleston, West Virginia, and southeastern Michigan, and he holds degrees from Wake Forest, Michigan State, and Johns Hopkins.

INDEX

Acosta, José de, 179
Adams, Nehemiah, 49
Addison, Joseph, 197, 203, 212n16
aesthetic theory, 195–204, 208–10, 212n16
Affleck, Thomas, 38
alligators, 205–6
ambergris, 181
American Indians. *See* Native Americans
American Revolution, 69, 76, 81; Mississippi Valley trade and, 144–48
Anderson, Virginia DeJohn, 4
Annales school, 4
Antigua: drought in, 69, 71–72, 74–76, 80, 81; famine in, 74–75, 78
Arcedeckne, Chaloner, 68
Arceneaux, Pierre, 141–42, 151n32
Archdale, John, 28
Archer, George, 92
Aristotle, 23–24, 26
Armitage, David, 15n7, 215
Ash, Eric, 177
Ashe, Thomas, 27–29
Ashley, Lord, 97
Athen, Edward, 188
Augusta, Ga., 202–3
Austrian Succession, War of, 75
Aztecs, 160

Banks, Jourden, 51
Barbados, 72; climate of, 22, 24–25, 30, 33; drought in, 69, 71, 73–75, 81
Barlowe, Arthur, 161
Barton, Benjamin Smith, 196–97
Barton, Edward, 41–43
Bartram, William, 12, 195–211, 217–18; on alligators, 205–6; on human nature, 198, 207; on rattlesnakes, 206–8, 214n49

Bashford, Alison, 15n7
beauty, 197–204, 208–10
Beecher, Catherine, 42
Berkeley, William, 99, 101
Berland, Alexander, 66
Bermuda, 12, 168, 174n48, 176–91, 217
Bernhard, Virginia, 188, 189, 193n32
Blackbeard (Edward Teach), 121
Bland, Henry, 50
Blome, Richard, 26, 27, 32
Bolster, Jeffrey, 114
Bonnet, Stede, 121
Boyle, Robert, 96
Braddock, Michael J., 15n7
Brafferton Indian School, 96, 104
Braudel, Fernand, 4
Brazil, 22, 164, 170
Breen, Benjamin, 8, 18n23
Brereton, John, 167
Brim, Clara, 50
Brown, Kathleen, 98
Brown, William Wells, 53–54
Buffon, Comte de, 198, 205, 206, 208
Bull, Stephen, 96–97
Bull, William, 80
Burke, Edmund, 197, 202–4, 209–10
Burrington, George, 118
Butler, Nathaniel, 176, 177, 183, 185–90, 193n37
Byam, William, 69
Byrd, William, 104

cacao cultivation, 160
Cahill, William, 196
Cañizares-Esguerra, Jorge, 8, 18n23
Carney, Judith Ann, 14n6, 158, 177
Carolina charter, 94
Carse, Ashley, 10–11

Cartwright, Samuel, 46–47
Catesby, Mark, 204
Cecelski, David, 121
Chambers, Robert, 46–47, 49
Chaplin, Joyce E., 36n41, 105n5
Charles II of England, 27
Charles V, Holy Roman Emperor, 178
Civil War, U.S., 5
"civilizing mission," 90–91, 94–95
Clark, Daniel, 148
climatic theories, 21–34; Aristotelian,
    23–24; Hippocratic, 23, 32
Clusius, Carolus, 169
cochineal, 179, 180
Colombia, 162, 164
Columbus, Christopher, 3, 159, 163
Coombs, John C., 176
corn cultivation, 73, 97; on Bermuda, 186,
    188–89, 190; Native American rituals of,
    102, 109n59
Cortés, Hernán, 160
Cotton, Robert, 169
Cromwell, Oliver, 24, 94
Cronon, William, 7, 10, 14n6, 90,
    136
Crosby, Alfred, 4, 14n6, 159
Cuba, 171
Curaçao, 139

Dalton, Joseph, 96
Dando, Marmaduke, 188
Dawson, Kevin, 182
Day, John, 188
deforestation, 67, 123, 215–16, 218
Descoudreaux, Charles, 140, 142–44
DeVilliers, Balthasar, 142, 143
Dominica, 81, 167
Drake, Francis, 160, 162
Draughon, Robert, 49
drought, 10, 65–83, 216–18; famine from,
    73–77, 79–80; hurricanes and, 67, 71,
    76–77, 217; inflation during, 73, 76;
    kinds of, 67
Dudley, Robert, 118
Dunbar, William, 145
Durham, Thomas, 188

earthquakes, 66–67, 217
Eason, George, 50
Edelson, S. Max, 35n25, 66, 70, 72–73,
    107n38
Eden, Richard, 159, 172n15
Edwards, Bryan, 82
El Niño phenomena, 68, 84n8
Elizabeth I of England, 177
Elletson, Roger Hope, 82
Eltis, David, 116
environmental determinism, 6
Ethridge, Robbie, 99

famine, 73–77, 79–80
Fastio, Isaac, 139
Fernández de Oviedo y Valdés, Gonzalo,
    159, 178
Ferrar, John, 190–91
Fitzpatrick, John, 140, 145
Florida, 161; Bartram's journey in, 199;
    Drake's raid on, 162; trade networks of,
    135–48; U.S. slave raids into, 99–100
Fontainebleau, Treaty of (1762), 135
Fothergill, John, 195
Frampton, John, 159–60
Francis I of France, 1
Franklin, Benjamin, 126–27
Fundamental Constitutions of Carolina,
    94
fur trade, 138, 140, 141

Galen, 23–25, 27
Gallay, Alan, 99
Gálvez, Bernardo de, 141
Gardyner, George, 157
Gaspar, David Barry, 71
gender roles, 90–105, 106n13, 202–3,
    209–10
Graham, Sylvester, 42
Grandberry, Mary Ella, 55
Gratz, Barnard, 145
Great Dismal Swamp, 117, 122, 129n16
Green Corn Ceremony, 102, 109n59
Grenville, Richard, 162
Grove, Richard, 4
Guadeloupe, 73, 74, 81

ENVIRONMENTAL HISTORY
AND THE AMERICAN SOUTH

Lynn A. Nelson, *Pharsalia: An Environmental Biography
of a Southern Plantation, 1780–1880*

Jack E. Davis, *An Everglades Providence: Marjory Stoneman
Douglas and the American Environmental Century*

Shepard Krech III, *Spirits of the Air: Birds and American Indians in the South*

Paul S. Sutter and Christopher J. Manganiello, eds.,
Environmental History and the American South: A Reader

Claire Strom, *Making Catfish Bait out of Government Boys:
The Fight against Cattle Ticks and the Transformation of the Yeoman South*

Christine Keiner, *The Oyster Question:
Scientists, Watermen, and the Maryland Chesapeake Bay since 1880*

Mark D. Hersey, *My Work Is That of Conservation:
An Environmental Biography of George Washington Carver*

Kathryn Newfont, *Blue Ridge Commons:
Environmental Activism and Forest History in Western North Carolina*

Albert G. Way, *Conserving Southern Longleaf:
Herbert Stoddard and the Rise of Ecological Land Management*

Lisa M. Brady, *War upon the Land: Military Strategy and
the Transformation of Southern Landscapes during the American Civil War*

Drew A. Swanson, *Remaking Wormsloe Plantation:
The Environmental History of a Lowcountry Landscape*

Paul S. Sutter, *Let Us Now Praise Famous Gullies:
Providence Canyon and the Soils of the South*

Monica R. Gisolfi, *The Takeover: Chicken Farming and the
Roots of American Agribusiness*

William D. Bryan, *The Price of Permanence: Nature and Business in the New South*

Paul S. Sutter and Paul M. Pressly, eds., *Coastal Nature,
Coastal Culture: Environmental Histories of the Georgia Coast*

Andrew C. Baker, *Bulldozer Revolutions: A Rural History of the Metropolitan South*

Drew A. Swanson, *Beyond the Mountains: Commodifying Appalachian Environments*

Thomas Blake Earle and D. Andrew Johnson, eds.,
Atlantic Environments and the American South